Christopher Brooke is Professor of History at Westfield
College, London University. He is a Major Scholar of
Gonville and Caius College, Cambridge, and was a Fellow
of this college from 1949 to 1956. He has published
extensively in scholarly journals and has written many books,
which include *The Dullness of the Past, The Saxon and
Norman Kings, Europe in the Central Middle Ages 962–1154*
and *Twelfth-Century Renaissance.*

Front cover: Coronation of St Edmund, from a
twelfth-century English manuscript of the *Life and
Miracles of St Edmund* (Pierpont Morgan Library, New York:
MS 736 f. 8v)

Back cover: Detail from the Bayeux Tapestry, showing
Harold's Saxon house-carles at the Battle of Hastings,
1066 (Photo: John Freeman)

Also in this series and available in Cardinal

THE CENTURY OF REVOLUTION by Christopher Hill

FROM ALFRED TO HENRY III
871-1272

FROM ALFRED
TO HENRY III
871-1272

Christopher Brooke

CARDINAL

CARDINAL edition published in 1974
by Sphere Books Ltd, 30/32 Gray's Inn Road,
London WC1X 8JL

First published in Great Britain
by Thomas Nelson & Sons Ltd, 1961
Copyright © Christopher Brooke 1961
First Sphere Books edition 1969

Set in Intertype Times

Printed in Great Britain by
Hazell Watson & Viney Ltd,
Aylesbury, Bucks

ISBN 0 351 15427 2

CONTENTS

MAPS AND PLANS

Grateful acknowledgement is due to the following for granting permission to quote: to Miss Margaret Ashdown and the Syndics of the Cambridge University Press for extracts from 'The Song of Maldon' (*English and Norse Documents*, 1930); to Professor G. N. Garmonsway, Messrs J. M. Dent & Sons Ltd, and Messrs E. P. Dutton & Co. Inc., New York, for extracts from the *Anglo-Saxon Chronicle* (Everyman's Library); to Professor Sir Maurice Powicke and the Delegates of the Clarendon Press for an extract from *King Henry III and the Lord Edward*; to Professor Sir Frank Stenton and the Delegates of the Clarendon Press for extracts from *Anglo-Saxon England* (1943); and to Professor Dorothy Whitelock, Professor D. C. Douglas, Messrs Eyre & Spottiswoode Ltd, and Oxford University Press, Inc., New York, for extracts from *English Historical Documents*, vols. I and II (1955, 1953).

The plan of Rievaulx Abbey is reproduced by permission of the Controller of H.M. Stationery Office (Ministry of Works).

TO MY WIFE

GENERAL EDITORS' PREFACE

Knowledge and understanding of English history change and develop so rapidly that a new series needs little apology. The present series was planned in the conviction that a fresh survey of English history was needed, and that the time was ripe for it. It will cover the whole span from Caesar's first invasion in 55 B.C. to 1955, and be completed in eight volumes. The precise scope and scale of each book will inevitably vary according to the special circumstances of its period; but each will combine a clear narrative with an analysis of many aspects of history —social, economic, religious, cultural and so forth—such as is essential in any approach to English history today.

The special aim of this series is to provide serious and yet challenging books, not buried under a mountain of detail. Each volume is intended to provide a picture and an appreciation of its age, as well as a lucid outline, written by an expert who is keen to make available and alive the findings of modern research. They are intended to be reasonably short—long enough that the reader may feel he has really been shown the ingredients of a period, not so long that he loses appetite for anything further. The series is intended to be a stimulus to wider reading rather than a substitute for it; and yet to comprise a set of volumes, each, within its limits, complete in itself. Our hope is to provide an introduction to English history which is lively and illuminating, and which makes it at once exciting and more intelligible.

C. N. L. B.

D. M. S.

AUTHOR'S PREFACE

My first aim in this book has been to make a remote period intelligible. In the Introduction I have tried to give a brief sketch of the materials with which our knowledge of these centuries is built, and a brief outline of what happened in them; and, above all, to describe some of the fundamental differences between the medieval and the modern world. Some of the chapters which follow are narrative; some describe and analyse social life, institutions, the Church, farming, trade and so forth. Planning the layout of these topics was no easy task; they could not be divided in a simple and logical way, as is possible in dealing with shorter, or later, periods. The history of the Church, for instance, falls naturally into three: the tenth-century reform (pp. 55–8), the century after the Conquest (chapter 8), and the thirteenth century (pp. 246–251). If the history of farming were divided in the same way, the first section would be a catalogue of insoluble problems, and the partitions would have hindered any rational explanation of the subject. It is much more satisfactory to treat it as a whole (chapter 7), and in close connection with the history of markets, trade and industry (pp. 125–33)—only so can one expound coherently these various aspects of economic life. Thus the plan of the analytical chapters is deliberately untidy; it has been devised for use, not for show. If anyone should get lost in the more devious passages, he should find help in the appendices and the index.

The errors in this book are my own; for the rest it is the fruit of a combined operation over many years by my father and my other teachers, my colleagues and my pupils, to give me some understanding of medieval England. I have also been much influenced by many of the books which I have listed, and by many books and articles which could not be included in the list. Such debts cannot be properly specified in a book of this character; but I am very much aware of them. In the preparation of the book, I am indebted to Mr Denis Mack Smith for his penetrating criticism and for translating many passages into English; to Mr Peter Hunter Blair and Dr George Holmes, who read the book at various times and gave me

13

valuable corrections; to my eldest son, Francis, who helped with the maps; to Miss H. Otto for typing my manuscript; to my colleagues in the Department of Mediaeval History at Liverpool for discussing some of the book's problems with me, and above all to Dr Alec Myers, who read the whole book in typescript and in proof, saved me from many errors, and gave me much generous help.

The dedication is a token of the many debts I owe to a fellow historian—and a colleague in countless other ways.

C. N. L. B.

PREFACE TO THIRD IMPRESSION

The opportunity has now been taken to make such corrections as a reprint permits. I am indebted to several friends, colleagues and reviewers for corrections and criticisms, and in particular to Professor Dorothy Whitelock and Miss Margaret Gibson.

C. N. L. B.

CHAPTER ONE

INTRODUCTION

(1) MATERIALS

A description of the materials from which the story is compiled may seem out of place in a book of this character. But it is one of its chief aims to act as an introduction and guide to more advanced reading. This should always include some reading of sources, however swift our study may be; and in this period many of the chief sources are literary histories and chronicles —vivid and readable narratives which tell the story better than it can be re-told. At the same time the sources are far from copious; they grow fuller as the centuries pass, but are still by modern standards exceedingly fragmentary. There is more material for a single week in the twentieth century than for several centuries in the Middle Ages. History, furthermore, is a peculiar science in that its materials are open to inspection by all: anyone can read a chronicle or a charter and understand something of its message. There is a great deal in historical reconstruction which requires expert treatment— learning, technical skill, experience, above all, knowledge of what other historians have done. But the materials are open to inspection; and in a period when they are both vivid and scanty they form the ideal mode of entry to the history of an age.

The great age of the 'literary' source—the chronicle and the history—was the twelfth century; this was the case all over Europe, and nowhere more than in England. Among the most distinguished authors was William of Malmesbury, who wrote a number of books which reflect the various interests of medieval historians very well. He wrote saints' lives and the histories of individual monasteries; he wrote a history of the English Church (*Acts of the Bishops*) and a history of the English kings (*Acts of the Kings*). Like all English historians of his day, he was aware of working in a great tradition. The Venerable Bede, most distinguished of all his predecessors, had been an Englishman.

15

'Bede, that man of great learning and deep humility,' wrote William in the preface to his *Acts of the Kings* (*c.* 1125), 'wrote a full account of the history of the English from their coming into Britain down to his own day, in a clear and graceful style. But I do not think you will easily find anyone after him who has given his mind to weaving the threads of English history in Latin. . . . There are indeed some fragments of antiquity laid out in annular form [with an entry for each year of grace], written like chronicles and in the vernacular. By their means the periods following Bede's death are saved from total oblivion.' In this patronising way William dismisses the *Anglo-Saxon Chronicle*. 'Concerning Aethelweard, a noble and generous man, who strove to render the Chronicle in Latin, silence is best'—a sarcastic reference to the extreme clumsiness of Aethelweard's Latin. 'Nor have I forgotten Eadmer's work, written in a quiet, pleasurable style; in which he dealt swiftly with the time from King Edgar to William I, then spread himself more freely down to the death of Archbishop Anselm (1109). . . .' Even so, William claims, there is no proper account of the period between Bede and Edgar, and this gap he sets out to fill, carrying his history on down to the time at which he was writing.

William was less than fair to his predecessors, and he ignores less formal kinds of historical writing. Thus we have a number of biographies: Asser's life of Alfred, numerous saints' lives and even occasional fragments of autobiography; above all, the unique description of the events leading up to the battle of Hastings in the Bayeux Tapestry. This splendid piece of embroidery was probably made by English needlewomen at the orders of Odo, Bishop of Bayeux. It was made to be hung in Bayeux Cathedral on the feast of the relics. It tells the story, not of the Norman Conquest, but of the decline and fall of King Harold. It ends with Harold's death and the English flight from the battle. Its central scene shows Harold swearing on the relics of Bayeux a solemn oath that he will not take the English crown. He takes it and the moral unfolds: swift retribution on the man who despised the Bayeux relics. But to us its great interest lies in the vivid portrayal of the central event of English history in this period, and of all the incidentals—armour, castles, ships, food, furniture—normally omitted from literary texts.

In spite of these qualifications, it remains true that there is

16

little in the way of narrative history between Bede and the Conquest apart from the *Anglo-Saxon Chronicle*. From then on we have the help of numerous writers from both sides of the Channel: men like the English Eadmer who wrote especially on St Anselm, and the Anglo-Norman Orderic, who was born in Shropshire, but spent his life in a Norman monastery, and wrote an immense history, covering Norman and English affairs and much of wider interest too. Eadmer is notable for his vivid account of Anselm in his *History of Modern Times* and in his life of the saint; and the *History* also contains striking descriptions of Anselm's relations with the English kings. Orderic's history is full of lively descriptions of persons and events; he was prolix and formless as a writer, but full of interest; it makes a good bedside book.

Histories and chronicles grew in quantity and fullness as the twelfth century went on, culminating in the immense semi-official chronicles of Roger of Howden, royal clerk under Henry II (died 1189) and Richard I (1189–99), which finally stopped in 1201. Literary sources of other kinds are also common, and unusually valuable to the historian in this century. The long quarrel between Thomas Becket and Henry II produced a massive body of literature. It was an age when men, following a classical model, collected their letters; and partly owing to literary vanity, partly to the desire of one or two of the participants to justify their cause or commemorate the martyr, large collections of the day-to-day correspondence of the crisis were preserved. Becket's murder and canonisation led to a flood of biography (some of it good, much indifferent) and of miracle stories. It is characteristic of this century that the life and death of Becket should be its best-documented event.

At the turn of the twelfth and thirteenth centuries lived and wrote one of the most popular of all medieval chroniclers, Jocelin of Brakelond, monk of Bury St Edmunds. His little book has been famous ever since Thomas Carlyle took Jocelin's hero, Abbot Samson (who died in 1211), as one of the central characters in his *Past and Present*. There are few more vivid and lively pictures of medieval life, and the account of Samson's election, with all the gossip and lobbying which preceded it, and of the abbot's personality, are particularly telling. As a picture of monastic life it is one-sided: Jocelin was the abbey cellarer, concerned with food, supply and administration, and he has much to say of worldly concerns, little of the spiritual or intellectual life of the abbey; and Samson, splendid man of business that he was, represents the shrewd, hard-headed merchants and estate-agents who made England prosperous in the thirteenth century, rather than the monastic tradition of St Dunstan or St Ailred of Rievaulx.

In the course of the thirteenth century literary histories declined both in quality and quantity. The most famous chronicler of the reign of Henry III was Matthew Paris, monk of St Albans, who died about 1259. Matthew was a character; a vivid and facile writer with a strong urge to write and no sense of discipline; a man of violent but very human prejudices; more of a journalist, perhaps, than a historian. Matthew was known in his own day as a writer of distinction. In marked contrast to him was the humble friar, Brother Thomas of Eccleston, who wrote about the coming of the Franciscan Order to England. Eccleston's chronicle is a collection of brief notes and stories. He differed from Matthew Paris in having no pretension to literary airs and graces; also in being remarkably accurate. His simple vignettes of Franciscan life make his chronicle a splendid source for the religious life of the time.

The great days of the literary source were departing. Neither Matthew Paris nor Thomas of Eccleston had successors of comparable interest. None the less the materials for thirteenth-century history are abundant. This is mainly due to a rapid growth in official documents starting at the turn of the twelfth and thirteenth centuries. Documents of some sort there had been throughout the period covered by this book, charters, for instance, official letters, and wills. Of one type of document, the royal writ, we shall have more to say when we study Anglo-Saxon and Norman government. In early days they were rare. One hundred and twenty royal writs (some spurious) survive from before 1066; about 500 between 1066 and 1100. Then the number grows: 1,500 for Henry I, and probably several thousand from the reigns of Henry II and Richard I. In 1199 the clerks of the royal Chancery began to make copies, kept on rolls of parchment, of writs sent out under the Great Seal of England. Before 1199 it is a matter very largely of chance whether a writ survives; after 1199, even if it does not, we can study its contents from the Chancery rolls. One of these sets of rolls, the rolls of letters patent, has been preserved ever since 1201. The proliferation of official records mean that we can trace the details of events far more fully than before; what we

18

lack in comment and vivid narrative we make up in formal, precise records of events.

Writs were not the only thing enrolled by the royal clerks in the thirteenth century, nor was the Chancery the only office in which rolls were kept. In fact, the other great organ of government, the Treasury, which from the early twelfth century had been controlled by its office of audit, the Exchequer, as we still call it, kept rolls of accounts, of which the earliest survivor dates from 1130. These rolls tell us much about royal finance; and their character is made intelligible to us by an elaborate account of the workings of the Exchequer, the *Dialogue on the Exchequer* (begun in 1177), written by no less a person than the royal Treasurer himself, the head of the office, Richard Fitz-Neal.

Records of law-courts always give us a somewhat raw picture of society; and the records of medieval cases are so prolific that medieval man has acquired the undeserved reputation of being incorrigibly litigious. But these legal records are not just a chronicle of the crimes and follies of mankind. They reveal something incidentally of the rich variety of everyday life; they can be made to illuminate a thousand dark corners of medieval society. They need patience in the unravelling. Their sheer bulk from John's reign on surpasses all other official records. But we are beginning to learn their value, and although only a small proportion have yet been excerpted, many tales from them have found their way into recent books.

Chronicles and official records, and documents of every kind, are the historian's traditional tools. But he has come in recent years to look for evidence wherever he can find it; and also to take an interest in every aspect of the life of the past. Survivals of every kind are useful to him: physical survivals, like fields and boundary walls, and the countryside at large; material survivals, churches, castles, and houses—the remains of town and village and monastery as they can be revealed by aerial photography or archaeology. We shall see when we talk of the Danish invasions how valuable is the evidence of place-names —the meaning and more particularly the language of the original name—in showing how the peoples who settled in this country were distributed. When we talk of Old English society, of the work of King Alfred, or the court of Henry II, we shall see how much of the life of the time is reflected in its literature. When we discuss the impact of the Norman Con-

19

quest on English life, we shall see how much essential evidence must be gathered from the fascinating history of the English language—of how it became Frenchified without becoming French; and also of how English skills in painting and design and English traditions survived, modified and moulded by Norman ideas and Norman energy. Finally, not least important, history is mainly the study of men and women, and at every turn the historian, attempting to describe and explain their actions, is compelled to use his knowledge of human nature. This has its dangers, since human nature is liable to change. Into this as into every type of evidence historians are tempted to read too much. But it is a vital basis for our reconstruction of the past.

This catalogue is not intended to bewilder or discourage. On the contrary, it shows the rich profusion of material from which the student of history can select. There is something here to suit every taste. That is the special value of history. It gives its students great freedom of choice. But for those who want to study history as it should be studied, imaginatively and for pleasure, three things are necessary: a well-stocked library, a readiness to explore, and eyes open to observe whatever they find, in or out of books.

(2) 871–1272

This volume covers just over 400 years, from the accession of Alfred to the death of Henry III; 400 years of great interest and importance in English history, and full of change. They saw the last three waves of successful conquest and extensive settlement: the two Danish invasions of the ninth and early eleventh centuries, and the Norman Conquest. Each conquest carried with it extensive political and social changes; profound alterations in the structure of English life and government. The Norman Conquest gave England an entirely new ruling class, and with it new social arrangements and customs. From any viewpoint, the Norman Conquest is the watershed in the history of these centuries. But there is another story unfolding behind these dramatic events. The main theme in ninth- and tenth-century history is the creation of an English monarchy out of the smaller units which had hitherto dominated the country. With the English kingdom grew up the first semblance of national institutions—institutions of central and local government which made the English monarchy among the most mature in the Europe of its time. It was not until the eleventh century that a united England really emerged, under the aegis of the Danish King Cnut; but its foundations had been laid in the hundred years after 871 by the dynasty of Alfred. These established institutions were not destroyed by the Normans; they adapted and developed them. There was a certain continuity of institutional life even through the Conquest. This, then, is the theme of the first four chapters of the book: the emergence of a united English monarchy.

In every sphere of life eleventh- and twelfth-century Europe was changing rapidly. The Church was finding new inspiration in monastic reforms and in the reform of the papacy. With these came new methods of Church government; and at the same time a great intellectual revival which culminated, in the late twelfth and thirteenth centuries, in the creation of universities. But it was not only the Church which was changing. Economic life was reawakening; the Mediterranean was once more freely used by western merchants, and in the twelfth century, by western soldiers on their way to the Crusades. Social codes, systems of government were changing; the code of chivalry was being devised. All these changes tended to enhance the impact of the Norman Conquest, which brought England into closer touch with European life, and made it politically very close to France, the centre of new fashions in thought and literature and art and war and, even then, in dress. Politically, the Norman Conquest made England the partner in an Anglo-French state; culturally, it speeded the process by which she became a partner in the new Europe. One of the most striking developments of the twelfth century was the emergence of a new kind of statecraft, of a government organised more elaborately and effectively than anything Europe had known for centuries. The two outstanding examples were both Norman creations: the Norman kingdom of Sicily and the Norman kingdom of England. These are the themes of chapters 5–11.

The Norman and early Angevin kings were in many ways remarkably despotic; they ruled by personal strength and through fear, and kept a close hold on the institutions of government. But they also ruled to some extent by consent; and the more they developed their judicial, administrative, and fiscal powers, the more some form of consent was necessary. It

21

was in the reigns of John (1199–1216) and Henry III (1216–72) that these tensions came into the open. Neither man was successful enough as a king to maintain the machinery of government without concessions to the magnates. At first, the concessions took the form of the issue and frequent re-issue of Magna Carta. As time went on government by consent began to take more self-conscious and elaborate shape in more formal arrangements for meetings of the King's Council, and in formal talks, 'parleyings', parliaments between kings and lords, and sometimes between king, lords, and representatives of the commons as well. Parliament as an institution was still remote enough when Henry III died; but new principles of government were astir. Henry III's court was a very active place. His civil service and his judicial system were growing; and the palace and abbey of Westminster reflected the taste of an artistic king in a great age of art and architecture. The new attitude to government is the theme of chapters 12–14.

(3) FUNDAMENTALS

It is my aim in this book to help anyone who reads it to understand a period of this country's distant past; to make it more real and less remote. England was a very different place in 1272, still more in 1066 or in 871, from what it is today; the understanding of these differences is the key to an understanding of its history. Not everything has changed. The geography, the climate are with us still; the barons and villeins of Domesday Book and Magna Carta were our ancestors. But in different conditions geography may have different effects; human nature may, and does, change; chance similarities may be most misleading. Medieval history demands imagination from its student; he must live himself into the past in order to appreciate a world of ideas, activities, and aspirations very different from his own. But the rewards are great. If we make the effort, we can meet our own ancestors working out their lives against the same physical background which we know; but on utterly different lines. Our first business as historians is to mark the contrasts; to make sure that we are not reading the present into the past, making our forbears in our own image. Once we have done that, the element of continuity, the links between past and present, will return in truer colours; we shall find that for all the changes the links are real; and both contrast

22

and continuity are profoundly interesting and profoundly in-structive—especially to anyone curious to know, as was King William in 1086, 'about this land and how it was peopled, and with what sort of men'.

There is an astonishing continuity in English institutions, which makes it possible for us in a way more immediately than any other European people to feel contact with our medieval past; and yet this continuity can be very deceptive. We have an institution which we call Parliament; its name has not altered since the thirteenth century. But the 'mother of Parliaments' today bears little resemblance to the confabula-tions between Edward I and his peers and councillors, to which it owes its name. If we listed the really significant things about our present Parliament—the things which give it meaning to us —it is highly unlikely that many or any of the points we should make would also have been true of its medieval ancestor.

We cannot study the Middle Ages without being constantly reminded of the elements of continuity and the profundity of the changes which have taken place. The continuity gives us contact, helps us to get in touch with our medieval ancestors. If we wish to study medieval life, we can learn a great deal by living in the present. The earth and stone walls which surround so many fields in Wales and south-western England are often of great antiquity; and sometimes the deep meandering lanes represent pre-Conquest boundaries of farms and estates, some-times boundaries still. These walls and boundaries are the product of social conditions; they are also related to farming needs which have not entirely disappeared, even in these days of tractors and combines and marketing boards. In a different way the enthusiasm with which medieval thought and medieval art are now studied reveals that the tastes and values which gave them birth are not in every particular foreign to us. If we are alive to it, our medieval past is always at our elbow; and its study is no remote esoteric adventure for the expert alone.

From time to time in this book we shall notice these contacts between present and past. For the moment we must concen-trate on the differences: on those attitudes which differentiate medieval from modern England, and make it a world apart. One cannot cover every difference in a brief introduction; what I plan to do is to select from various aspects of medieval life, and to give a few examples. If we could visit a medieval village or a medieval town we should be struck immediately by the difference in physical environment. As we lived with the people, we should perhaps in course of time be even more struck by the difference in their unspoken assumptions, their attitudes, and beliefs. We shall start, then, with a look at their houses and furniture and ideas of physical comfort. Since this is a book on English history, we shall next inquire, was there such a thing as England? How was it viewed by Englishmen and foreigners? Since this is a book about the Middle Ages, the ages of faith, we shall go on to inquire about the Church and its place in men's lives; and finally, about how men's attitude to God affected their attitude to the material world—about their notions of science.

In the Middle Ages men built in mud and wood and stone. Since stone is durable, and stone buildings more easily adapted to changing fashions of internal furnishing and decoration than removed altogether, it is the stone buildings which survive. To us medieval building means stone churches, cathedrals, and castles, although we may have seen the impressive wooden nave in the church at Greenstead in Essex, or the timber structures of a few old barns and houses. Today the great English cathedrals are surrounded by modern cities. There is still a notable contrast between the architecture of the cathedral and of the modern secular buildings close at hand. But the contrast must often have been sharper when the cathedral was first built. Here and there in the city might be the stone house of a lord or a prominent citizen, like the ancient stone houses still to be seen on the hill leading up to Lincoln Cathedral. But the majority of the houses would be small structures of wood and wattle and daub, clustering along narrow streets and around courtyards. In the villages the houses would not be so tightly packed, but their structure might be even more primitive. The peasant commonly lived in a mud hovel with one room, or at best two; and these apartments would house his whole family and some livestock besides. We know very little about them; hardly any survive before the very end of the Middle Ages. But we do occasionally find inventories of their contents. If they were crowded with living things, not much space needed to be reserved for furniture. This was of the barest and simplest, and the personal possessions of a peasant rarely went much beyond the pots and pans with which his wife did her cooking, a rough bench and table, and the essential tools of a small farmer.

24

What we miss immediately in any description of a peasant's house is any sign of privacy and comfort. Before the twelfth and thirteenth centuries the same is as true, by and large, in the houses of the wealthy. Indeed, it is not before the sixteenth century that the English gentry began to turn the hens out of doors and build private rooms for the various members of their family; and it was the Industrial Revolution which first brought notable improvement in the houses of the labouring poor.

The houses of the English kings and nobles in the early Middle Ages were substantial enough, but almost as innocent of comfort as were the cottages. The great halls described in Anglo-Saxon poetry, like the halls of the Northumbrian kings excavated at Yeavering, were large open structures with a single room in which the whole court ate and slept. The Norman Conquest saw the introduction of the characteristic symbol of feudal lordship, the castle, built both for defence and as a home, but more suited to the necessities of war than to the comforts of peace. At first the castle keep was usually of timber, on the summit of a mound; the Norman kings set the fashion for building more permanent keeps of stone on solid foundations. From the first some buildings lay in an outer court, and in the late twelfth and thirteenth centuries the great rooms of the keep were less and less used. But even the royal court in Henry II's day (1154–89) might meet in the hall and chamber of the Tower of London or Dover Castle; and the dramatic encounter of Henry and Archbishop Thomas Becket in October 1164 took place in the great keep at Northampton (now the site of a railway station). Hall and chamber: these were the two essential living rooms of a great house. In the hall the whole household ate and slept; the chamber was at first the more private apartment of the lord or king and his immediate household. The riff-raff was excluded; but even so there was little privacy. Gradually the castles and palaces grew, and more private chambers were provided. This had happened earlier in the great royal palaces at Winchester and Westminster, and in the late twelfth and thirteenth centuries it became the case in many large houses up and down England. The early Norman castle, as portrayed in the Bayeux Tapestry, had an outer court, or bailey, and an inner keep, the mound or 'motte'. The motte grew into the great stone keep; the bailey acquired more and more buildings to be used in times of peace. And as peace became more normal and more generally expected, the buildings

25

of the bailey came to replace those of the keep in importance. The palace of Westminster sprawled over an even wider area; and the castles of king and nobles up and down the country grew in proportion. The great stone keep of the Tower of London or Dover Castle gave way to the more elaborate castles of Edward I, which can still be seen in many corners of Wales: the fortifications are more elaborate and more sophisticated, and consist of a series of curtain walls with towers and turrets and battlements and barbicans. The chambers of the keep have given way to more convenient apartments; these are scattered over the larger space enclosed within the walls of the inner and outer courtyards.

Beside the changing fashions of architecture there took place a corresponding change in furnishing and decoration. As in so many things, the Church led the way. First, sumptuous hangings were provided for the altar, for shrines, and for the walls of the greater churches. Then the windows (hitherto frequently open to wind and rain) began to be filled with glass, often exquisitely painted; then the more important inmates—bishops, monks, canons, and leading laymen—were provided with seats; and even, as the centuries passed, with cushions and carpets on which to kneel. All these things gradually made their way into palaces and great houses. Often they were provided more for magnificence than for comfort. In this period there were benches and tables for meals, thrones for kings, and a few stools; but chairs were rare, and chairs and beds, by our standards, exceedingly hard and uncomfortable.

In dress, especially ladies' dress, the Church strove to avoid setting the fashion, but it was not entirely successful. The twelfth century saw new standards of comfort and luxury in many things; notably in the use of furs by great ladies. An English Church council in 1138 had to forbid nuns the use of vair, gris (probably miniver), sable, marten, ermine, and beaver—and this is the first known mention of some of these articles in an English document. Fashions were shifting; standards of living were rising, and affecting even the religious Orders. Monastic reformers of this age laid a quite new stress on simplicity and austerity in clothing and food and comfort, and this was in part because these things were improving in the secular world. In earlier ages there had been little of comfort and luxury in the lay world for the monk to avoid.

Fashions of every kind often had their origin in France. They remind us that from 1066 England was ruled by a dynasty of Norman origin, that the English kings were usually lords of large dominions in France; that French was the language most commonly heard in castle and palace; and that England and the Continent were closely bound together.

The ideas of nationality and nationalism are linked in our minds today with our sense of loyalty. We all have many loyalties—to our family, to our friends, our town, to a host of other groups with which we may be connected in one way or another, and finally, to our country. This last loyalty is connected with the idea that there is something which sets all folk of British nationality apart, or rather ties them together; most of us assume the existence of this, even if we cannot analyse its nature. National frontiers are sometimes identical with natural geographical frontiers, like the shores of this island; sometimes with linguistic frontiers, like the Pyrenees or the boundaries of France and Germany. But it is very rare for all the possible factors which can contribute to a sense of nationality—geography, race, language, politics, religion and, above all, the sense of a common history—to meet together in any single nation. All these ingredients play their part; but the modern idea of nationalism is something which exists apart from these and in some ways overrides them. Nationalism of such an overpowering kind is a very recent thing; and with its rise in the last 150 years loyalty to state and nation has assumed a place in the hierarchy of our loyalties that it never claimed before. That is not to say that there was no sense of nationhood or Englishness in medieval England; but it was something quite different from what we mean by the word. Let us take a look at some of the elements—geography, language, and politics—and see where the difference lay.

Frontiers are troublesome things; they are always shifting, and sometimes an obvious 'natural frontier' is translated into a highway overnight. 'Natural frontiers' are of two kinds. First, there are barriers, boundaries either difficult to cross, like the Pyrenees or the Himalayas, or so obvious as to be a convenient line of demarcation to successive negotiators, like the great rivers of Europe or North America. The second kind of 'natural frontier' may include no barrier of any kind, but may represent the shift from one kind of country to another; say, from hill to valley or from chalk to clay. In the history of Europe the second kind has been of greater importance than the first. To a maritime people a sea or a river is a highway, not a frontier. Mountains have passes, and even elephants can be transported across the Alps. But for a people used to living in the hills to take to the plain, or a people used to cultivating light soil to take to heavy clay, is to change a whole way of life. The most stable frontier in the history of this island has been that between the lowland and the highland zone; very roughly, between land below and land above 600 feet. The lower land is usually suitable for large-scale intensive arable farming, especially in the heavy clay lands of the Midlands; the higher land only for dairy farming, sheep grazing and lighter, scattered arable farming, The boundary between the two is nowhere very precise, and has never very precisely conformed to the political frontiers of the country; but it is none the less important for that. The Romans divided their British provinces into two sections, the civil and the military; and the civil, with its centre in London, conformed pretty much to the lowland zone of the south-east. The Anglo-Saxon invaders were arable farmers, and liked heavy soils. They occupied the lowland zone more thoroughly than it had been occupied before, reclaiming large areas of land from the forest. The old British populations, in great measure excluded from the lowland zone, were happy to cultivate areas of the country with lighter soils; they had always avoided the heavy clay. The Celtic lands—Wales, Cumberland, and Scotland—lie wholly in the highland zone; the main core of England lies in the lowland zone. The frontiers between England and Wales and between England and Scotland were never settled in the period covered by this book; but this basic distinction between England and non-English Britain is fundamental to an understanding of the island's history. Compared with the distinction of lowland and highland, the English Channel was less a barrier than a highway. A barrier to some the Channel has always been; but in an age which knew no railways and when most roads were worse than anything we can readily imagine, water provided the main means of transport; and water transport, for an island, very largely meant sea and coastal transport. The Channel was never in the Middle Ages, in any profound sense, either a political or a cultural frontier. Our twelfth- and thirteenth-century kings held sway over large tracts of France and spent much of their time trying to govern and to extend them. Much was lost to the English kings in the thirteenth century; but they were never entirely excluded from French territory until the sixteenth century. From 1340 until 1802,[1] indeed, the official title of our monarchs, which appeared on every formal document issued in their name, was 'King of England and France'. They knew the difference between England and France, but at least until the late fifteenth century an English king crossing the Channel thought of himself as passing from one part of his dominions to another; and over much of the period between 1066 and 1272 a number of his leading subjects also held extensive properties on both sides of the water.

In some ways the role of the Irish Sea, and the long stretches of water which lie to the south and south-west of it right down to the Bay of Biscay, was more striking still. Throughout the Middle Ages this was the highway of a group of peoples with common traditions and a language basically one, yet never politically united. The shores of this great highway were peopled with all the Celtic peoples, the Irish, Scots, Welsh, and Bretons, who had a sense of unity among themselves based on common language, common traditions, and trade, which was very persistent in spite of the very different political allegiances which they owed.

Before 1272 England was invaded so many times that we have no possible means of counting the number of the invasions. It was invaded by a variety of prehistoric tribes and armies, by the Romans, by countless bands of Angles, Saxons, 'Jutes', Irish, Norse, Danes; and by the Normans and their confederates. Even 1066 is not the end of the story. The Norwegians came again, Henry II had invaded the country three times before he was recognised as king in 1154; when King John died in 1216 a French army was at large in the kingdom, and it was by no means clear whether the infant King Henry III or the Dauphin would succeed; quite possible that the French kings, who had already swallowed most of the Angevin [2] inheritance in France, would swallow England too.

The Roman invaders, the Norman Conquest, and the Angevin Empire remind us how often England was a part of a continental empire: a distant province of Rome; the most stable element in the diffuse empire of the Danish Cnut; the glittering prize of the Norman expansion of the late eleventh century; less than half of the great expanse of the Angevin Empire in the twelfth. These facts were the play of political circumstance; of deeper significance perhaps was the close relation between England and Europe in religion and civilisation. A history of

29

English art or religion from the seventh to the twelfth century which ignored Europe would be meaningless; and a history of the western, Catholic Church in the same period would be meaningless if it ignored England. Why did Henry III succeed and not the future Louis VIII? There were many reasons; one was that Henry was supported by an Italian cleric called Guala, who was without roots or connections or intimate friends in the country. But his word was none the less effective, because he was the pope's legate. England at this date was a papal fief.

The Channel was no frontier, but its influence was none the less crucial. It was between the accession of Alfred in 871 and the twelfth century that England achieved political unity and something like its present frontiers with Wales and Scotland. The foundations of this unity had been laid long before. The unity was based, as we have seen, on the geography and the soil of the lowland zone; 'England' conformed in great part to the civil provinces of the Romans; it represented the area over which the Anglo-Saxons found it congenial or possible to settle —hence its name, Angel-land. But if we look at the English kingdom at the height of its greatness under Henry II, we find a kingdom with its capital in London and a Church with its headquarters in Canterbury, both in the extreme south-east of the country. These things owe something to the Romans, who established the capital in London and built a network of great roads from London to the main cities of the kingdom—roads which were never effectively replaced until the eighteenth century. They owe something to the accidents of politics of the sixth century, which established St Augustine and the Roman mission in the kingdom of Kent. But Rome and the kingdom of Kent were very distant memories long before the Norman Conquest. The survival of the road system and the main network of towns on Roman lines—or rather their revival, because many had almost disappeared in the interval—was due in great measure to the recurrence of a situation similar to that which had given them birth. Norman England was not an outpost of a great empire; but it was ruled by a king as much at home in France as in England. The lowland zone in England lay opposite a lowland zone in northern France, and the exigencies of government and commerce made a system of towns and communications radiating from London once again natural and convenient.

The Channel was a key factor in English history as a centre

of communications. That it was far less of a barrier then than now will be apparent in many chapters of this book. Feudal institutions and social organisation of every kind, especially the 'manor', were the local expression of forms of organisation common to much of northern Europe. The castle was imported from the Continent, and so were many themes of our art and architecture. This does not mean that English art was purely derivative; in some ways the use the English made of their continental models, especially in Norman and Gothic architecture, was of crucial importance for continental development, and in the art of illuminating manuscripts the balance of trade was very often in England's favour. The Channel was one of the main arteries of Europe.

And yet there is a paradox in what has just been said. Can it really be true that the triumphs of modern science have done nothing to bring the Continent nearer to us? Speed and ease of communication have increased enormously, and it is now possible for a far higher proportion of the English population to visit the Continent than ever before. But there is something in the paradox none the less. It was partly that to a small proportion of the population England and the Continent really seemed to be less apart than they do today; and partly that for most of the population even England was a concept too vast to be grappled with. The man from the next village or the next shire was as foreign as a visitor from abroad. By such folk the existence of 'England' as a country or a nation was scarcely felt at all.

Medieval England was a country of villages, towns (most of them, by our standards, slightly swollen villages), castles, and monasteries—small communities living very much isolated from one another. Such communities entirely lacked modern means of communication. There was a certain compensation: news could travel remarkably fast and often quite accurately, as is observed today in backward countries. But this is only a slight qualification to the fact that most men's horizons would be bounded by the small group of villages which they knew personally. And if they did move, it was as easy to move by water as by land—if you were carrying heavy goods, far easier.

I have often tried to visualise what picture of England a man would have who had never seen a map. Maps, in the modern sense, were extremely rare and usually most inaccurate. They certainly formed no part of the mental equipment of most men

31

before the sixteenth and seventeenth centuries. It is hard to believe in something of which one can form no mental picture. One might acknowledge loyalty to distant potentates whom one had never seen—to king and pope; but the man living in West-minster or Rome meant little. In the later Middle Ages there were beginning to be some of those instruments of government which make us aware of government as an abstract thing, to be disliked, perhaps, but obeyed—organs of jurisdiction, taxation, and so forth of a permanent kind, the beginnings of bureau-cracy. It is this abstract conception of government to which we give the label 'the state'; and in this sense the state scarcely existed in England before the fourteenth century. Loyalty re-mained still at heart a personal matter, and few medieval monarchs really stirred the sense of loyalty of the majority of their subjects unless they were constantly travelling. Pageantry was tremendously important to the medieval king. It was the means by which he showed himself to his people; by which they became aware of him as a person to whom one could feel loyalty and allegiance. The pageantry itself expressed in sym-bolic language the power of the king and his relation to the people.

It is interesting to compare a medieval and a modern corona-tion. In ceremonial, in their symbolic significance, they are much alike. In recent years the similarities have been self-consciously fostered. But there are two profound differences. On the one hand, the medieval coronation was a symbol of actual power—of the divine blessing on a man who was himself going to exercise authority. On the other hand, the medieval audience was infinitely smaller. The second difference is really the less profound. Medieval England was not a democracy. The king had to reckon on the consent and co-operation of a large number of people—large, but not beyond counting; less, for example, than the number of voters in a modern constituency. A significant proportion of them could actually witness his coronation.

By constant pageantry an able monarch could become per-sonally known to a fair proportion of his subjects, to a large proportion of those who counted. But he never became the focus of loyalty which the monarch is today. Horizons were far narrower, local patriotisms more local, and sheer lack of communications made government, state, and nation far re-moter things. That is the negative side of the picture. To differentiate England from Europe presupposes a fairly sharp image of what England is and what Europe is. Neither existed in the minds of most medieval Englishmen.

Nor did a common language separate Englishmen from their neighbours on the Continent. The English language of today is a hybrid with many ancestors. Chiefly it is a mingling of one Germanic and one Romance language, of Old English or Anglo-Saxon and Norman French (or 'Anglo-Norman'). The arrival of Anglo-Norman was one of the many consequences of the Norman Conquest; but in the two centuries which followed, the languages were still distinct. Indeed, there were at least three languages currently spoken in England after the Conquest, excluding the Celtic tongues of Cornwall, Wales, and Scotland: English, Anglo-Norman, and Latin, the international language of the Church—at least three, because doubtless in the north and east the Scandinavian dialects of the Danes and Norse settlers still survived, though decreasingly. In 1100 a common tongue united the upper clergy of England and western Europe at large; a common tongue united the lay aristocracy of England and north-western France. These languages divided the upper classes from the great mass of the English people, who spoke their various dialects of English. Doubtless by this time many of the laity were bi-lingual and many of the clergy tri-lingual. But it is evident that language could not be a coherent factor in English nationalism. Between 1066 and 1272 Latin and French were the languages of the court, and the English kings could talk more easily with their French than with their English peasantry.

One possible ground of nationhood, and that a very powerful one, did exist, and was recognised by men of learning and reflection. Long before the birth of Alfred, Bede had written his *Ecclesiastical History of the English People*, one of the finest and most widely read of medieval histories. In Alfred's time the more modest, but equally significant *Anglo-Saxon Chronicle* was begun; copies were circulated, and these copies added to in various monasteries until after the Conquest. The eleventh and twelfth centuries saw a host of historical writers at work, some on national histories, some on world histories; but many of them revealing an intense patriotism. Most popular of these was the *History of the Kings of Britain* by Geoffrey of Monmouth (c. 1138). There is a nice ambiguity about this book,

ENGLAND
871 ~ 1066

Newcastle and Battle were founded
soon after 1066

Frontier unsettled

(Newcastle)
Durham

NORTHUMBRIA

Stamford Bridge
York
Fulford

Humber

Wirral
Doncaster
Eddisbury   Lincoln
Chester Bakewell
Derby   Nottingham

MERCIA
Tettenhall   Stamford
Leicester
Warwick   Northampton
Bedford

Offa's Dyke

St Albans   Hertford
LONDON   Maldon
Chippenham   Isle of Sheppey
Edington   Canterbury
Carhampton WESSEX The Weald Dover
Athelney   (Battle)
Porchester Hastings

since Britain and England are not, and were not, interchange-
able terms. It deals with a long line of kings starting many centuries B.C., passing via King Lear and King Arthur to the
seventh century A.D. Then it ceases. Were these British kings
meant to be the predecessors or the rivals of the kings of the
English? The problem is not made easier by the character of
the book. It was cleverly written, and almost everyone took it
seriously at the time; but in fact it was almost entirely fictitious.

The legend of King Arthur, which had formed the centre of
Geoffrey's book, became the common possession of western

34

European literature, much as the siege of Troy had been the common possession of the Greeks. In so far as it served a political end, it enhanced the prestige of the Anglo-Norman kings, Arthur's ultimate successors. It did little to draw together the English and the Welsh; but its fictions puffed up the English with a sense of the greatness of their past. Above all, its legends were used by the reigning dynasty to make itself a glittering reflection of Arthurian glory. This was done self-consciously by Edward I and Edward III, and again by the Tudors; and when an intelligent Italian historian in the reign of Henry VIII coolly observed that the whole story was nonsense, something very like national resentment was aroused.

There have been men in every age who understood something of the elements of nationality and their significance. Among other signs of this, the game of describing national characteristics was already well established. Then as now, much of it was crude. To English and Norman alike the Welsh and Scots were *barbari*, partly because they spoke a foreign language. An Englishman writing to a French friend said in fun, 'You know that their assiduity in drinking has made the English famous among the foreign nations'. And he goes on to state the age-long contrast between the French who drink wine and the English who drink beer. 'I however am fond of both wine and beer, and do not abhor any liquor that can make me drunk.' The friend to whom he wrote, a French monk with many English friends, felt moved on another occasion to draw a more sophisticated distinction between the races. In the eleven-seventies he became involved in a theological controversy on the Immaculate Conception of the Blessed Virgin, then a novel idea in the West, which was being strongly supported by a group of English monks. 'And so I come to your fantasies, alluring and attractive in their way, but quivering on a tenuous foundation; for whatever is not supported by the authority of Scripture is not soundly based. Do not be put off if Gallic maturity prove more soundly based than English levity. Your island is surrounded by water, and the inhabitants are not unnaturally affected by the qualities of that element, and by its constant movement drawn to the most slender and subtle fantasies, comparing, not to say preferring, their dreams to genuine visions. Can we blame their nature, the country being what it is? Certainly I know from experience that the English are more often dreamers than the French. In a damp climate the brain is swiftly caught up in vapours from the stomach—to be attributed to physical as much as spiritual causes . . . ; and what is so produced, and falls short of sound conviction, is properly called a fantasy or dream. My France is neither hollow nor watery after this fashion: there the mountains are made of stone, there iron is found, there the land is *terra firma*.' [3]

The word 'Europe', though it was known, was very little used in the Middle Ages. The nearest equivalent was 'Christendom', *Christianitas*. This expressed a sense of unity, even of community, based on religious and cultural bonds. It gave expression to the most potent factor in medieval unity and modern disunity, the religious factor. There is a sense in which all the English monarchs and many English nobles felt themselves to be members of a European rather than just of an English ruling class. In this they differed little, perhaps, from their descendants in more recent times, in the eighteenth and early nineteenth centuries. But far more powerful was the sense of common values, interests, language, and education which bound together the higher clergy of England and Europe.

Medieval society was fundamentally and ineradicably hierarchical, though the class structure was never rigid. One of its most fundamental divisions, indeed, was not horizontal at all, but vertical—the division between cleric and layman. We may simplify a complex picture by saying that there were four principal classes in medieval England: the upper clergy, the lower clergy, and the two classes of lay-folk, knights and nobles on the one hand, and yeomen and peasants on the other—those who fought and those who worked. The upper clergy were bishops, archdeacons, canons, and monks—and also the high civil servants. We might define them as the educated clergy. From the twelfth century on, the leading schools, later to become universities, were manned by and primarily designed for the upper clergy, and an increasing share of the Church's wealth was organised so as to be at their disposal. It was they who spoke and wrote the language of learning, Latin; and in whatever country they lived they represented the standards and values of the Catholic Church—or, as they themselves often called it, the Holy Roman Church—of western Christendom. The schools and universities were open to men of every nation, and scholars came and went freely between them. The English (or Anglo-Norman) Thomas Becket began his education at a grammar school in London, then studied at Auxerre, Paris, and Bologna;

and he visited Rome. In these centres he learned the theological doctrines of the time; and also something at least of canon law, the law of the Church. This revealed to him, as to countless thousands of other scholars of his day, the great structure of Church government, and the doctrines which both supported and depended on the primacy of the Roman see. He rose to prominence after his return to England in the service of Theobald, Archbishop of Canterbury, and then of the King, Henry II. For eight years he was a very faithful henchman and minister of Henry II; one of the architects of royal power. But after his elevation to the archbishopric of Canterbury in 1162, his early training and the clerical principles absorbed in his earlier career reasserted themselves. If it came to the point where he had to choose between his allegiance to the pope and his allegiance to the King, the strength of his clerical education, his vision of the churchman's first duty and first loyalty, overcame his loyalty to the King and his personal friendship with him. His murder in Canterbury Cathedral in 1170 summed up in extreme form all the various tensions which could exist between layman and cleric. Most people agreed in principle that it was the duty of the twin authorities of Church and state to co-operate in doing God's work on earth; but on the precise limits of the two authorities there was a good deal of disagreement. And when difficulties arose they were made worse by the social cleavage of clerical and lay, between the upper clergy with their very elaborate education and sophisticated theological and legal learning, and the lay aristocracy, uneducated or half-educated at best in the sense in which we use the term, bred for the arts of war and (in a rudimentary way) of government. To them allegiance to the king had a religious aura all the more deeply felt for being allegiance to a man they all knew and could see. The authority of the pope they acknowledged; but it was a remote loyalty for most of them, and it seemed like treachery if it were invoked as an excuse for not obeying the king. Under certain circumstances the nobles were themselves prepared to break their fealty to the king—it was part of the feudal code that under certain circumstances they might—but they were not prepared for anyone else to disobey him. On occasion the tension between clerical and lay assumed something of the problem of a colour bar, of two races within one kingdom; but with this difference, that layman and cleric came from the same homes, that each had brothers and cousins in the

37

other camp; that social disputes, when they arose, were fought out against a background of personal intimacy between many individuals of the two groups. In the end we must not overstress the conflicts between clergy and laity or between royal and papal authority. The conflicts are famous and fill a large place in our history books; but they were always the exception, and most of the time kings, popes, and bishops agreed to co-operate or agreed to differ.

These divergences of interest and background between laymen and churchmen provided perhaps the most striking qualification to local separatism or nascent nationalism in medieval Europe. They are, in a sense, the keynote of the Middle Ages. When they cease to be more fundamental than the difference between Englishman, Frenchman, and German, when government and literature come to be conducted in the vernacular, then we know that the Middle Ages are on the way out. This characteristic of medieval society arose out of the way in which the Middle Ages came to birth. In the break-up of the Roman Empire the tenets and standards of the Christian faith, and with them something of the learning of the ancient world, were preserved by churchmen in an increasingly barbarian and barbarised Europe; and in such a world it was inevitable that education and the standards of Christian life and thought should become a specialised possession. The great achievement of the Church in the early Middle Ages was to preserve the faith and something of the civilisation of the Christian Roman Empire, and to convert the barbarian peoples to Christianity. In the ninth and tenth centuries this work was still very actively in progress. The cultural inheritance was still precarious; with the Danes in occupation of large areas of the country, the English Church became once again a missionary church. By the twelfth and thirteenth centuries all this was over. Medieval civilisation had staked its claim to what it could absorb of ancient culture; a great medieval revival of learning had taken place. The Danes, too, had been converted, both in England and in Denmark. Almost every corner of Europe was nominally Christian. To the east lay the world of the Byzantine (Eastern Orthodox) Churches, now usually out of communion with Rome, and the great expanse of Islam. But in western Europe, however kings and popes might dispute, the Catholic faith was a secure possession; and in England, before the fourteenth century, the outbreaks of heresy were no great matter.

This background of assured faith is commonly taken to be the supreme characteristic of England and Europe in the Middle Ages. Faith, indeed, did not preclude inquiry. The most characteristic activity of the educated clergy of the later Middle Ages was the application of reason and logic to the investigation of the faith. The logical and metaphysical systems which they produced were among the maturest fruits of medieval culture; and however we regard them, we cannot but admire the toughness and subtlety of mind of these great technicians who taught Europe how to think, or rather, re-taught her, because their work was made possible by the rediscovery of ancient Greek thought, enriched by the systematic efforts of the leading Arab (and Jewish) thinkers of the preceding centuries to adapt Aristotle to the special needs of a religion of Semitic origin. But our present concern is with the world of ordinary attitudes and assumptions, rather than with the more rarefied speculations of the schools. The scholastic systems were *tours de force* of abstract thinking. Abstract thought was alien to most men; they expressed their thoughts in concrete symbols.

In a modern Roman Catholic church the most important and the most sacred object present is the tabernacle and its contents, the Reserved Sacrament. In the period covered by this book the sacrament was sometimes reserved; God was always supreme among the inmates of his churches; the celebration of the Eucharist, the Mass—the re-creation, by symbolic act, of his Body and Blood—was always the central event of the church's day. But the most conspicuous objects in the church were more commonly connected with its other most distinguished occupant, the saint to whom it was dedicated. This is especially true of the eleventh, twelfth, and thirteenth centuries. In a church of any size a shrine would be built to house the relics of the saint behind the high altar. In numberless churches a solemn 'translation' of the relics to a new shrine took place in this period. If the relics were substantial, the shrine might well become a centre of pilgrimage—and a source of great prestige and prosperity to its possessors, as was the shrine of St Thomas Becket at Canterbury.

The Eucharist itself was the supreme symbol; the symbol of God himself, and of the whole drama of the Passion. The cult of relics reflected the belief that spiritual power was symbolised, mediated on earth in concrete physical objects. There were numerous cases in which one of the great saints of the Church was eclipsed as patron of a particular cathedral, abbey, or parish church by a lesser man, simply because the church was more amply provided with the supplanter's remains. The saint whose presence the relics symbolised was very much alive. He owned the church; its head—be he bishop, abbot, or rector—acted as his representative. On occasion the saint found it necessary to intervene, to help the pilgrims who came to his shrine, to heal the sick, to comfort the oppressed, to destroy the oppressor. In a parish, the patron saint was the most important person in the village; a sort of super-squire. His house, and the house which God himself was to visit, was not unnaturally the most magnificent building in the village. But the saint was not the only supernatural resident; the devil had his representatives too. The supernatural was close at hand in countless forms, not all of them pleasant.

There was very little science in the Middle Ages, in our sense of the word. The later scholastics provided the necessary intellectual apparatus for the beginnings of empirical inquiry; some quite elaborate machines (like clockwork) were brought in from the East in the later Middle Ages; some new ones were developed. But the world of ideas was radically unsuited to scientific inquiry as we understand it. Science proceeds by the application of scepticism—of disbelief in the accepted explanation of some natural phenomenon. To the man of science and to modern man in general, an event, however old, is presumed to have a natural or scientific explanation until proved otherwise. This does not necessarily involve a total disbelief in miracles; but most of us agree not to call a thing a miracle until we have exhausted the possibilities of giving it a 'natural' explanation. The medieval attitude was quite opposed to this. There were not lacking those who applied critical principles to the investigation of miracles. In 1100 William Rufus was buried under the tower of Winchester Cathedral; in 1101 the tower collapsed. 'I forbear to tell the opinions which were held on this event,' said William of Malmesbury, 'lest I seem to believe in trifles—especially since it could have collapsed in any case, even if he had not been buried there, because it was badly built.' But on the whole, medieval man preferred to give an event a supernatural explanation if he possibly could. He went about looking for events to which a supernatural explanation could be given. We may think this excessively credulous, and no doubt there was much credulity and superstition in the

40

Middle Ages. But he was encumbered with a view of the 'natural' world so absurd and improbable that his pursuit of the marvellous was not so irrational as it may sound. Whatever the explanation, medieval books of miracles are full of stories which we should never think of calling miraculous—strange coincidences, striking dreams—and so forth—as well as stories which we cannot pretend to understand or explain.

'In the region of Chiusa (in Italy) there is a kind of wine which is particularly red, like blood; and this wine is used for mass in preference to white, lest white wine be confused with water, which is easily done, and water offered instead. This red wine has the property of staining linen so that it can in no wise be washed out.' Thus opens the pathetic story of the young clerk who spilled wine on the corporal and was filled with panic; then, seeing no way to clean the cloth or undo the damage, he prayed with special fervour to the Blessed Virgin, and the stain disappeared.[4] It is a trivial story, as many miracle stories were not; but otherwise wholly characteristic.

What had Chiusa to do with England? The author of this story, the young clerk himself, was called Anselm; he was a nephew of St Anselm of Aosta and Bec, the second Archbishop of Canterbury after the Norman Conquest (1093–1109). The younger Anselm followed his uncle to England, and became abbot of Bury St Edmunds. The uncle was one of the great figures of the medieval church: monk and scholastic, a profound theologian and devotional writer, before circumstances made him an ecclesiastical statesman. In a more humble way the nephew was a more typical product of his age. Though an Italian and a cosmopolitan churchman, he quickly absorbed many English traditions. In writing down the *Miracles of the Virgin*, he was engaged in an activity especially characteristic of English churchmen at this time. In championing, as he did in later life, the Immaculate Conception, he was engaged in an activity which our French monk regarded as a natural aberration of the foggy-minded English.

Many morals can be drawn from the study of the two Anselms. He who wishes to emphasise the lofty nature of Christian theology and devotion in this period can find much comfort in the uncle. He who wishes to emphasise the growth of 'Mariolatry' can find many texts in the writings of the nephew. The Immaculate Conception was at this date a local English devotion. No-one could find nascent Protestantism

41

in that. But the way in which it was fostered in spite of the Norman Conquest and then spread abroad by cosmopolitan churchmen shows that local traditions could prosper; it also shows, as does every detail of the career of both nephew and uncle, how cosmopolitan the Church was becoming in the late eleventh and twelfth centuries.

1. Except between 1360 and 1369.
2. See p. 196, n. 3.
3. Cf. R. W. Southern in *Mediaeval and Renaissance Studies*, IV (1958), pp. 204–5.
4. *Ibid*, pp. 190–1.

CHAPTER TWO

THE REIGN OF ALFRED

(1) ENGLAND IN THE NINTH CENTURY

Alfred is commonly thought of today as a great pioneer: a man who planned many aspects of a united English kingdom, although he did not live to see his plans completed. But to contemporaries he must often have appeared more like the last heir of a doomed kingdom, a man struggling to save something from the kingdom of Egbert and the inheritance of the Anglo-Saxon monarchs of the eighth century.

By 871 most of the old-established English kingdoms had collapsed. Hitherto England had been divided into a number of kingdoms—tradition says seven, that England had been a 'heptarchy'; but it is impossible to point to any period in which there were precisely seven kingdoms in the land; and the word 'heptarchy' suggests a division of the country far tidier than ever existed in the centuries following the departure of the Romans and the Anglo-Saxon conquest. Over the three and a half centuries preceding 871 the fortunes of the country had mainly depended on the heads of three confederations, of the Northumbrians, the Mercians, and the West Saxons. Each in turn had held hegemony in England—Northumbria in the seventh century, Mercia in the eighth; last of all Wessex, for a short space under King Egbert, had been recognised as the first kingdom in the country. But within thirty years of Egbert's death the other kingdoms had been overwhelmed by Viking hosts: Kent and East Anglia were Danish bases, Northumbria on the verge of becoming a Norse kingdom, Mercia divided between the Danes and English, with the English kingdom reduced to a mere satellite.

The first mention of Viking raids on this country is in 789; but it was not until the later years of Egbert, King of Wessex, who died in 839, that they became frequent. From then on the tale of attack and disaster is continuous. The movements of heathen hosts—of Danes and Norsemen—is the constant theme of the *Anglo-Saxon Chronicle*. In 843 'King Aethelwulf

[Egbert's son] fought at Carhampton against thirty-five ships' companies, and the Danes had possession of the place of slaughter'; in 855 'the heathen for the first time wintered in Sheppey'; in 865 'Ethelred [Aethelwulf's third son] succeeded to the kingdom of Wessex. And this same year came a great host to England and took winter-quarters in East Anglia.' In 866 the host moved into Northumbria, in 867 into Mercia; 'and Burhred, king of Mercia, and his councillors begged Ethelred, king of Wessex, and his brother Alfred to help them fight against the host.' The two brothers came into Mercia the next year, but without decisive result, and 870 saw desperate fighting in Wessex itself. Three major engagements failed to give the West Saxon leaders an advantage, and after a series of minor conflicts they were compelled to make their peace with the host. It was in these circumstances that King Ethelred died, and his brother, Alfred, succeeded to the throne (871).

In spite of the great energy with which Wessex was being defended in this year, it might have seemed only a matter of time before this kingdom, too, succumbed. The events of the following years could only confirm this impression; and in 878 'the [Danish] host went secretly in midwinter [when Alfred and his followers felt secure from attack] after Twelfth Night to Chippenham, and rode over Wessex and occupied it, and drove a great part of the inhabitants oversea, and reduced the greater part of the rest, except Alfred the king; and he with a small company moved under difficulties through woods and into inaccessible places in marshes.'[1]

878 proved not to be the end of English history, but, in a way, its beginning; and it is our business in this chapter to understand how this could be. When Alfred died twenty-one years later, his kingdom was still precarious; the Danes far from subdued. But Wessex was more settled, more powerful than when Alfred succeeded to the throne; he was the acknow-ledged leader of the English survivors throughout the south and west of the country; he had shown that Vikings could be defeated, and even baptised. The creation of a united kingdom of England was begun by Alfred's successors, and not fully achieved before the eleventh century; but many essential foundations had been laid. Much of this was due to the unique personality of Alfred. But he was helped by some of the tendencies of the situation; and also, paradoxically, by the Danes themselves.

44

The Danes were farmers and pirates. Like many pirates, they became in course of time great traders. But it is a mistake to think of Alfred's opponents as traders in any orthodox sense. They valued the things which merchants valued—money, gold (which was very scarce at this time), silver in any form, and all the materials which went to make a man wealthy and proved him to be so. It is clear that the population of the Scandinavian countries was growing in these years; and that their own lands were becoming insufficient to support these peoples by the elementary agriculture and fishing on which they had hitherto depended. But 'land-hunger' can be only a part of the explanation of the rapidity with which they spread all over northern and western Europe, raiding, settling, forming principalities in Russia, northern France, the British islands, and ultimately in Iceland and Greenland; even (in all probability) visiting North America. The deeper explanation of these extraordinary movements lies in the social organisation and the social ideals and aspirations of the Viking peoples. By custom and training they enjoyed adventure, travel, and war; and their upper classes had learned to live by plunder. When on the move they were organised by war bands, with the ship's company as the basic unit. The leaders of companies and hosts had to reward their followers with lavish gifts; and yet to retain still greater wealth in their own hands. The splendour of their armour and their halls, and the ornaments and jewellery with which they could adorn their wives and daughters, were the symbols of their greatness. A man who failed in generosity or became impoverished was lost. Small wonder that it is in the Scandinavian homeland and the Baltic islands that the most wonderful finds of silver coins and silver ornaments of this period have been discovered. They come from the Arab world, from Byzantium, from many parts of Europe, and from England.

The bulk of this wealth was acquired by tribute and by loot. The Viking leaders valued above all a rich country which could be plundered year after year; the raids gave their men exercise, occupied them in their proper and favourite pursuits, and provided for both men and leaders generous pay at no cost to either. A really sophisticated pirate is deeply concerned for the welfare of the trade on which he preys. But pirates are rarely sophisticated, and loot and plunder seem to have been the only concern of the Danes at this time. None the less, they were not out for a speedy conquest of the whole country. For decades they came as raiders and plunderers, and it was only slowly that they conceived the idea of settling. When the host first wintered in Kent and East Anglia, it settled in old fortified places, which it used merely as bases for long-distance plundering in the winter. It was natural that prolonged acquaintance with the country should suggest to the Danes other ways of exploiting it; the decline of its wealth was bound sooner or later to force them to more creative activities, or to abandon the country altogether; and the breakdown of authority tempted the Danish leaders to replace the old monarchs with themselves. The Danish invasions of the ninth century thus passed through many phases. They started as occasional plundering raids. Then large hosts established themselves under kings and jarls (earls) on a more permanent footing. Finally these hosts began to settle in various parts of the country, and the leaders took to rewarding their followers with land as well as loot. In Yorkshire, Lincolnshire, and the north-east Midlands hundreds of place-names deriving from Old Danish roots show us where the Danish peasantry settled thickly at this time; the English had lived in hams and tuns (our 'homes' and 'towns'), the Danes colonised bys and thorpes. Among the Vikings in England Danes were in the majority; in Ireland, Scotland, and the Western Isles, Norwegians. But in the north of England the two met and mingled. The north-west is thickly studded with Norse place-names, from Irby, Thingwall, and others in the Wirral peninsula up to the gills, fells, and thwaites of Cumberland.[2] East Lancashire and Yorkshire were more Danish than Norse, though the kings of York were sometimes Norwegian (i.e. Norse from Ireland), and the links between the two peoples were close.

It was only slowly, then, that the Vikings conceived the idea of replacing the native dynasties with their own kings; and only sporadically that they tried to replace existing systems of government with their own institutions. The slow transition gave the kingdom of Wessex a breathing-space; it also gave the leaders of Wessex time to prepare against the challenge of the Danish attack. In these two ways Alfred was helped by the habits of the Vikings to take advantage of what survived of his inheritance in Wessex.

His inheritance consisted, first of all, of a society, of human material moulded by the ancient custom of the English. There were many signs of what we should call civilisation in English

46

life in the eighth and early ninth centuries. The Christian conversion had struck deep roots; with it had come a renaissance of art; literature and learning (after the fashion of the Dark Ages) had flourished in Northumbria in the days of Bede and in the country at large in the mid and late eighth century. More superficial were the traces of a money economy, of permanent markets, of literate government. All these things were to recover and develop during the period covered by this book beyond what anyone could have imagined in the ninth century. Nor were the Anglo-Saxons or Vikings savages: both had lived for centuries in some kind of contact with civilised peoples and civilised standards, and were not unaffected by them. But all this does not alter the fact that English society in the eighth and ninth centuries knew little of what we should call civilisation; that the lay aristocracy consisted of fundamentally barbarian warriors who did not differ greatly from their Viking enemies in aspirations, in methods of war, and way of life.

The qualities of Anglo-Saxon lay society are revealed to us more clearly than those of any other Teutonic people of the period, owing to the survival of a quite large quantity of Old English literature—of poems written to be sung to the harp in the great halls of the English warriors; the staple of entertainment in the early Middle Ages, and, more than that, a vital form of education, moulding the tastes and ideals of generations of warriors. The lay upper classes were illiterate; that is to say, they had no education as we understand the term. But they were brought up to a knowledge of the traditional crafts of their class—the arts of war, justice, and government, hunting and hawking; and their outlook was moulded by the heroic lays of the minstrels. The best known of these poems is an epic, *Beowulf*, probably of the eighth century. *Beowulf* must be read and re-read by anyone who wishes to understand Old English society: it is full of insights into the minds of our ancestors, insights of a kind normally very difficult to obtain. In one way it is probably untypical. Most of the early lays and epics were tales of blood feud and human glory; blood and thunder stories of war and plunder and revenge. *Beowulf* is the work of a Christian cleric determined to point a moral: blood feuds are kept well in the background, and Beowulf slaughters dragons and not men—indeed, it is specifically noted that Beowulf's own people were astonished at his prowess, because

47

he had none of the previous record of slaughter which usually preluded a glorious career.

But if the author of *Beowulf* has attempted to suppress the more barbarous elements in such stories, he none the less makes Beowulf display very clearly the proper heroic qualities courage and prowess in war, and loyalty—loyalty to his kin, loyalty to his chief, and loyalty and generosity to his followers; and after Beowulf has become king he maintains justice and the rights and privileges of his people. Here we are shown the characteristics of Anglo-Saxon society at its best. It is a society in which kinship and personal loyalty are the principal bonds. It is an aristocratic society: above the clans of kindred are the tribal chiefs and the kings; and every chief and every king is surrounded by a company of followers, the 'following' or *comitatus*. This crucial institution in all Germanic peoples meets us in the first century A.D. in the *Germania* of Tacitus, meets us in the military following of barbarian leaders in the fifth and sixth centuries, in royal and princely courts of the seventh, eighth, and ninth; meets us again in the knights of a feudal lord in the tenth and eleventh centuries, and in the knights of the Round Table as they were described in the twelfth. Followers were drawn from a number of sources, from the chief's own kin, from the leading warriors of his land, and from other tribes or kingdoms: it was a common practice for kings and nobles to send their younger sons to the courts of neighbouring princes to be brought up and to learn the art of war and the skills of a warrior. These followers gave their chief unstinted support in his enterprises, and in return he asked their advice, protected them and kept them. It was a similar relationship which compelled the Viking leader to shower gifts upon his followers; and even in the more settled Anglo-Saxon courts gifts were still vitally important, although the followers of an Anglo-Saxon lord expected first and foremost a landed estate.

There are in *Beowulf* two common synonyms for a king— 'the giver of treasure' or 'the lord of rings'. In the poem, the treasure consists of gold cups and gold ornaments; the rings are golden rings. But there was very little gold in eighth century England. In this as in other respects there is an archaic flavour about the poem: it holds up the past as a mirror to the present. And since it was already about a century old before Alfred was born, it may seem to have little bearing on the relations of

48

Alfred and his followers. But for two reasons this is not so. First of all, it is the representative of an oral literature which changed comparatively little over the generations. Alfred was apparently brought up on just such heroic stories, although we cannot tell if he knew *Beowulf* itself. 'He listened attentively to Saxon poems day and night,' writes his biographer, 'and hearing them often recited by others committed them to his retentive memory.' Although his taste in literature developed and matured, he never lost his fondness for the heroic lays of his own people. Furthermore, the minstrels were still busy composing their own versions of this kind of poem, and some of the meagre survivors from the ninth and tenth centuries reveal that the same emotions and qualities were preserved in them as appear in *Beowulf*. Finest of all is the poem on the battle of Maldon, which describes very movingly the last stand of an English leader against the Danes. The incident took place much later than Alfred's time, in the second wave of Danish invasions at the end of the tenth century; Ealdorman (or earl) Brihtnoth fell in 991. Thus the poem serves to show the continuity in the ideals of English warriors. It is very short. It opens with an account of the preparation for the fight; it tells how Brihtnoth deployed his men: 'he rode and gave counsel and taught his warriors how they should stand and keep their ground, bade them hold their shields aright, firm with their hands and fear not at all. When he had meetly arrayed his host, he alighted among the people where it pleased him best, where he knew his bodyguard to be most loyal.

'Then the messenger of the Vikings stood on the bank, he called sternly, uttered words, boastfully speaking the seafarers' message to the earl, as he stood on the shore. "Bold seamen have sent me to you, and bade me say, that it is for you to send treasure quickly in return for peace, and it will be better for you all that you buy off an attack with tribute, rather than that men so fierce as we should give you battle. There is no need that we destroy each other, if you are rich enough for this. In return for the gold we are ready to make a truce with you. If you who are richest determine to redeem your people, and to give to the seamen on their own terms wealth to win their friendship and make peace with us, we will betake us to our ships with the treasure, put to sea and keep faith with you."

'Brihtnoth lifted up his voice, grasped his shield and shook his supple spear, gave forth words, angry and resolute, and

49

made his answer: "Hear you, sea-rover, what this folk says? For tribute they will give you spears, poisoned points and ancient sword, such war gear as will profit you little in the battle. Messenger of the seamen, take back a message, say to your people a far less pleasing tale, how that there stands here with his troop an earl of unstained renown, who is ready to guard this realm, the home of Ethelred my lord [the King], people and land; it is the heathen that shall fall in the battle. It seems to me too poor a thing that you should go with our treasure unfought to your ships, now that you have made your way thus far into our land. Not so easily shall you win tribute; peace must be made with point and edge, with grim battle-play, before we give tribute."

'Then he bade the warriors advance, bearing their shields, until they all stood on the river bank.' There the two armies waited as the tide went out and left them dry land on which to fight. For all their heroism, the English company was defeated and their leader killed.

'Brihtwold spoke and grasped his shield (he was an old companion [follower]); he shook his ash-wood spear and exhorted the men right boldly: "Thoughts must be the braver, heart more valiant, courage the greater as our strength grows less. Here lies our lord, all cut down, the hero in the dust. Long may he mourn who thinks now to turn from the battle-play. I am old in years; I will not leave the field, but think to lie by my lord's side, by the man I held so dear."' Another member of the following also encourages them to battle, leads his men against the Vikings, falls in the strife; and there, as suddenly as it began, the poem ends.

The old follower's speech is one of the most moving things in Anglo-Saxon literature; it also catches to perfection the finest spirit of the German heroic lay—courage in defeat. This was no doubt the theme of many of the Saxon songs which Alfred learned by heart; and it was this element in the tradition of the English warrior families which enabled them in the end to react so powerfully to the Danish challenge.

But the warrior aristocracy was itself only one element in English society, and not the only one which played its part in King Alfred's success. His armies were partly manned by peasants; and in any case, as Alfred himself said, a king needed 'men who pray, and soldiers and workmen'. It is time to look at those who prayed and those who worked.

50

The conversion of the English had been accomplished in the seventh and early eighth centuries; from then on, England was a nominally Christian country, even if some of the missionary work had to be done again after the coming of the Danes. With Christianity came literacy, at least for the small band of educated clergy. In the Byzantine Empire in this period, and especially in the capital, Constantinople—incomparably the greatest centre of culture and learning in the Christian world before the twelfth century—literacy was widespread among laymen as well as among the clergy. In contrast, there existed throughout western Christendom a sharp distinction between the literate, educated, Latin-speaking clergy and the lay aristocracy, illiterate, bred for war. The upper clergy were at once the mediators of the Christian tradition and of the learning and civilised standards of the ancient world. They were usually very few in number, and partly for that reason their standards of learning were precarious. Learning and the knowledge of Latin liteature rose and fell in the early Middle Ages with astonishing rapidity, largely because they depended on a small number of good teachers and their pupils. In the days of Bede and Alcuin, in the eighth century, England was famous for its learned men. But there is no reason to think that Alfred was exaggerating much when he said of his own youth: 'So completely had learning decayed in England that there were very few men on this side of the Humber who could apprehend their [Latin] services in English or even translate a letter from Latin into English, and I think that there were not many beyond the Humber. There were so few of them that I cannot even recollect a single one south of the Thames when I succeeded to the kingdom.' The upper clergy were few, and the educated clergy almost non-existent.

Who were the upper clergy? In the last chapter I defined them as bishops, archdeacons, canons, and monks; and distinguished them from the lower clergy, the parish priests, most of whom were socially and economically much less privileged, often of peasant stock and semi-literate at best. This general picture is true of the period after the Conquest; for the ninth century it needs two major qualifications. Before the Conquest the upper clergy were small in numbers. The staffs of bishops and cathedrals were usually modest compared with what they later became; no hierarchy of officials separated the bishop from the parish clergy—there was no-one comparable to the later archdeacon or rural dean. In 1066 there were well under 1,000 monks. In Alfred's time the figures must be scaled down still further. Outside the small and struggling community he himself established at Athelney, there were no monks at all— no monks, that is, in the formal sense of men living in community according to a monastic rule. On paper there were about sixteen bishoprics. Of these, at the time of Alfred's death, four or five were in places occupied by the Danes and had long been vacant; two (Dunwich in Suffolk, later surrendered to the sea, and Leicester, revived only in very modern times) were allowed to lapse. The rest reappeared in the course of the tenth century. How active the remaining cathedrals were we have little means of knowing; but they were certainly not centres of vigorous intellectual or religious life. The disappearance of most of the old monasteries meant that the libraries, on whose shelves books might survive for centuries, even if no-one read them, were tending to be lost. The future of learning in England depended on a thin trickle of tradition, or on the chance of a great patron appearing who could restore links with the scholars and the libraries of Europe. The only gleams of light in the island at the beginning of Alfred's reign were the frequent visits of Irish scholars to the court of Gwynedd in North Wales, and their journeys through England on their way to the Continent; and it was to Wales and Ireland—whose schools still retained much of their ancient tradition of learning —as well as to the Continent that Alfred looked when he tried to revive English schools and libraries.

Compared with later times, the lower clergy were also few. The parish system was only beginning to be formed. Christianity had originally been a religion of the town, based on the cities of the Roman Empire; and it was slow to accommodate itself to the needs of the village-dwelling peoples. At first the cathedral clergy were the clergy of the diocese; then other large churches, 'minsters', were built, where small communities of clerks could live and serve the needs of a large area. This might suit a missionary church, but was a makeshift in a settled Christian country. And so local lords and the leading men of the villages laid out the money to build churches, and paid their tithes for the support of priests. Gradually the parish system spread about the country. Even by the Norman Conquest it was far from complete, especially in the north and west. In Alfred's day the parish church was far from being the common sight it later became; and in the areas occupied by the Danes, it must have been virtually unknown. Paradoxically, it is precisely in the Danelaw that churches were built most rapidly in the tenth century; and partly for this reason, partly on account of the availability of stone for building, Lincolnshire and Northamptonshire have more visible traces of Saxon architecture than any other county. The English Church was weak; the English monarchs therefore possessed very few tools for creating even the first beginnings of literate government.

About the great mass of the English peasantry, 'those who work', we are singularly ill-informed. A few glimpses reveal to us a peasantry divided into *geneatas, cotsetlan*, and *geburas*; and in Domesday Book (1086) we are given a rich vocabulary of peasant groups. The *gebur* was the normal peasant of early medieval society, much like the Roman *colonus* or the later villein in status; provided with a plot of land on which he and his family could maintain a living, though sometimes a meagre one, in return for services often very burdensome; personally free, but often tied to the land he held. The *cotsetla* was a cottager, with or without a small holding of land; a man whose livelihood could not entirely depend on what he grew, but must expect some supplement from wages earned by occasional or regular labour on other men's estates. The *geneat* was the aristocrat of the Anglo-Saxon peasantry; the 'free man' or 'sokeman' of Domesday Book or even something more. He was sometimes a substantial small farmer. The boundary between him and the *gesith* or *thegn*, the lord or the lord's companion, was not always very great or impassable.

The *gebur* was personally free: he could not be bought and sold; he lived on his own plot of land. But there were also in eleventh-century England large numbers of slaves—25,000 of them are recorded in Domesday Book. The number was declining: the freeing of slaves was a work of mercy, and the *gebur* or villein suited the farming ideas of the Norman lords better than did the slave. The slaves performed the function later carried out by the wage-labourer, and one reason for their disappearance was that the increasing use of money in late Saxon and early Norman times meant that it was easier for a lord to pay for labour when he wanted it than to feed and care for a team of slaves in and out of season. But throughout Saxon times the slaves must have been a familiar sight in many

English villages; and even in the late eleventh century it required a special mission to Bristol by the Bishop of Worcester, St Wulfstan, to suppress the trading of English slaves to Ireland.

(2) 878–99

At the end of March 878 Alfred and his following established themselves in a secret base among the marshes of Somerset, at Athelney; and from there resistance was planned. Alfred summoned the 'fyrd' or militia of Somerset, Wiltshire, and western Hampshire—that part of Wessex with which he could still keep in touch—to be ready for a rapid attack on the Danes early in May. And with these forces he fell on the Danes at Edington, pursued them to their camp, and after a fortnight's siege compelled them to surrender. Three weeks later the Danish king, Guthrum, and thirty of his leading followers were baptised in Alfred's presence.

Decisive as was the battle of Edington in saving Wessex from total destruction, it did not lead to any lasting peace. In the mid eight-eighties war was renewed, and this time Alfred had the opportunity to take the initiative. In 886 he captured London, and put it in charge of his close ally, Ethelred, Ealdorman of the Mercians, who shortly after married Alfred's daughter, Aethelflaed. Soon after 886 another truce was made between Alfred and Guthrum, which established a temporary frontier between English and Danish England. It divided the lowland zone into two, by drawing a line along the Thames from its mouth, skirting north of London, then running northwest to Bedford, and so along Watling Street (now the A5) to the Welsh border. But it did not lead to peace. From 892 to 896 a new Danish army was at large in England; and throughout the last decade of Alfred's reign there was the threat of raids from the Danish kingdom of York.

Alfred was never free from wars or rumours of wars. But in the last ten years of his life he was able to reorganise the English defences and establish a military organisation which saved the country from a repetition of the disastrous winter of 877-8, prepared the way for the successes of Edward the Elder and Athelstan, Alfred's son and grandson, and in some respects provided the model on which another distinguished Saxon, Henry the Fowler, repaired the defences of German Saxony against the Magyars a generation later.

The Danes had the great advantage that they were highly mobile, could move great distances by sea, and very frequently achieved surprise. Alfred was concerned to meet them on their own terms. First of all, he built ships, large and swift, 'neither after the Frisian design nor after the Danish, but as it seemed to himself that they could be most serviceable'. The interest Alfred took in designing the ships is characteristic of his restless inquiring mind and searching imagination, and also reveals the attention to detail of the fine administrator. But the Danes were not only mobile by sea. Their armies were always in being, and could be swiftly mobilised. The disaster in 877–8 had occurred because the English militia took so long to mobilise. Alfred simplified its organisation and divided it, so that manpower was available to supply the militia, man the fortresses, and till the soil at the same time. Hitherto the militia, the 'fyrd', had been exceedingly reluctant to remain under arms for more than a short campaign, or to move any distance. This division meant that their work at home was not totally neglected, although we do not know how the arrangement worked in detail. A large, and perhaps increasing, part of the English army consisted of nobles and their retinues, the more permanent military class, the thegns and their followers. A division of the thegns similar to that of the fyrd made longer campaigns possible for them too.

The militia was not a new instrument, but an old royal right reorganised. Another public obligation developed by Alfred was that of building and repairing fortresses—a duty incumbent on almost all holders of land. Alfred in fact began, and Edward the Elder completed, the construction of a national network of fortifications. By the early tenth century no village in Sussex, Surrey, or Wessex was more than twenty miles from one of these fortresses. They provided defence in depth against an enemy who might come from any direction—from land or sea; and they provided refuge for men and cattle against an enemy whose chief motive was plunder. The fortresses were normally large enclosures, walled towns rather than castles; and many of them were sited in, or later became, towns. Indeed, the building of the *burghs* (our 'boroughs') by Alfred and his son marked an important stage in the recovery of English towns and so in the long run of trade and economic life generally.

Alfred's achievement in saving Wessex from the Danes and

laying its defences on a more stable base was remarkable enough. What is even more remarkable is that in the brief intervals of war and defence he showed so much concern for the general welfare and for every aspect of the life of the kingdom whose very existence still lay in the balance. He had a vision of a kingdom more stable, more peaceful, and more civilised than anything he could hope to live to see. These points are remarkably illustrated by his *Laws* and his translations.

The written laws of Anglo-Saxon kings were not comprehensive codes. The main body of the law was customary and unwritten. When custom had to be altered, or clarified, or emphasised, it might be put in writing. The result is that the law-books from the time of King Ethelbert of Kent to King Cnut are at once very particular and precise and very fragmentary. It appears that Alfred, in issuing his code, was reviving a custom which had not been exercised for a century. During this period law-making as a royal right disappeared in the French kingdom; the revival in England under Alfred may have saved it from a similar oblivion.

Human law was felt to be a reflection of divine law. Alfred had the conviction that the divine law was the source of first principles; and that the Bible, which contained the divine law, might provide texts of more particular application too. Alfred's laws have a long introduction attempting to tie English law on to Biblical (Mosaic) law and the law of the early Church, as deduced from the Acts of the Apostles. The rest of the book is an attempt to select and record what was valuable and necessary from earlier collections. 'Then I, King Alfred, collected these together and ordered to be written many of them which our forefathers observed, those which I liked; and many of those which I did not like, I rejected with the advice of my councillors, and ordered them to be differently observed. For I dared not presume to set in writing at all many of my own, because it was unknown to me what should please those who should come after us. But those which I found anywhere, which seemed to me most just, either of the time of my kinsman, King Ine [688–726]), or of Offa, King of the Mercians [757–96], or of Ethelbert [King of Kent, 560–616], who first among the English received baptism, I collected herein, and omitted the others. Then I, Alfred, King of the West Saxons, showed these to all my councillors, and they then said that they were all pleased to observe them.'

This is the first description of English law-making, and it is altogether more informal than later processes. The custom of his predecessors, for the most part, was treated with great respect; nothing was done without the advice of his councillors. Yet Alfred knew his own mind. 'I, King Alfred, collected these together and ordered to be written . . . those which I liked.' Especially significant is his use of the Mercian laws. He was King of the West Saxons; but he felt a responsibility to all the English—even to the English subjects of King Guthrum, whose interests he protected in the peace treaty.

'Judge thou very fairly. Do not judge one judgment for the rich and another for the poor; nor one for the one more dear and another for the one more hateful.' This sentiment was introduced by Alfred into the introduction to his *Laws* from the Book of Exodus; but the sentence has been a good deal elaborated in the course of translation, and has become a full expression of one of Alfred's basic beliefs. In a similar way in his translations Alfred interprets the thought of his source, expands, annotates, and illustrates it; makes it his own.

'His unique importance in the history of English letters,' writes Sir Frank Stenton, 'comes from his conviction that a life without knowledge or reflection was unworthy of respect, and his determination to bring the thought of the past within the range of his subjects' understanding'. Here is Alfred's own account of the genesis of his translation of Gregory the Great's *Pastoral Care,* a manual on the office of a bishop. 'When I remembered how the knowledge of the Latin language had previously decayed throughout England, and yet many could read things written in English, I began in the midst of the other various and manifold cares of this kingdom to turn into English the book which is called in Latin *Pastoralis* and in English *Shepherd-book,* sometimes word for word, sometimes by a paraphrase; as I had learned it from my Archbishop Plegmund, and my Bishop Asser, and my priest Grimbald and my priest John. When I had learned it, I turned it into English according as I understood it and as I could render it most intelligibly; and I will send one to every see in my kingdom.'

This describes, in a nutshell, Alfred's concern and his method. His subjects were ignorant of Latin. The treasures of ancient literature must be translated. He himself had neither time nor the fluency in Latin to translate alone; so he presided over a seminar of learned men who assisted and advised him. It is an astonishing story. A warrior king on his own initiative feels the lack of learning in himself and his people; struggles to learn to read and write; collects scholars; presides over their work and as time passes himself takes a hand in it; founds schools in which not only churchmen but laymen, too, may learn. His immediate success was slight—there was too much ground to be covered; his lay followers were not accustomed to learning and not seriously amenable to it. But on a longer view the achievement was extremely impressive.

Alfred's own childhood had accustomed him to the existence of a great European heritage: as a small boy he had twice been on a pilgrimage to Rome. But it was only gradually that he worked out his programme and collected his band of scholars. He had to search widely for them. Plegmund and Werferth (not included in the list in the *Pastoral Care*), were native Englishmen. Grimbald came from the north of France, John from the north of Germany, Asser from Wales. All took a hand in the work of translation.

Gregory's *Pastoral Care* was throughout the Middle Ages the fundamental book on the duty of a bishop—and of special interest to Alfred in stressing the responsibility of a bishop for educating laymen. Gregory's *Dialogues*, translated by Werferth, contained miracle stories, especially the miracles of St Benedict, author of the famous monastic rule. Its choice reflected Alfred's desire to see monasticism re-established. The library of translations also included two distinguished works of history, the English history of Bede, and the world history of Orosius. To Orosius Alfred added his own reflections on the countries and peoples of Europe, especially on the Scandinavian and Baltic countries unknown to Orosius (who had lived in Spain), but of special interest to Alfred, whose whole life was spent fighting the Vikings. This geographical lore shows again the width of his interests, his passion for inquiry. Finally he turned his hand to two books of more personal interest to him. Boethius had written his *Consolations of Philosophy* while awaiting execution at the hands of the Goths. Its comforts seemed specially appropriate to Alfred's own circumstances. And in his rendering of St Augustine's soliloquies, the book in which he departed most freely from his original, Alfred expounded his philosophy of learning. It marks the end of the road whose beginning he had described in the *Pastoral Care*. He tells how he had been, as it were, a forester cutting timber in the wood of ancient knowledge.

'Then I gathered for myself staves and props and bars, and handles for all the tools I knew how to use, and cross-bars and beams for all the structures which I knew how to build, the fairest pieces of timber, as many as I could carry. I neither came home with a single load, nor did it suit me to bring home all the wood, even if I could have carried it. In each tree I saw something that I required at home. For I advise each of those who is strong and has many wagons, to plan to go to the same wood where I cut these props, and fetch for himself more there, and load his wagons with fair rods, so that he can plait many a fine wall, and put up many a peerless building, and build a fair enclosure with them; and may dwell therein pleasantly and at his ease winter and summer, *as I have not yet done*. But he who advised me, to whom the wood was pleasing, may bring it to pass that I shall dwell at greater ease both in this transitory habitation by this road while I am in this world, and also in the eternal home which he has promised us through St Augustine and St Gregory and St Jerome and through many other holy fathers; as also I believe he will, for the merits of them all, both make this road more convenient than it has hitherto been, and also enlighten the eyes of my mind so that I can find out the straight road to the eternal home, and to the eternal mercy, and to the eternal rest which is promised to us by the holy fathers. So be it.'

1. To this period of Alfred's career tradition has attached the famous story of how he was sitting in a cowherd's cottage, preparing his bow and arrows and other weapons, when the cowherd's wife saw her cakes burning in the hearth, and scolded the luckless king for not paying attention to them. The story first appears in a saint's life written a generation or two after the Norman Conquest; it may be based on ancient tradition, but it may equally well be the author's invention, like many other things in the book. (See W. H. Stevenson, *Asser's Life of King Alfred* [Oxford, 1904], pp. 136, 256ff.)

2. Irby is 'the *by* (village) of the Irish', reminding us that the Norse came by way of Ireland; Thingwall, 'the field of assembly', the place where the local court or assembly of Wirral (forerunner of the 'hundred' court), the 'thing' familiar to readers of Icelandic sagas, met. *Gill* (ravine with a stream) and *fell* are Norse words; *thwaite* (clearing in woodland) was used by Norwegians and by Danes.

CHAPTER THREE

THE MAKING OF THE ENGLISH KINGDOM, 899–1035

(1) 899–959

Though Alfred was never free to dwell in his enclosure at ease winter and summer, and though Danish raids continued right to the eve of his death, the most serious threat to the survival of Wessex had passed. His practical measures and his great prestige had strengthened the material and psychological defences of his kingdom. The impetus of the Viking attacks, meanwhile, had weakened. In Ireland, Scotland, England, and northern France, as the ninth century turned into the tenth, the Viking bands were turning from pillage to settlement; they had reached the limits of their expansion.

The end of the great Viking offensive did not mean an end to the problems of English defence. Alfred's son and successor, Edward the Elder (899–924), was as frequently engaged in war as his father; and, in his way, as notable a warrior. Kingship was a very personal thing in the Middle Ages. However strongly one king might build up the bases of his power, his successor's position always depended to a great extent on his own achievements. Alfred's positive achievements, however sensational, did not give Wessex stability or permanent security. His work would have foundered if he had not been succeeded by a line of able kings. It was carried on, and in certain respects completed, by his remarkably able descendants, notably by his son Edward, his grandson Athelstan (924–39) and his great-grandson, Athelstan's nephew, Edgar (959–75). After Edgar's death the throne passed to lesser men, and the long rule of Ethelred II (979–1016) coincided with the renewal of Danish attacks. With Ethelred the dynasty collapsed, though not, as we shall see, the kingdom.

For the first ten years of Edward's reign no further progress is recorded in the recovery of English territory from the Danes. Danish armies indeed supported a cousin of Edward in rebellion against him. Apart from this there were signs that relations between English and Danes were becoming more peaceable, that Edward and his thegns were finding opportunities for peaceful infiltration. In 909 the armies of Wessex and Mercia attacked the Northumbrian Danes and dictated terms of peace to them. In the following year the Danes retaliated by raiding English Mercia, but their army was caught on its way home near Tettenhall in Staffordshire, and annihilated. From then on the leaders of Wessex and Mercia were free to reconquer the southern Danish kingdoms without serious interruption from the north. Ethelred, Ealdorman of Mercia, died in 911, but co-operation did not cease with his death. His place was filled by his wife, Edward's sister, Aethelflaed, 'Lady of the Mercians', who continued her husband's work in close association with her brother until her own death in 918; from then on Wessex and Mercia were united.

The *Anglo-Saxon Chronicle* had hitherto devoted most space to the doings of the 'heathen', the 'host'—that is, the Danes. First compiled in the reign of Alfred, not perhaps under his direct inspiration, but clearly reflecting the literary revival of his time, its main entries for the mid and late ninth century tell the tale of attack and disaster in plain, unemotional, but effective prose. In Alfred's later years more is said of the King's activities; one senses the feeling that at last the initiative is shifting. But the hosts are frequently the subject of annals still. In 914 a great pirate host of Danes came from Brittany and attacked south and central Wales, but it was turned back on the English border. This apart, the main burden of the annals from 911 to 925 is the steady progress of Edward's reconquest.

After the Ealdorman Ethelred's death in 911, Edward took over London and the south-east Midlands, leaving the rest of English Mercia to Aethelflaed. The building of fortresses and the advance east and north went on steadily through the following years. In 914 Aethelflaed built a fortress at Eddisbury (Cheshire) and at Warwick; in 917 she captured Derby; in 918 Leicester, and but for her death that year she might have received the submission of York. In 912 Edward built a *burh* at Hertford, and prepared for campaigns to east and north. In 914 and 915 he received the submission of Bedford and Northampton; in 916 he built a *burh* at Maldon in Essex; in 917 he and his followers defeated a great counter-offensive mounted by the Danes, and occupied Essex and East Anglia, restoring the *burh* at Colchester. In 918 he was at Stamford and Nottingham.

These places had been two of the crucial Danish centres of power south of the Humber; it is likely that a third, Lincoln, also submitted to Edward in this year. By these surrenders he became lord of the Danelaw up to the line of the Humber; by his sister's death he was lord of Mercia; and in the same year the kings of several leading Welsh kingdoms accepted his over-lordship.

The offer by the Danes of York to submit to Aethelflaed—an offer not repeated to Edward after her death—and the rapid submission of the Danish armies of the north Midlands and of Lincolnshire was partly inspired by the progress of another Viking power, this time of Norse origin and leadership. Many of the place-names in the Wirral peninsula in north-west Cheshire, in the angle between Wales and the Mersey, are of Norse origin; and the Norse settlements in this area date from the first decade of the tenth century. The Norsemen came, immediately, from Ireland. If the Wirral was their chief point of entry, their settlements must have spread all along the coast of Lancashire and Cumberland and south-western Scotland. In 919 the most powerful of the Irish-Norse leaders, Raegnald, established himself as King of York.

The Norse kingdom of York acted as a check on the English advance for a number of years, but it forms only a slight quali-fication to Edward's remarkable tale of success. His last years saw the rebuilding of more *burhs*, and as a final coping-stone to his prestige, after the building of the *burh* at Bakewell in the Peak of Derbyshire in 920, 'the king of Scots and the whole Scottish nation accepted him as "father and lord": so also did Raegnald [King of York] and the sons of Eadwulf and all the inhabitants of Northumbria, both English and Danish, Nor-wegians and others; together with the king of the Strathclyde Welsh and all his subjects.'

In 924 Edward died, and was succeeded by his eldest son Athelstan. Athelstan had been brought up in the household of the Lord and Lady of the Mercians, and was as readily accepted as king in Mercia as in Wessex. In his time the local particu-larisms of these two countries were rapidly breaking down. But it is still too early to talk of a united English kingdom. The north of the country was only slowly conquered; and Athelstan was lord over an assemblage of peoples, English, Danes, and Norse, with diverse traditions and diverse motives for allegiance and disaffection. The royal scribes pronounced the unity of his kingdom in Latin of immense portentousness and obscurity. They protested too much; though the words of one of the charters, 'most glorious king of the Anglo-Saxons and the Danes' came near the truth. But true unity was not to come to the English peoples until a Dane sat on Alfred's throne, in 1016.

The first years of Athelstan's reign saw him established as king in almost every part of England, and received as overlord by the border kingdoms in Wales and southern Scotland. His relations with the Welsh princes were closer and more effective than had been established by any of his predecessors. The methods of his government, his coinage, and his laws all seem to have influenced the most distinguished of these princes, Hywel Dda of Dyfed, whose name became traditionally attached to later editions of Welsh law-books. Of more immediate importance to the English kingdom was Athelstan's conquest of the Norse kingdom of York.

His relations with the Scottish kings soon broke down. In 934 he paraded a large army through Scotland as a demonstration of power, but the Scots avoided battle. In 937 an Irish king, son of the last king of York, joined the kings of Scotland and Strathclyde in a combined invasion of England. Their army was met by a large English force led by Athelstan and Edmund, his brother; and the decisive English victory at Brunanburh (the site has not been identified) is recorded in the *Chronicle* in stirring verse. 'With their hammered blades, the sons of Edward clove the shield-wall and hacked the linden bucklers. . . . There the prince of Norsemen . . . was forced to flee to the prow of his ship with a handful of men. . . . There, likewise, the aged Constantine [King of the Scots], the grey-haired warrior, set off in flight, north to his native land. No cause had he to exult in that clash of swords, bereaved of his kinsmen, robbed of his friends on the field of battle.'

When he died in 939, Athelstan was recognised as one of the leading princes of western Europe. The composition of his court from time to time reflected his sway over the princes of Wales, the Scottish border, and Scotland. The solemn language of his charters evidently reflects a court conscious of its distinction, concerned to cut a figure in the world. In 926 one of his sisters married the Duke of the Franks. This was the response to an embassy carrying rich gifts to the King, including jewels, perfumes, and relics—of which Athelstan was a princely collector. In 928 another sister married the heir of

64

Germany, the future Otto the Great, reopening traditional links between old and new Saxony, between the English and their Saxon homeland. These were the most impressive symbols of the European reputation of Athelstan, which involved him in the affairs of Brittany and Lotharingia (Lorraine), and brought him also friendship with the King of Norway. We should like to know more about him as a man: what we do know suggests some likeness to his grandfather.

With Athelstan's death in 939 English rule over the Norse kingdom of York became extremely precarious; and a great part of the reigns of his brothers Edmund (939–46) and Eadred (946–55) was spent in the attempt to re-establish Athelstan's supremacy in the north. The key to much of the fighting of this period is the growing antagonism between Norse and Dane in the kingdom of York, and the close links between the Vikings and their Scandinavian homeland. Norse war-lords were established between the Humber and the Tees, and Norse settlers in the north-west. But in the Danish areas south of the Humber the Norse kings of York were never popular, and never won more than a temporary supremacy. Late in Edmund's reign and early in Eadred's, the English kings were successful for brief periods in mastering the north. But in the middle years of Eadred's reign two distinguished Vikings, one from Ireland and one from Norway, held sway at York. Eric Bloodaxe indeed had been King of Norway for a time, and had made a considerable name for himself for violence and adventure. After his expulsion he twice succeeded in winning the kingdom of York (948–9, 952–4). But it was difficult even for a great Viking leader like Eric to establish himself on English soil for any length of time. In 954 the Northumbrians expelled him, and Eadred ruled over the whole of England. In the following year he died.

Thus, after some vicissitudes, the inheritance of Edward the Elder and Athelstan passed into the next generation intact and well established. It was well that it did so, because the next generation was represented by Edmund's sons, of whom the elder, Eadwig, cannot have been more than fifteen and the younger, Edgar, was twelve. Eadwig lived only four years after his accession; long enough to acquire an evil reputation in those circles to which we owe record of his reign, not long enough to redeem it by any notable act. It is noteworthy that several of the leading associates of his brother, Edgar, had already been promoted under Eadwig; but that Eadwig quarrelled with the greatest of Edgar's colleagues, St Dunstan. It was probably to this quarrel, whose true origin is quite obscure, that Eadwig owed his bad reputation.

(2) 959-75 : EDGAR AND THE MONASTIC REVIVAL

Edgar began his reign while still a boy and died in his early thirties; the prestige he acquired is all the more remarkable. As a soldier, Edgar acquired little glory, because, as one version of the *Chronicle* has it, 'God granted him to live his days in peace'. But his reign was not weak, and his prestige stood very high. In 973, at the age of thirty—the age when a man might be ordained priest—Edgar was solemnly anointed and crowned king by Archbishop Dunstan, in a ceremony which laid special emphasis on the analogies of kingship and priesthood, and provided for the first time in England a fully elaborated coronation service on the Frankish model. The coronation emphasised the divine source of royal authority, and the close bonds between king and Church. Later in the same year, in an equally famous scene at Chester, Edgar received the submission of seven Welsh and Scottish kings—who rowed him, as legend has it, on the Dee, between his palace and the church of St John. This show of power was accompanied by an act of policy which was probably characteristic of Edgar. The King of Scots became Edgar's man; in return Edgar granted him Lothian, the land between the Tweed and the Forth, a country always remote from English authority and difficult to control. The grant was the first step towards establishing the present frontier of England and Scotland. Within England itself, Edgar recognised that English and Danes lived by different customs, and he allowed the Danes to regulate their own customs; thus recognising the existence and native rights of a vital minority in his kingdom.

The coronation ceremony in 973 was the climax of the collaboration between the King and his chief councillor, Dunstan, Archbishop of Canterbury. Like Lanfranc and Stephen Langton in later days, Dunstan combined the fullest appreciation of the spiritual aspect of his office with political statesmanship of a high order. The dual capacity of a bishop's office, on the one hand, that of royal councillor and leading subject, on the other, that of spiritual leader, was often an embarrassment to a conscientious medieval bishop. Dunstan, like Lanfranc, lived both lives to the full. In Dunstan's case the difference was hidden by his strong conviction that Church and state were one; that the king was natural ruler of the Church, 'king and priest'. This union of offices did not give the king the specifically clerical function of performing the rites and administering the sacraments of the Church; but it meant that in return for protection and patronage the Church recognised in him God's instrument for controlling its government. The close liaison of king and Church gave a special character to the English Church; and the Church's support made possible the dramatic developments in English government in the tenth and early eleventh centuries.

In 940 King Edmund had nearly perished while hunting the stag in the Cheddar Gorge in Somerset. Saved, as it seemed, by a miracle, he at once set about re-establishing the church at Glastonbury, not far away, as a regular monastery, and put Dunstan at its head. Circumstances were different from the days when Alfred had to fetch monks from abroad to furnish a community. Foreign influence was strong in the monastic reform inaugurated by Dunstan; but its personnel was almost entirely English, and its leaders were quickly supplied from Dunstan's early disciples at Glastonbury. In spreading his movement in the early years Dunstan met difficulties; though highly born and exceedingly well connected, he had enemies at court. But after Edgar's accession in 959 events moved swiftly. Dunstan himself became archbishop in 960, and the diocese of Worcester, which he had held for a brief space, was given to his disciple, Oswald, who from 972 to his death in 992 combined Worcester with the archbishopric of York (an act of pluralism made necessary by the poverty of York). In 963 Dunstan's other leading disciple, Ethelwold, became Bishop of Winchester. From these key positions the three colleagues directed a great revival and reformation of the monastic order in England. Between 940 and the Norman Conquest some sixty houses of monks and nuns were founded or revived. Compared with later figures the number of houses and the number of religious in them (about 1,000 in 1066) were not sensational; but the influence of the monks on English life was out of all proportion to their numbers.

Behind the English reform lay two active movements on the

67

Continent, one centred in Lorraine, the other in the celebrated Burgundian monastic house of Cluny. Cluny was founded in 910; Brogne and Gorze, most important of the houses of Lorraine, were refounded about 920 and 933. These foundations lay between the age of Alfred and the age of Dunstan; they provided Dunstan with a background that had been lacking in Alfred's day. Alfred's attempts at cultural revival and his successors' steady patronage of the Church and learning had slowly taken effect. And Dunstan himself was peculiarly well qualified to found a monastic revival. Brought up near Glastonbury, he was in contact with such elements of monastic tradition as still lingered in the area, and also in touch with the dual tradition of Celtic and Saxon monasticism which gives Glastonbury its special interest and partly explains why it became so powerful a centre of legend. Dunstan and Oswald both spent a few years in continental houses, Dunstan at Ghent and Oswald at Fleury on the Loire. Ghent had recently been reformed from Brogne and Gorze, Fleury from Cluny; so that the English movement came early into contact with both streams of continental tradition.

Gorze and Cluny differed in a number of respects; most obviously in that houses reformed from Gorze retained close bonds with the lay patron who had organised the reform, while Cluny favoured at least a legal independence of secular control. In part this reflected the divergence between the settled monarchy of tenth-century Germany, where the 'connection' of Gorze flourished, and the feudal anarchy of France. In England we have a situation more similar to Germany's than to France's, and close alliance with the king and other lay patrons became the English tradition.

In other respects Gorze and Cluny were much alike; especially in owing a profound debt to the constitutions which St Benedict of Aniane had promulgated for all the monasteries of the Frankish dominions at Aachen in 817, under the patronage of the Emperor Louis the Pious, Charlemagne's successor. This piece of history was well known to Dunstan and his colleagues. In or about the year 970, at a great gathering modelled on that at Aachen, Edgar and the bishops and the whole synod promulgated a set of constitutions for the English monasteries, the *Regularis Concordia*, a 'monastic agreement' or agreed norm for the religious life, to be the basis for the practice in all the English monasteries. It is a nice mingling of influences from

68

Lorraine and Burgundy with native traditions. Its final form probably owed more to Ethelwold than to Dunstan. In the later stages of the revival the details of reform were more in the hands of Ethelwold and Oswald, who were very active in and out of their dioceses—and especially in the east Midlands and East Anglia, which the Church was quickly recovering from Danish paganism, in close alliance with the local ealdormen.

The English Church was becoming thoroughly monastic. Between the accession of Edgar and the Conquest a high proportion of the bishops were monks; under Edgar and Ethelred II (died 1016) almost all. Fundamentally a monastery is an inward-looking community, a haven apart from the world. But the monasticising of the English Church did not mean a separation of Church and state; quite the contrary. The English monasteries retained a tradition of more normal contact with the life of the world than was usually favoured by monastic reformers. In the reign of Alfred the higher clergy had been few in number. They were more prolific by Edgar's time; but very largely because of the increase in the number of monks. A secular [1] higher clergy of any proportions was still lacking. The broad character of the English monastic order, and with it of the English Church in general, reflected the wide interests of St Dunstan. He had been a statesman, a monk, a man of great learning by the standards of the day; and, curiously enough, an artist as well. In art and sacred literature the monastic reformation was tremendously fruitful. Close links between lay patrons [2] and the monasteries; a powerful monastic influence at court, and every kind of link between Church and king; and a monastic tradition especially notable for its artistic creativity; these were the marks of the English Church in the time of St Dunstan.

(3) 975–1016: ETHELRED II AND THE DANES

Edgar died suddenly, while still a young man, in 975, and was succeeded in turn by his two sons, Edward (975–8) and Ethelred (978–1016). Edward was very young, yet he managed in his brief rule to alienate a number of his subjects by his insufferable manners and bad temper. In 978 he was treacherously murdered, and replaced by Ethelred, who was then still a boy.

The crime which brought him to the throne cast a shadow over the reign of Ethelred and may partly explain the stunted weakness of his character throughout life. It was not the violence of the murder but the treachery of it—betrayal of a lord by his subjects—which shocked contemporaries. In 1008 Ethelred issued a code including this clause: 'The councillors have decreed that St Edward's festival is to be celebrated over all England on 18 March.' In this ironical fashion Ethelred was compelled to celebrate the event which had made him king. The name Ethelred means literally 'noble-counsel'. We do not know whose wit first devised the pun 'no-counsel', 'unræd', for the unfortunate king; the nickname is first recorded in the thirteenth century. But the word had other meanings too, including 'evil counsel', 'a treacherous plot'. If it was devised in his lifetime, it would certainly have got home. The subtlety of the nickname has been lost in the modern corruption 'Ethelred the Unready', though that too is not inappropriate.

The death of a king of high prestige was commonly followed by disorder among leading nobles hitherto held in check by fear or respect for the dead man. To the disorder following Edgar's death was added the horror of Edward's 'martyrdom'. But greater misfortune than these was in store for the unfortunate Ethelred. The mainland of Scandinavia, remarkably quiescent since the fall of Eric Bloodaxe, was ready for another wave of expansion; Viking attacks began again; and the unsettled politics of England combined with England's growing wealth to make it a favoured target.

The second wave of Danish attacks began, like the first, with plundering raids. But the attacks of the period 980–1016 differed fundamentally from those of the ninth century. From the early nine-nineties they became large-scale, highly organised raids, planned by the leading figures of the Scandinavian world, conducted by highly professional armies. This phase lasted until 1013, when Swein, the Danish king, decided to take over the government of his prey, and came in person.

The first of the great leaders of the Vikings in the ninenineties was Olaf Tryggvason, who came in the raid of 991 which led to the battle of Maldon, celebrated in the poem quoted in an earlier chapter. Olaf shortly after became the first Christian King of Norway; but he never ceased to be a Viking adventurer. In 994 he came accompanied by Swein, heir to the throne of Denmark, at the head of a formidable host. There was talk of making Swein King of England; but his alliance with Olaf was precarious and his campaign not wholly successful, so he agreed to peace for a payment of £16,000. In most years after this, down to 1006, a Danish host attacked England and levied plunder or tribute—the 'Dane-geld'—or both. Then came a gap of two years, when Ethelred and his councillors made feverish attempts to prepare the country's defences against further attacks. From 1009 the attacks were continuous, and aimed for the first time at the conquest of the kingdom.

More than one of the Icelandic sagas describes the legend of how Harold Bluetooth, Swein's father, had built a great fortress at Jomsborg, near the mouth of the Oder, on the German mainland. It consisted, so they tell us, of a fort and fortified harbour; a large military base, accommodating several thousand professional soldiers, on a permanent war footing. The leaders of these troops in the fortress included Thorkell the Tall, and Swein himself. It has long been disputed how much truth there is in the legend, and the existence of Jomsborg is still in doubt. But the part of the story which was at one time most generally doubted was the size and nature of the camp. In recent years the general truth of this picture has been dramatically confirmed by archaeology. Four forts similar in character to that described in the sagas have been discovered in Scandinavia itself. Three of them, capable of holding about 2,000 men each, probably belong to Swein's own time; the fourth and largest was constructed somewhat later. Clearly a large professional army existed in the time of Swein; and this formidable force would have daunted a more capable warrior than Ethelred.

Swein's armies in 1009 were led by three experienced Vikings, including Thorkell the Tall and one of his brothers. From 1009 to 1012 they raided many English shires systematically. In 1012 they made peace with the English in exchange for an immense ransom, assessed in the *Chronicle* at £48,000. But before the Danes would disperse, they demanded an extra ransom from their most illustrious prisoner, Aelfheah, Archbishop of Canterbury. Aelfheah first agreed, then felt this concession to be wrong and withdrew it. Thorkell struggled to control his men; but they were in ugly mood and murdered the Archbishop in barbarous fashion. Before the end of the year Thorkell and forty-five ships from the Danish fleet went over to Ethelred. It is likely that the two incidents were connected.

In 1013 Swein himself came to England for the third and last time—he had raided in the country in 994 and 1003. This time he was determined on conquest, and after a rapid campaign described in brief but vivid phrases by the chronicler he was accepted as king over most of the country. Then in February 1014 he suddenly died. The period between the death of Swein and the final acknowledgement of his son, Cnut, as king, at the end of 1016 is exceedingly confusing. At the time of his father's death Cnut was about eighteen, and the sudden acquisition of responsibility was evidently too much for him. He withdrew hastily from England; and when he returned, he was supported by three great Viking leaders, his elder brother, Harold, King of Denmark, Eric, the Regent of Norway, and Thorkell the Tall, who had returned to his old allegiance. At one point Cnut held Wessex and Mercia, while Edmund 'Ironside', Ethelred's son, held the northern Danelaw—both in defiance of King Ethelred, who was still holding out in the south-east. It was Cnut's unheralded withdrawal which had alienated the Danelaw and made Edmund's intrusion there possible; while in spite of the momentary recovery of Ethelred in 1014 and 1015, there was treachery in the English court, which aided Cnut to over-run Wessex and Mercia. Ethelred died in April 1016; a few months later Edmund was decisively beaten by Cnut, and the uneasy truce which followed was quickly ended by Edmund's sudden death. The events of the civil war had shown that there was no simple division of loyalty between English and Danes, and that a number of leading thegns and jarls were prepared to support a monarch from either side, if he proved more competent than Ethelred, and capable of holding the allegiance of his subjects. It was this circumstance which made possible the notable success of the young Cnut.

(4) 1016–35: THE REIGN OF CNUT

King Edgar had recognised that his subjects lived by two divergent sets of customs, English and Danish. The events which followed his death had shown that Viking leaders from Scandinavia could still find allies in the Danelaw; and that under exceptional pressure, both English and Danes were prepared to submit to a Viking lord. At first sight it seems surprising that the first ruler of a really united England should have been a Dane; but on closer inspection the paradox is easy to understand. Divergent customs and language, links with the north and memories of past glory would tend to make the Danes and Norwegians uneasy subjects of a native English king. The Danes in England, however, had had some generations' experience of English rule—of the rule, that is, of the most considerable monarchy, apart from the German, in northern Europe. They had experienced some of the benefits of a régime more stable than those to which they had been accustomed in Scandinavia, while suffering as much as the native English from the constant passage of armies and levying of tribute in Ethelred's later years. Cnut was thus doubly attractive to them: as a Danish overlord and as a man who could restore peace and stable government. In other ways too Cnut was ideally placed for binding both peoples together in allegiance to himself. Swein had been accepted by a large proportion of the thegns as king; and, as Swein's son, Cnut had some show of legitimacy. This he confirmed by marrying the young widow of King Ethelred, Emma, a Norman princess, whose advent foreshadows the events of fifty years later. In 1019 he became King of Denmark on his brother's death, and to this he added Norway for a time, and even claimed some part of Sweden. He was for most of his reign in England far and away the greatest lord of the Viking world, and so a natural centre of loyalty for English Scandinavians, and a guarantee of peace to his English subjects.

In the north he reigned as a Viking king; in England as the successor to King Edgar. In England he was a model of piety and good government; in Denmark the regency of his English concubine, Aelfgifu of Northampton, and her son, symbolised an irregularity of life not uncharacteristic of the Viking world shortly after its conversion to Christianity. At Oxford in 1018, 'King Cnut with the advice of his councillors completely established peace and friendship between the Danes and the English and put an end to all their former strife,' as the official record describes it. The councillors 'determined that above all things they would ever honour one God and steadfastly hold one Christian faith, and would love King Cnut with due loyalty and zealously observe Edgar's laws.' As well as requiring exhortation to piety the Danes had to be paid off, and a levy of Danegeld which the *Chronicles* assesses at the enormous figure of £82,500 was necessary for this. Forty ships and a number of Viking leaders remained with Cnut; the rest sailed for Denmark. From then on Cnut's reign in England saw remarkably little incident. He was very well served, both in defence and lay administration by his Danish earls, led by Thorkell and Eric, and in all the aspects of government requiring literacy by his bishops and the clerks of his chapel, led by Wulfstan II, Archbishop of York (1002–23). Through the influence and writings of this distinguished preacher and statesman the character of the English Church and of English government as laid down by Edgar and Dunstan was preserved. Wulfstan first made his mark in the reign of Ethelred, whose laws he framed, denouncing the while the chaos and wickedness of Ethelred's England. Under Cnut he continued to be a leading councillor, to draft laws and to represent in other ways the continuity of English government. Monastic influence in Church and government was still strong; but there were beginning to be signs of an influential secular (i.e. non-monastic) element in the upper clergy. The clerks of the royal chapel, the men who sang daily mass before the king and maintained all the services of the royal court, and also wrote his letters and charters and carried out any business demanding a literate or an educated hand, were beginning once again in Cnut's later years to find their way to bishoprics. But in most respects the English Church maintained the traditions of Edgar's day; including the tradition of royal patronage and royal authority. In other respects, too, Edgar was regarded as the model of English kingship. The councillors at Oxford in 1018 'determined that . . . they would . . . zealously observe Edgar's laws', thus ignoring Ethelred and the period of anarchy and misgovernment which had intervened since Edgar's death.

In some respects English traditions of government were developed; in one respect considerably modified. In Denmark and Norway the authority of the kings had always been qualified by the considerable measure of freedom which they were compelled to allow to their leading jarls or earls. A strong king kept his earls in check, won their steady support. A weak king was ruled by them, or ignored or deposed by them. In conquered England, Cnut owed a great deal to his leading supporters. They naturally expected a corresponding reward. A number of them attained high positions in Cnut's court, and he was regularly attended by his Danish bodyguard, his housecarles, who from this time formed the permanent nucleus of the English

74

army. It is a symptom of the change in personnel that the title of the Old English ealdorman came to be replaced by the Scandinavian jarl, or earl. Six of the sixteen earls of this time whose names are known were English, but only one family maintained through Cnut's reign the power it had had under Ethelred. Leofwine, Ealdorman of the Hwicce (Gloucestershire and Worcestershire), was succeeded by his son Leofric, Earl of Mercia, and Leofric's grandsons survived into the reign of William the Conqueror. Another Englishman, Godwin, who became Earl of Wessex, owed his position to his loyal service to Cnut. (Godwin's sons in due course became earls also of Northumbria, East Anglia, and the home counties, and the most famous of them, Harold, was to be the last of the Old English kings.) In Cnut's time the other great earldoms, Northumbria and East Anglia especially, were in Danish hands. Northumbria went first to Eric of Norway, later to Siward, 'old Siward' of *Macbeth*, whose long reign on the northern border ended only in 1055, and whose son survived the Norman Conquest. Thus the great earls, at first primarily the pillars of Cnut's court and leaders of his army, gradually acquired immense possessions and a territorial power comparable to that which they might have held in Denmark or Norway. In every way but this, Cnut's reign was a constructive period in the history of the English monarchy. When his strong hand was removed by his early death in 1035, the earls came near to dismembering the state.

In 1027, like several of his predecessors, Cnut went on pilgrimage to Rome, to visit the tombs of the apostles and all its many other sanctuaries and holy places. He chose his time well. His visit coincided with the coronation of the Emperor Conrad II by the Pope, and all the princes of the Empire were there; 'and they all received me with honour, and honoured me with lavish gifts' as Cnut himself proudly said in a letter which was sent on his behalf to England to describe the scene. At the same time he won privileges for English pilgrims to Rome, and no doubt took the chance to hold conversations with the Emperor, since the frontier between Denmark and Germany was uneasy. The pilgrimage was the characteristic act of a man of conventional piety, and a distinguished patron of the Church; it also underlined Cnut's determination to act in the tradition of the English kings—and to cut a figure in European society. He was the greatest monarch in northern Europe in his

75

day, and was evidently much flattered to be well received by Pope and Emperor.

1. The word 'secular', when used of clergy, distinguishes those who were not committed to a specific rule, i.e. the majority of the cathedral and parish clergy, from monks (and later, friars) and 'canons regular'; the 'secular' clergy were those who lived in the 'world' (*in saeculo*).

2. The founder of a monastery became its patron: he protected it and supported it, in return for prayers and for certain rights and privileges. The office of patron was hereditary; and in early days the patron had great influence in the affairs of a monastery.

CHAPTER FOUR

ANGLO-SAXON INSTITUTIONS

(1) LAW AND JUSTICE

In one of his most brilliant studies, *Domesday Book and Beyond* (1897), F. W. Maitland tried to penetrate behind the description of England made in 1086 and to discover the structure of English society and English law before the Norman Conquest. 'Unless we have mistaken the general drift of legal history,' he wrote, 'the law implied in Domesday Book ought to be for us very difficult law, far more difficult than the law of the thirteenth century, for the thirteenth century is nearer to us than is the eleventh. The grown man will find it easier to think the thoughts of the schoolboy than to think the thoughts of the baby. And yet the doctrine that our remote forefathers being simple folk had simple law dies hard. Too often we allow ourselves to suppose that, could we but get back to the beginning, we should find that all was intelligible and should then be able to watch the process whereby simple ideas were smothered under subtleties and technicalities. But it is not so. Simplicity is the outcome of technical subtlety; it is the goal not the starting point. As we go backwards the familiar outlines become blurred; the ideas become fluid, and instead of the simple we find the indefinite.' [1]

Anglo-Saxon law is difficult and obscure; but none the less worth study for that. There is no better way of penetrating the minds of our remote forefathers than by trying to imagine what was their attitude to law. Partly this is because they viewed law quite differently from us; partly because it played a bigger conscious part in their lives than it does in ours.

Modern society is so settled that it takes law for granted most of the time. We assume a community normally peaceable and obedient, directed, but not (in the main) forcibly controlled by a corps of policemen. We assume that the law on any topic, however absurd or obscure it may be, is reasonably fixed; that it can be known; that much of it can be read. Even if we ourselves do not know it, there are solicitors to consult, policemen to

77

obey, barristers to convince the world of our innocence, judges to sum up the results of all this learning—a large professional body, in fact, dedicated to administering the law.

None of these things existed in England before the Conquest —no habit of obedience comparable to ours, no comprehensive code of laws, no class of professional lawyers whose sole business it was to know the law and enforce it. Society was 'lawless', not in the sense that it had no law—very far from it—but because crime and violence were regarded as normal excesses, not as occasional signs of ill-health in the society. The surviving law-books frequently recur to the problem of how to enforce law—how to detect criminals, how to compel powerful offenders to come to court, how to enforce the judgments of the court. By our standards, government was exceedingly weak, and throughout the Middle Ages the enforcement of law was a haphazard business. This had been particularly true during the Danish invasions, when the cumbersome machinery had almost broken down. It was one of the chief tasks of Alfred and his successors to revive it; and they faced the challenge so squarely that royal justice emerged stronger than ever before. The royal rights, especially in controlling the courts of shire and hundred, were sufficiently established to survive the second Danish onslaught unscathed.

Such codes as there were dealt with what was exceptional, or odd, or specially needing to be written down; or else they stated large legal principles in the hope (often vain) that they would become established. One of the reasons why Anglo-Saxon law was excessively complex is that it came from many different sources. It arose out of attempts to codify and rationalise numerous laws of clans, peoples, and kingdoms. We have seen how Alfred used old codes from Kent, Wessex, and Mercia and tried to put together 'those which I liked'. Soon after the Norman Conquest it was said that there were three laws in England; the Danelaw, the law of Mercia, the law of Wessex. This was a desperate generalisation. The old codes attempted to canalise, to direct the progress of legal ideas; they attempted to stamp a certain measure of uniformity on the diversities of English law. But they were not codes in the modern sense. They were not in the least comprehensive. Indeed, they fail to answer most of the questions we should like to ask about English law before the Norman Conquest.

There was no comprehensive code; equally, there were no

78

professional lawyers. Some men knew the law better than others; there have been 'barrack-room' lawyers in every age. But no-one was a lawyer and nothing else. There were judges, but the judges were kings, ealdormen, bishops, lesser officials, and the lords or their representatives in private courts.

The Anglo-Saxon court had no jury, in anything like the modern sense. None the less, the jury is the one survivor of early methods of legal procedure; it is the one survivor from the days when the law was essentially unprofessional. Some of the books tell us that the jury system came over with the Conqueror, and is descended from late Carolingian sworn inquests —from those small groups of local worthies who gave information on oath to royal officials in the Frankish kingdoms. Others tell us that it originated in the Danelaw, in the twelve senior thegns of the wapentake (the Danish 'hundred'), who produced a list of the notorious scoundrels in the neighbourhood to provide a basis for criminal proceedings. This has a Scandinavian background, and is very close in principle to the later 'jury of presentment', which performed the same office in the courts of Henry II. But the vital point about the origin of the jury is that it represented a compromise between the way in which courts were generally conducted in early times, and the convenience which all societies have discovered in delegating essential business to small committees. There are plenty of cases in the years immediately after the Norman Conquest of folk being collected in little groups of four or seven or twelve to give specific information. The Danelaw thegns are the only case known before the Conquest; but there is no reason to suppose that they were unique. Later on we shall see these committees at work, and study the growth of the jury more closely. Our present interest is in the popular courts from whose practice it originally grew.

The essence of early English law is that it was 'popular' law. The people at large were the repositories of law; they were the judges in the public courts. Law represented custom, of which any man with a good memory might be the repository, and local opinion; it was the one quasi-democratic thing about our early society. The judgments of the 'hundred' court, says Sir Frank Stenton, 'represented the deliberations of peasants learned in the law, who might be guided but could never be controlled by the intervention of the king's reeve, their president.' [2] Guidance was often very important in medieval deliberations. But it

79

was never forgotten that these court were popular courts.

What was the function of these 'peasants learned in the law'? If we look closer, we find they did almost everything except what a modern jury does. They provided local knowledge. They answered such questions as: Who has held this land in living memory? Is this man a notorious criminal? They were witnesses and counsel, so to speak. They also, in theory, stated the law, although they must normally have had to submit to guidance on this point. But they did not normally say whether the party in a criminal suit was innocent or guilty. With a becoming humility they confessed they did not know. Indeed, in many cases it must have been extremely difficult to discover. (Even in the more settled conditions of the thirteenth century hundreds of unsolved crimes might be committed in a single year.) The pre-Conquest court had solid grounds for leaving this question to higher authority. A solemn oath, often on sacred relics, in which the accused man would normally be supported by a team of 'oath-helpers', cleared him of the deed; or rather, exposed him to the judgment of God, which would be kindly to the innocent, but might later undo the guilty. In early days the oath-helpers came from the kindred of the accused; in later times from his neighbours and friends, and so constituted a less partial panel of witnesses. The other method of proof was a more direct appeal to divine judgment. 'Among our own forefathers,' wrote Maitland, 'the two most fashionable methods of obtaining a *iudicium Dei* were that which adjured a pool of water to receive the innocent and that which regarded a burnt hand as a proof of guilt.'[3] In the former case the accused was thrown into the pool; if he floated, he was guilty, if he sank, he was innocent. In the latter case, he was given a red-hot iron to hold; if he came away unmarked, he was innocent. How these ordeals were conducted, we do not precisely know; but contrary to what one might expect, it appears that in both cases a suspect had an even chance of escape. Both, no doubt, were open to human intervention as well as to divine.

'The iron which belongs to the three-fold ordeal is to weigh three pounds.' So runs one of the jottings attached to an ordinance of the mid-tenth century; and its fellow reads: 'A cow's bell, a dog's collar, a blast-horn; each of these three is worth a shilling, and each is reckoned an informer.'[4] The commonest kind of theft was cattle stealing, and a bell attached to the cow helped the pursuers. So did a good dog. Since there was no police force, the whole neighbourhood had to be roused to the 'hue and cry' when a thief was to be pursued; and it was roused by a bugle or 'blast-horn'. The cow's bell, the dog's collar and the blast-horn were symbols of justice as natural and familiar as the policeman's helmet is to us today.

(2) LOCAL GOVERNMENT

Medieval government knew no clear distinction between justice and administration—between the judicature and the executive, as the eighteenth-century theorists had it. The independence of the English judges is the result of a long and tortuous development. They began as the king's representatives; and in early days the king himself often presided in his own court. Equally, the presidents of local courts were royal officials, as much concerned with enforcing royal rights, levying taxes, and the other paraphernalia of administration, as with justice. It is for this reason that one cannot discuss the courts and the lawsuits in which they engaged without first surveying the general structure of English local government.

Nothing reveals the continuity of English life and institutional development more clearly than the history of the English shires. With the exception of Lancashire and the four counties to its north and the pocket shire of Rutland, all the English shires or counties were established in or before the tenth century. Some represented older units—the kingdoms of Kent, Sussex, Surrey, Essex, Middlesex; some were of great antiquity as units of local government, like the shires of Wessex. Some grew up round the headquarters of Danish armies—notably round Lincoln, Derby, Nottingham, and Leicester. These were four of the 'five boroughs' used by the Danes as military centres. Some, including most of the shires of the west Midlands, were artificially created as the power of the kings of Wessex spread north in the tenth century. Recent local government Acts have broken some 'counties' into smaller units; but this apart, the boundaries of the major areas of local jurisdiction are still today much as they were in the days of Athelstan, Edgar, and Ethelred.

At the same time the smaller unit of jurisdiction, the hundred, was also becoming fixed. The hundreds had grown up in early days in Wessex, haphazardly, and there they were of many different shapes and sizes. In Kent and Sussex they never

ousted the older regions, called lathes and rapes, which were
of rather larger size than a normal hundred. In the west Midlands they were created at much the same time as the shires;
and here and in other parts of England one finds hundreds of
a more uniform size, revealing the origin of the name. There
was a much smaller, more ancient unit of land called a hide,
traditionally supposed to be land sufficient to support a family.
In the course of time it had become the basis of assessments for
taxation, and like all assessments for taxation in medieval times
it tended to become fossilised. More land might come under
cultivation, prosperity might fluctuate; but the taxpayer found
ancient assessments less burdensome than up-to-date ones, and
the tax-gatherer found the labour of trying to enforce a new
assessment not worth the effort and danger involved. Anglo-
Saxon tax-collectors seem to have imagined that they knew
what a hide meant in terms of land; but all we know is what it
meant in terms of tax. Since the 'hundred' court was the place
where royal officials and local worthies met to decide how the
burden of taxes was to be distributed, there was great administrative convenience in arranging for a 'hundred' to contain
roughly or exactly 100 hides. And so hundreds containing 100
hides—or 200 or 300—were common in the west Midlands.

To us the hundred is an antiquarian memory. The hundred
courts have long ceased to meet, though it is not so long since
all trace of them died away. The shires are very far from being
a memory. These two facts reflect two basic tendencies of late
Anglo-Saxon history, which become clearer to us if we contrast
what was happening in the Frankish kingdom at this time. In
the early ninth century, in the days of Charlemagne, the
whole empire was divided into a number of comparatively
small local units, called counties. They were units of local
jurisdiction; they were governed by royal officers called counts
whose rights and duties resembled those of the later English
ealdorman and sheriff. Within the county was a smaller unit,
called the *centena,* a word very close to our hundred, though it
is doubtful if they were directly connected. When Charlemagne's empire broke up, and the strong controlling hand was
relaxed, the counts became hereditary, independent nobles,
and often ceased to be royal officials in anything but name.
They absorbed into their own body of private rights most of
the royal rights they had been set up to administer; and they
and other local notables swallowed the rights and perquisites of

82

the *centena* so that all trace of it disappeared. Many of the counties survived, but as the names of independent principalities, not as units of royal jurisdiction. Private enterprise took over from royal control, and the old organisation was rapidly forgotten.

In England this never happened. Many shires owed their shape to ancient tradition or to the activities of Danish armies. But once the pattern of administration had been established in the tenth century, the main lines of local geography remained without alteration for hundreds of years. There were some signs in the eleventh century that the creation of the great earldoms by Cnut might start a movement which would lead to the disappearance of the shires. But this was prevented by the Norman Conquest. The English monarchy was sufficiently strong to prevent the local courts from being swamped by a territorially based nobility. Moreover, the growth in dignity of the ealdorman or earl meant that he became too busy to preside at the court of every shire in his earldom, and in the eleventh century more and more of his duties were delegated to a new official, the shire-reeve or sheriff. At first commonly a protégé of the earl, the sheriff was brought by strong monarchs wholly under the king's direct control; in his turn the sheriff threatened to become over-powerful, but the Norman kings were able to dominate him, and so make him the pivotal official of English local government.

The story of the hundred courts is not quite so free from ambiguity as that of the shires. The hundred courts began by being, like the shire courts, both royal and popular; the king had the power of appointing their president, the people were suitors and judges. But in two ways great lords of the neighbourhood might absorb or compete with the king's rights in the hundred. Apart from the royal, shire, and hundred courts there was an ancient body of private courts, 'seignorial' courts, controlled by lords other than the king. From the tenth century onwards the kings were strong enough to limit and define the jurisdiction of these courts. The courts had very various kinds of jurisdiction—described in the famous jingle 'sac and soc, toll and team and infangenetheof'. 'Sac and soc' referred to the basic jurisdiction of a seignorial court, especially the right to deal with land disputes; 'toll and team' granted jurisdiction over cattle as well as over men—the right to levy tolls on cattle sales and the right to give men accused of stealing cattle a

83

hearing. 'Infangenetheof' gave power to do justice on a thief caught red-handed on the estate. They were elements of a crude judicial system, perhaps; but essential to a lord for two good reasons. They gave him the power to keep elementary order and do elementary justice among his tenants, which was an essential part of any medieval conception of 'lordship'; and they provided him with money. Justice, as the medieval proverb had it, was a great source of revenue: *magnum emolumentum iustitia*.

Such was the private court; and the private court of a great estate could compete with the official hundred court, could even swallow it. Sometimes this was done by open means, and from the tenth century on a great number of hundred courts were granted away, or their usurpation confirmed, by the king. This happened more often after the Conquest than before; feudal justice in early Norman times was very greedy. But in most shires in the last century of Anglo-Saxon history the hundred organisation flourished as the meeting place of local worthies and royal officials—the first breeding ground of the English tradition of administration by discussion and consent.

The special character of English government in the Middle Ages has been called 'self-government at the king's command'. This meant that the king had to listen to what his subjects said; but it gave him an unusually good opportunity to tell them what to do with some shadow of confidence that they would do it. Only the great met the king in person, in the great council, 'the moot of the wise men' as it was euphemistically called, the Witenagemot or Witan. But every thegn and many freemen had a chance to meet the royal representative in shire and hundred. Before the Conquest this meant much to the king; little to the subject. Later on it came to mean more to both.

(3) CENTRAL GOVERNMENT AND THE MONARCHY

In the museums of Scandinavia may be seen great quantities of English coins of the late tenth and early eleventh centuries, all that remains of the immense tributes levied by the Danes from Ethelred and his government. The sums raised in any particular year, varying from £10,000 to £80,000, may not seem startling in modern terms. But the pound now has a tiny fraction of its tenth-century value; and in the tenth and eleventh centuries, in every European country, the scale of operations

84

was infinitely less than it is today; even in the twelfth century an English king had normally to be content with an annual revenue of less than £30,000. Towns and markets were small and only slow in growth. A part of the royal revenues was still levied in kind. The first regular silver currency since Roman times had been struck in the eighth century, and its use in everyday life, for buying and selling, for paying rents and for paying taxes, was only slowly spreading. The Dane-geld was paid in what was virtually the only English coin of the day; the silver penny.[5] If we try to imagine Ethelred's subjects going through the process of coining and distributing these pennies, then assessing each hide and hundred for its contribution and collecting these barrowloads of pennies with considerable speed when the Danes demanded payment, we come to appreciate that English government, for its day, had some remarkably sophisticated tools at its command. The mints which struck the coins were subject to an elaborate organisation—perhaps the most elaborate in western Europe. The whole process of taxation, down to the moment when the coins entered the treasury at Winchester in the form of taxes, required large-scale organisation and co-operation between royal officials and the leading thegns of hundreds and wapentakes. All this we may take for granted. But in the early Middle Ages it could not be taken for granted; that a king could tax directly with a reaonable expectation that most of his subjects would pay up and be fairly treated was a portent.

The Dane-geld was the most direct tax and illustrates the system most clearly. But it was not at this time the most regular or normal source of royal revenue. The Dane-geld was an occasional tax to meet a crisis; though once the Danish menace was removed, the king levied it for other crises, or imagined a crisis to excuse him for levying so admirable a form of revenue. In principle, as in the sixteenth century, the king lived 'of his own', that is, out of his private income. As king he was the greatest landowner in the country, and the normal expense of maintaining the royal household was met out of the ancient system of food-farms. Each royal manor or group of manors was responsible for feeding the king's household for one or more days and nights a year—the unit of payment was quaintly called 'the farm of one night'. In early days this is quite literally what happened: a law of King Ine (late seventh century) says precisely how many cheeses and how many pounds of butter

85

and how many eels a lord can demand from ten hides. In practice such highly detailed lists must have been a rough guide rather than a precise tally. Sometimes the food was consumed on the manor, if the king happened to be visiting that part of the country; more often it would have to be carted to wherever the court was staying. When the King of Wessex became King of England, and his court travelled all over the kingdom, the system must have been hard to maintain; more and more often a part or the whole of these farms came to be commuted for money. This money was collected by the local sheriff, who also collected other items of royal revenue, including profits of justice in royal courts, and brought them to the treasury.

There is no reason to suppose that sheriffs or treasurers were literate: so far as we know, accounting and auditing at Winchester was done without written records, by means of the tally. The tally was simply a notched stick; the notches registered sums of money. When a sum had changed hands a tally was cut, then split down the middle so that each half showed the identical notches; one half was given to the man paying in as his receipt, the other stayed in the treasury as its record. Further progress in financial arithmetic, so far as we know, did not come until after the Norman Conquest.

None the less, the sheriff had to have men about him who could read, because he and the other great men of the shire were liable to receive letters from the king containing essential instructions. Before the tenth century messages were mostly sent by word of mouth; a message or a letter was authenticated by a ring or some other token of the sender. The only formal written instruments of government were charters establishing land ownership, the 'land-books' as they are called. Most land grants took place without charters; but under special circumstances, even before the Conquest, written evidence was needed, and institutions whose inmates were literate, like monasteries, were specially keen to possess and preserve written evidence of their most valuable properties and privileges. The charters were usually in Latin, and as time passed their language became increasingly elaborate and increasingly obscure. They reached the height of elaboration in the time of King Athelstan, whose charters describe at length the vileness of the world, and the fearful disasters in this world and the next that will overtake anyone who tampers with the grants described. Formidable documents were produced in many parts of Europe at this time; but none can compare for pretentiousness and absurdity with Athelstan's. 'If ... anyone puffed up with the pride of arrogance shall try to destroy or infringe this little document of my agreement and confirmation,' runs one clause from an immense charter, 'let him know that on the last and fearful day of assembly, when the trumpet of the archangel is clanging the call and bodies are leaving the foul graveyards, he will burn with Judas the committor of impious treachery and also with the miserable Jews, blaspheming with sacrilegious mouth Christ on the altar of the Cross, in eternal confusion in the devouring flames of blazing torments in punishment without end.'

When Athelstan granted a large area, Amounderness, in what is now Lancashire, to the Archbishop of York, extreme statements were needed if the grant was to take effect. But the same type of language was also used for quite small grants of land—for anything indeed for which a 'book' was deemed necessary. It may well be that it was the exceptional contrast between the terms of these fantastic charters and the workaday character of normal business which suggested the use of a simpler document. Whatever the reason, there is no doubt that it was in the English court that the idea was devised of using the simplest kind of document—a mere letter written in English—for grants and instructions to which special thunders did not need to be attached. There could be no greater contrast than that between the old land-book and the new 'writ', as we call a charter in this simple form. Here is one in which Edward the Confessor greets his successor-to-be: 'Edward the king greets Harold the earl and Tofi his sheriff and all his thegns in Somerset in friendly fashion. And I make known that Alfred has sold to Giso the bishop [of Wells] the land of Litton peacefully and quietly: he did this in my presence at Perrott, and in the presence of Edith, my wife, Harold the earl and many others who were there present with us. We also wish that the same bishop shall hold that land with all its appurtenances which the bishop possesses with sac and soc as freely as any of his predecessors as bishops ever held anything. And if anything be taken away from it unjustly we ask that it may be restored. Nor shall it be done otherwise.'

The writ was a remarkable instrument in its day. It was a real exercise in literate government in an illiterate age. Being in English, it could be read out to Tofi the sheriff and all the thegns assembled in the shire court of Somerset without any translation or interpretation. It carried, furthermore, large and imposing evidence of its authenticity. The land-book had carried 'signatures', which were merely crosses supposed to be added by the witnesses of the charter. But the crosses could easily be forged, and a scribe's copy—in which he himself made all the crosses—carried as much weight as an autograph. By the eleventh century the writ carried a seal: a large lump of wax with the impress of the Great Seal of England, which could be shown to an audience to whom a signature would have meant nothing.

Even so, surviving eleventh-century writs are rare, and they were probably never very extensively used before the Conquest. When the custom began we do not know. When we first meet the writ in the late tenth century it had become a bureaucratic instrument of a primitive kind. It was written by one of the clerks of the royal chapel, who were building up what was later to become the royal chancery—the royal writing office, from which came all documents issued under the Great Seal.

It may seem strange to us, who assume the letter as the basis for literate government, that medieval man was so slow to use it. But his assumptions were different; and the entry of literacy into government was a more difficult and a more fundamental process than is often realised. The writ may have been comparatively little used before the Conquest. But it had a tremendous future before it, and not only in England. Even before the Conquest it symbolised the first real beginnings of literate government, made possible by the specially close alliance of king and Church.

There were in the tenth century only two monarchs in western Europe who possessed power comparable to that of the English kings. Both called themselves kings of the Franks. One of them was king of the area which broadly coincided with what we call France; king in name that is, because over most of France he had no more stable sway than the English kings in Wales and Scotland. Outside the narrow extent of the royal domain, the 'Île de France', his influence was slight and fluctuating; there was certainly no effective structure of royal officials and royal courts. The other Frankish king, the king of what we call Germany, was a far more powerful monarch, the most powerful in Europe. His influence was felt in every corner of Germany; he ruled through an elaborate hierarchy of royal officials; his links with the Church were almost as close as

Edgar's. There are many interesting parallels between the German and the English monarchies. Both were trying to break down local particularism and the diversity of tradition of the different parts of their kingdom; both had to struggle against a few great subjects who were determined to carve the kingdom up into duchies or earldoms. In the long run England emerged the more closely knit, the more durable kingdom; in particular, the structure of royal courts and royal officials was never destroyed, or seriously weakened.

The power of the English monarchy, like that of all medieval monarchies, depended to a great extent on the personality of the king. One can analyse many deep foundations of power—divine right, the force of custom, the idea that the king was in a special sense the people's representative in all his dealings, and the actual instruments of government which we have been describing. It is true that a succession of weak kings between 975 and 1016, and again between 1035 and 1066, failed to undermine these foundations; that in certain respects the power of the monarchy was even increasing. But it is most unlikely that this could have happened without the strong rule of Cnut from 1016 to 1035; and it is probable that some aspects of royal strength would have disappeared had a weak king succeeded in 1066. Every monarchy had to face the problem; either it must ensure a succession of able kings, or face the possibility of collapse.

All medieval kings, in some sense or another, were 'elected'. But when we have said that we have said very little, because no historical label has been susceptible to more different interpretations than the word 'election'. To us it means free choice of a representative by a specified body of electors, a choice determined by some kind of majority principle. All these ideas were foreign to the world of thought of the early Middle Ages. Election did not mean free choice, for two good reasons. First of all, the choice lay with God; the king, once chosen, was king by God's grace. God worked through human agents and above all through the custom of the land. It was custom which dictated how a man became king and who should be chosen. Once again we come up against the maddening indefiniteness of primitive law. When a king died it was usually obvious to the Witenagemot who should succeed him. The leading councillor presented the king-to-be to the Witan, the wise men, who nodded their assent. All early medieval elections seem to have consisted in some form of 'designation' and acclamation. Who made the designation is another matter. All the documents will tell us is that this or that king was 'elected by the magnates'. How they did it we can only deduce from later cases or continental analogies—or from the result. In 1087, when William the Conqueror lay dying in Rouen, he designated William, his second son, as King of England, and sent instructions to Lanfranc to see to the succession. Lanfranc, as Archbishop of Canterbury, the King's first councillor, and Regent in William's absence, received the instructions from the younger William shortly after the father's death. He summoned the magnates in great haste. In a formal assembly—no doubt preceded by a certain amount of lobbying such as we know to have taken place when Henry I became king—Lanfranc presented William to the magnates. They duly elected him, or, as we should say, acclaimed him; whereupon Lanfranc set the seal of divine sanction on the new king by anointing and crowning him according to the traditional English rites.

Continental analogies suggest that this would be the normal process. There was no election in our sense. The new king was expected to be next in succession to his predecessor, unless there was some special reason for avoiding the principle of primogeniture. But in practice it was very frequently avoided, and a whole series of somewhat indeterminate notions governed the reasons for overriding it. This meant that there was an element of choice, on somebody's part. But there was no question of a determinate body of electors choosing on a majority principle. Often the choice must effectively have been made in the old king's lifetime. We may be sure that tenth-century kings sometimes designated their successors, as did many of the German kings of this period, and as the Norman kings usually tried to do. When the old king died, a formal election would still be necessary, some leading magnate would doubtless propose and the Witan accept, as they accepted William Rufus; and then the archbishop would crown, unless as in Edgar's case, there were special reasons for delaying the coronation. When there was serious doubt—as in the anarchy before Cnut's accession—the magnates had to exercise a certain freedom of choice, though doubtless the formal process would be the same. This freedom of choice might or might not have a profound influence on the future of the monarchy. In Germany similar conditions led in the end to the formation of a real body of electors, who chose freely. But in England in the early eleventh century freedom of choice seems to have been an embarrassment, from which one escaped as soon as convenient. There was an element of 'election' in many king-makings in later medieval England. Sometimes the magnates used these occasions as opportunities to exact special promises from the king. But the English monarchy was never elective in the modern sense of the word.

Nor was it, strictly, a limited monarchy. The king consulted his Witan, and as the monarchy became more civilised and its institutions more complex, effective rule came to depend on the co-operation of more and more people. The more they co-operated, the more the king could govern, the more powerful he was. This formed in a sense a limitation on his autocratic powers. Nevertheless, the Anglo-Saxon king could be a very powerful man. Custom limited his autocracy, but in the vaguest of terms. Churchmen might treat Cnut as a pious protector, a paternal monarch. But to the men who remembered him as the savage young Viking who slaughtered his enemies, his power rested on a different set of qualities. No medieval monarch was wholly successful who could not inspire fear as well as respect in his subjects; a monarch whom everyone feared could become almost unassailable.

1. *Domesday Book and Beyond*, p. 9.
2. *Anglo-Saxon England*, p. 296: 'never' is perhaps an overstatement.
3. Pollock and Maitland, *History of English Law*, II, pp. 598–9.
4. *English Historical Documents*, I (ed. D. Whitelock), p. 394.
5. Apparently coins of the value of one-third of a penny were struck in Alfred's time and throughout the early Middle Ages half-pennies and farthings might be made by cutting a penny into halves or quarters. Apart from coins, payment could be made by weight of silver (or of gold, when gold was available). This explains the pound, the shilling, and the mark, which were in origin weights, and so came to be used very commonly as coins 'of account' (i.e. in accounting). The mark was two-thirds of a pound, i.e. 13s. 4d.

CHAPTER FIVE

THE NORMAN CONQUEST, 1035–87

Across the English Channel, at its narrowest point, lay another great Viking state, the duchy of Normandy. A Norman princess, Emma, had successively married both Ethelred and Cnut. A Norman duke, Robert I, amiably known to later tradition as Robert the Devil, had gone through a form of marriage with a sister of Cnut. Duke Robert was naturally interested in English politics, all the more because the young sons of Ethelred, Alfred, and Edward, were exiles living in his duchy. Had Robert not died on his way back from a pilgrimage to Jerusalem in 1035, it is highly probable that he would have staged an invasion of England on these young men's behalf.

In 1035 Duke Robert died, and his illegitimate son, William, succeeded at the age of seven. His chances of survival seemed slender. His early years were spent in dealing with troubles at home: first with rebellious subjects and then with a dangerous overlord. His duchy was not free from internal and external dangers until 1060, and even then his attention was concentrated on the conquest of Maine until at least 1063. In that year he began to look seriously at his chances of the English throne. He had been in touch with England since his childhood friend, Edward the Aetheling, had become king in 1042; he may have visited it in 1051 or 1052, but before 1063 he was too closely engaged in the affairs of his own duchy to think much of foreign adventure. Nature and his fearful upbringing had made William a stern practical man, who ruled by force and not by dreams. But he was also provided with imagination—the imagination needed by a great constructive ruler.

England had been conquered by a Viking leader in 1016, and Cnut's success, and his care to rule in the tradition of his English predecessors, might seem to have left his kingdom secure against another similar conquest. But there were potential weaknesses in Cnut's England which might, if occasion offered, have given a foreign pretender a chance to succeed.

In the first place Cnut died young (1035), and left an uncertain succession. His throne was disputed between his two

93

sons: Harold, his son by his concubine, Aelfgifu, and Hartha-cnut, his son by his queen, Emma. Each was strongly supported by his mother. In addition, Ethelred's sons, Alfred and Edward, were awaiting their chance. In the event, Harold and Hartha-cnut succeeded in turn, and Alfred, attempting to intervene, was arrested and cruelly maltreated, and shortly afterwards died. Cnut's two sons each died very young after a short and violent reign, and the way was clear for Edward, later known as Edward the Confessor (1042–66).

Edward the Confessor stepped into an exceedingly difficult inheritance. He had spent most of his life in Normandy and elsewhere on the Continent, and was not personally known to the English leaders. This meant that he could not hope, in his early years at least, to outshine in personal prestige the great earls whom he had inherited from Cnut. In fact they were bound to dominate him until he had proved himself. Edward had some ability, but lacked perhaps the energy and ruthless determination of a successful king. He was not a great warrior, and he never succeeded in mastering the earls. This did not mean that his throne was insecure. He never consummated his marriage, and had no close heirs or rivals—his one nephew died well before him, and his great-nephew was never seriously considered for the throne. There were in fact only two possible alternatives to Edward seriously canvassed before the last years of his reign, the Duke of Normandy and the King of Norway. Duke William was Edward's own choice for his successor, and there was no question of William's trying to usurp Edward's throne. So far as we know, the King of Norway, Harold Hardrada, was not favoured by any of the earls before 1065. It may even be true that it was the threat of foreign invasion which kept them loyal to Edward.

But their loyalty did not make his government easy. In his early years the most powerful of the earls was Godwin of Wessex, the king-maker: the man who had secured the succession of Harold I to Cnut, and probably played a leading part in Edward's own succession. He and his family dominated the south of England and ruled the King; Godwin's daughter, Edith, was married to Edward. It is clear, nevertheless, that Edward was eager to throw off the tutelage. In itself it was doubtless irksome; and he knew Godwin to have been responsible for the death of his elder brother, Alfred. Edward waited, gathering round him a group of followers, both lay and

94

clerical, from all over north-western Europe, especially from Lorraine, Brittany, and Normandy. The English court was cosmopolitan as never before. Half the clergy of the royal chapel were recruited from abroad, and it was recognised over a wide area as a place in which an ambitious man might seek wealth and promotion.

In 1051 a Norman, Robert of Jumièges, Bishop of London, was promoted to the see of Canterbury, and Edward received a visit from a leading Norman count, Eustace of Boulogne. These events did not rouse a feeling of national distrust, as some historians have thought; but they made clear to Godwin and his family that Edward was deliberately surrounding himself with influences more congenial than themselves. Trouble arose between Godwin and the King; Godwin raised an army and tried to force Edward's hand. But Edward was supported by the earls of Mercia and Northumbria in this crisis, and by skilful manoeuvring he forced the family of Godwin into exile —all save Queen Edith, who was sent into enforced retreat among the nuns of Wherwell. Within a few months Edward had promised Duke William the crown.

Before 1052 was over, Earl Godwin had managed to return and dictate his terms to the King. These included the restoration to the family of their earldoms and to the Queen of her place in court. The brief spell of personal government was over. Godwin himself died in 1053, but his earldom and his standing passed to his eldest surviving son, Harold. The King was no mere cypher in his last years, as he has sometimes been pictured. It is true that he appeared less prone to intrigue, and even less active than before; that his central interest was the re-founding and rebuilding of Westminster Abbey. He was also compelled in 1052 to dismiss some of his Frenchmen from court, including the Archbishop of Canterbury. But other events seem to show Edward still in control, and a part of Godwin's earldom went to Edward's Norman nephew, Ralph, who organised Herefordshire on the model of a Norman frontier province. Harold, however, was undoubtedly the first man in the kingdom, the 'under-king' as one writer calls him, the leader of the English army. Necessity or circumstances had led to something like a true reconciliation between Edward and his wife's family. It may even be that Edward had partly reconciled Harold to Duke William's succession. For some reason now past explaining Harold crossed the Channel in 1064, was captured by the Count of Ponthieu, and rescued by William. Then followed the mysterious arrangement so graphically portrayed in the Bayeux Tapestry. Duke William somehow found the opportunity to cajole or compel Harold into an oath, sworn on the relics of Bayeux Cathedral, to support William's claim to the throne.

The crisis of 1066 came swiftly and with only the slightest of warnings. Tostig, Harold's brother, had been Earl of Northumbria since old Siward's death in 1055. But the Northumbrians owed no natural allegiance to a son of Godwin, and they proved intractable subjects. In 1065 they rebelled and forced the King to appoint Morcar, brother of Edwin, Earl of Mercia, and grandson of Cnut's earl, Leofric, in Tostig's place. At the end of the year the King was known to be dying, and the vultures began to collect. Three men were known to have the ambition to be king: Harold Hardrada of Norway, William of Normandy, and Harold of Wessex. What happened in the King's court at Christmas we shall never know. But in the end he designated Harold of Wessex as his successor; and on the day after the King's death (6th January 1066) Harold was duly accepted by the magnates and crowned. We do not know what caused the King to change his mind. Either he or those about him must have reckoned that the confusion of the country, the uncertain state of Northumbria, and the threatened invasion of Harold Hardrada, demanded a king who could instantly command the allegiance of a great part of England.

Their calculations were very nearly justified. In his brief reign Harold revealed his skill, determination, and generalship to the full. He is first recorded at York in the early months of the year. Then in May he dealt with an attack by his brother, Tostig, on the south-east coast. This raid was presumed by Harold to be the precursor of an invasion from Normandy, and he mobilised all the military and naval resources at his disposal to meet an attack by William. But these forces could not be held in readiness indefinitely. Early in September the militia was disbanded, and the ships were moved towards London— many of them being lost on the way. Before the end of the month both Harold Hardrada (now in alliance with Tostig) and William of Normandy had landed in England.

The Norwegian came first, and somehow achieved surprise. Earl Edwin and Earl Morcar gathered an army against him, but were checked in a violent battle at Fulford. From now on

Harold of England had to rely on his own resources. He was in the south, organising the dispersal of the militia, when the news was brought to him of the Norwegian landing. He marched north with great rapidity, and fell on the enemy before they could have expected him at Stamford Bridge, near York. Three hundred ships or more brought the Norwegian host to England; twenty-five sufficed to take away the survivors of Fulford and Stamford Bridge. Both Tostig and Harold of Norway were among the slain. Harold of England had won a great and decisive victory. The threat which had hung over the country for twenty years was removed, and rebellion from within his family had been scotched. Harold might well look forward to the fruit of so great a victory: to the prestige of a great warrior and the unquestioned obedience which had been the lot of Athelstan and Cnut after their victories. A few days later he learned of the landing of William of Normandy.

William's preparations had been very swiftly made. He needed ships and supplies, an army more considerable than could be levied in Normandy alone, and needed moral and spiritual support. To many his scheme must have seemed a desperate adventure. With the resources of a single duchy William was planning to attack one of the richest and most powerful kingdoms in northern Europe, controlled by a soldier as experienced and competent as himself. The odds were heavily against him, and clearly some of his followers told him as much. His critics were what we should call realists, but the destinies of Europe have rarely been decided by *Realpolitik*. William was allowed to go ahead with his plans, and set about gathering support from outside the duchy. The army which assembled on the Norman coast in the summer had been recruited from Normandy, Brittany, Maine (recently made a subject principality), and Flanders, the county of his father-in-law; with a sprinkling from all over northern France and even from the recently formed Norman states in southern Italy. It was the greatest adventure of the day, and William had given it a coat of respectability by winning papal support. He had claimed at Rome that England was rightly his, that Harold was a perjurer and usurper: The nominal leader of the English Church, Archbishop Stigand, had acquired his see irregularly on the removal of his predecessor in 1052 and held it in plurality with that of Winchester and in defiance of a papal sentence of deposition.[1] William had already won the reputation of being friendly to reform in the Church; he was in a position to tempt the papacy. The idea was gaining ground in papal circles that even apparently aggressive wars, if fought in a just and holy cause, could be blessed; the Pope, urged on by Hildebrand, the future Pope Gregory VII, gave William his blessing, and so made the campaign of Hastings something very like a Crusade. The Duke's material preparations—the felling of trees, the building of ships, and gathering of arms and other stores—are very vividly shown in the Bayeux Tapestry. For a number of weeks in August and September the army was held up on the Norman coast by contrary winds. At last, on 27th September, two days after the battle of Stamford Bridge, the wind changed, and William was able to slip across the Channel. He landed at Pevensey, but rapidly established his base at Hastings.

The battle of Hastings was fought on Saturday, 14th October, sixteen days after William's landing, nineteen days after the battle of Stamford Bridge. The campaign was extraordinarily rapid. After the briefest of pauses Harold hurried south. He left himself no time to collect a substantial army; but apparently marched into Sussex with his own and his brother's house-carles, such thegns as had been able to answer his hasty summons and the local levies of the immediate neighbourhood. Nobody has ever explained his haste; had he waited, he could have collected a far larger army. He may have doubted the loyalty of the southern counties; he may have wished to protect his own estates, so many of which lay near Pevensey and Hastings. We do not know what intelligence he had; nor do we know how large a force William had landed. William was reinforced very soon after the battle; it may be that he had landed only a part of his army, and that Harold calculated on pushing it into the sea before reinforcements came. It is probable in any case that Harold underestimated the Norman strength, and that his great victory in the north had made him over-confident.

The decisive battle was fought between very small forces. Harold had camped his army for the night in a natural defensive position on the edge of the Weald, the great forest of Kent and Sussex and Surrey, nine miles from Hastings, where the town of Battle now lies. It was camped on a promontory or hill, with the forest behind it, and a front of only 500 or 600 yards. Beyond this front lay slopes of varying steepness, up which an advancing enemy must come. It was a strong position, but a very narrow one. Its size suggests that the English army was not much more than 3,000 strong; and it is unlikely that the effective Norman strength was very much greater. The battle of Hastings was an altogether slighter affair than Stamford Bridge.

Early in the morning of 14th October the Normans began the attack. It seems that they had achieved tactical surprise. Harold hastily organised his camp as a defensive position, placing his best troops, dismounted, shoulder to shoulder along the crest of the hill. Their shields formed a solid and impenetrable wall, and the axes of the housecarles were formidable weapons against the chain mail of the Norman knights.

The battle continued from early morning until dusk. The Norman attacks were beaten off as steadily as the French charges at Waterloo. At one moment the Normans retreated in some confusion, and were only rallied by Duke William's prompt intervention. This retreat proved the undoing of the English army. A number of the English broke ranks and pursued the Normans, who, when they had recovered, turned and cut them down. Later in the day, we are told, the Normans twice repeated the manoeuvre: they feigned retreat, and then turned on their pursuers. By such means the English 'shield-wall' was gradually whittled away; and its morale was constantly impaired by showers of arrows from the Norman archers. As dusk was falling King Harold himself was killed. This was decisive. The English resisted some time longer, and even in their retreat did much damage to the Norman attackers. But in the end 'the French had possession of the place of slaughter'.

The death of Harold and his two brothers in the battle was a vital stroke of fortune for William. If Harold had still been at large after the battle, William would have had many difficulties to face. Even so, the English Witan did not immediately take William as seriously as he had hoped. The legitimate adults of the large house of Godwin were now virtually extinct, and the only native heir was Edward the Confessor's great-nephew, Edgar the Aetheling, whom no-one had seriously considered hitherto. The Archbishop of York, the Archbishop of Canterbury, the Earls of Mercia and Northumbria, and the citizens of London all declared for Edgar. At this stage they seem to have regarded William as little more than a lucky adventurer.

William meanwhile returned to Hastings, 'and waited there to see if there would be any surrender', and also to collect his reinforcements. He then began a long roundabout march on London, via Dover and Southwark, the middle Thames, and Berkhamstead. This gave him time to subdue the land between his coastal bases and the city, and to give England due notice of his methods. William was a pious man; but he was also utterly ruthless. He knew from experience that a successful ruler had to be feared, and he reckoned that this was even more true of a successful usurper. He harried the countryside as he went, and twenty years later in the signs of declining value and devastation recorded in the description of the manors in Domesday Book, the route of his march can still be traced. By the time William reached Berkhamstead most of the English leaders had decided to submit, and on Christmas Day he was anointed and crowned in Westminster Abbey. The ceremony was performed by the Archbishop of York. Stigand of Canterbury had submitted to William, and was left in possession of his see until 1070; but as his irregularities had been one of the grounds of papal support for William, the new King could hardly accept anointing from him.

William claimed to have stepped into his rightful inheritance, and at first he took some steps to maintain continuity of rule, as Cnut had done. The main points in the old system of local and central government were continued, but rapidly adapted and developed. For a time the native English earls and thegns mostly remained in possession of their properties. A sufficient number of them had fallen at Hastings to provide the King with land to reward the most outstanding or grasping of his followers. He and his lieutenants began at once to build castles at key places and in many of the larger towns; symbols to the Normans of normal military organisation, to the English of the beginnings of foreign domination.

William's hopes of succeeding as an English king accepted by the English leaders rapidly disappeared. From 1068 to 1070 he had to deal with almost continuous rebellion in Northumbria and sporadic outbreaks in Wessex and Mercia. The revolt in the north in 1069–70 was made all the more serious by Danish intervention. It was joined by Waltheof, old Siward's son, now the chief power in Northumbria, and royal suspicion drove Edwin and Morcar into the alliance. In the end Waltheof and most of his associates submitted, Edwin was killed by his own men, and Morcar became a fugitive. After 1070 resistance was reduced to guerilla warfare under such leaders as the celebrated

Hereward the Wake, who held out for a time in the Isle of Ely. William's subjection of Mercia and the north was sealed in the same fashion as his original conquest of the south-east, by devastation. His army harried extensive areas in the west Midlands, and he laid waste the vale of York so effectively that large areas of it had to be re-colonised in the twelfth century.

By 1070 England had been conquered and had learned to fear its conqueror. This did not mean that William was free from wars and rebellions. In France, his position in 1066 had been made secure by the minority of King Philip I, the alliance of Flanders, the submission of Brittany and Maine, and anarchy in Anjou. None of these circumstances was lasting, and in his later years war with Anjou, difficulties in Maine, and the rebellion of his eldest son, Robert, often supported by King Philip, kept him occupied in indecisive campaigns. In England the northern frontier was never entirely quiescent until Robert (in an interval between rebellions), led a punitive expedition in 1080 into Scotland, and strengthened the defences of Northumbria by building a fortress on the north bank of the Tyne at the place still called Newcastle. In England as a whole, the only serious rebellion after 1070 came in 1075. In that year Earl Waltheof allied with the Earl of East Anglia, a Breton whose family had been settled in England by Edward the Confessor, and the Earl of Hereford, son of William's leading viceroy on the Welsh marches, William FitzOsbern; and the three earls expected support from the Danes, which came too late to help them. Their rebellion was swiftly suppressed. The Breton fled to Brittany; the Norman, according to Norman custom, was imprisoned and lost his lands; Earl Waltheof, according to English custom, was beheaded. With him the last of the native earls disappeared from the scene, and although the title of earl has survived from that day to this, the power of Cnut's earldoms was never revived outside the frontier marches of Wales and Scotland.

In 1085 the Conqueror prepared to face the last serious threat to his authority in England, a final attempt at invasion from Scandinavia. Internal troubles in Denmark prevented the attack from developing. But it may well have been this crisis which led William to the great stock-taking which formed the climax of his reign, and underlined the strength of his control over England and the magnitude of the changes he and his followers had made.

In this year the King spent Christmas at Gloucester, and there 'had important deliberations and exhaustive discussions with his council about this land, how it was peopled, and with what sort of men.' Then he sent groups of commissioners to every part of England to collect details of each village from sworn inquests of local men—details which included not only who held what land, but much information about the value of each holding and its stock. These details were collected county by county and then digested in local centres; and the digests were sent to Winchester for the final version to be made. One of the digests, that for East Anglia, apparently came too late to be included. And so the great survey—'called by the natives "Domesday" ', as a twelfth-century writer tells us, because it was reckoned to be the final court of appeal in questions of tenure—has been preserved ever since in the national archives in two volumes. Volume I contains the final version of most English counties, volume II is the local digest of East Anglia, never finally revised. There are errors, inequalities, omissions, and incoherences in Domesday Book. But it remains the most impressive record of royal administration in the Europe of its day. It makes modern English historians of the period the envy of continental colleagues. It reminds us that in every sphere of government the elaborate foundations of the Anglo-Saxon monarchy were retained and expanded by the vivid energy of the Normans. Last and not least it is a monument to the imaginative vision and energy of the Conqueror. He may not have conceived the idea, or worked out all its details himself. But only he could have had the energy and confidence to organise so vast an inquiry so swiftly. It is likely that Domesday Book was completed in substantially its present form in little more than a year. While it was being compiled, William confirmed his authority in another way, by a great gathering of landowners at Salisbury, who did homage and renewed their fealty to him. At the end of the year 1086 he left England for his last war in Normandy; on 9th September 1087 he died.

William was more feared than loved in his lifetime, and his English subjects remembered his oppression, his castle-building, his exactions, his avarice. They remembered, too, some more human qualities: his love of the chase—'he loved the stags as dearly as though he had been their father'—and his love of justice, his piety, and rectitude. 'Though stern beyond measure to those who opposed his will, he was kind to those good men who loved God'—and the chronicler goes on to describe William's benefactions to monasteries, in particular his foundation of Battle Abbey on the site of his victory over Harold. The chronicler might have added that William was the only one of his line who was faithful to his wife. To his enemies he was utterly relentless; but the final impression is not one of unrelieved oppression. Successful kings in the eleventh century were rarely admirable in their public dealings. But in government William showed the imagination of a creative statesman —crude perhaps, but none the less remarkable for that. Only a fuller analysis of the effects of the Norman Conquest can reveal his essential achievement.

1. There was precedent for holding two sees at the same time in the career of St Oswald in the tenth century (and of more than one of his successors), who combined the bishopric of Worcester with the archbishopric of York. But the circumstances were entirely different. York in the tenth century was a very poor diocese, with a strong Danish element in its population, still in process of conversion to Christianity. Worcester gave Oswald a secure base in the Christian West Country and an income suited to his standing in the kingdom. Stigand had no such excuse: the see of Canterbury had an income sufficient for its needs, and Winchester was probably the richest in the land.

CHAPTER SIX

FEUDALISM AND THE NORMAN SETTLEMENT

(1) ANGLO-NORMAN FEUDALISM

In the next three chapters we turn aside from our narrative to analyse English society and the effect on it of the Norman Conquest—concentrating first on the ruling class, from knight to king, then on the life of village and town, and thirdly on the life of the Church. To make the analysis clear we shall cast our eyes back before the Conquest, and forward over at least the first three generations of Norman rule. The life of the village is viewed over the period of the book as a whole. After these chapters we resume the narrative in 1087, and only after we have reached the reign of Henry II shall we try to sum up the whole effect of the Norman Conquest.

Normandy was, so to say, the French Danelaw, the one great French principality which owed its origin to Viking leaders alone. In the days of Alfred and Edward the Elder, Danish and Norse settlers had tried to establish themselves at many points along the French and Flemish coast. But profoundly as they affected the whole of this coastline, the only place where the settlers were powerful enough to oust the local hierarchy for more than a short time was Normandy. In 911 the most considerable Viking chief in Normandy, Rollo, was given some measure of recognition as a subject count by the Frankish king. At first, however, it was easier for the counts of Rollo's dynasty to obtain recognition from their overlord than from their subjects. Rollo was the most powerful of a number of semi-independent Viking leaders, and it was only gradually that his successors enforced their rule in Normandy as a whole. The dukes (or counts, as they were usually called) of the turn of the tenth and eleventh centuries were men of piety, after the rough conventions of their race. They were patrons of monasteries and set their followers an example of lavish generosity. But it is a measure of the uncertainty of their authority, even then, that western Normandy was still largely pagan, and that the bishops of Coutances made no serious attempt to occupy their see before the middle of the eleventh century.

By 1066 Normandy was one of the most highly organised feudal states in northern France. The Norman leaders had accepted the fashions of the day in war, administration, and society as well as in the affairs of the Church. But the duchy had very recently achieved this standing, and accepted these standards. When the Conqueror succeeded to the duchy, there was a tradition of strong ducal rule already established, and a tradition of close liaison between duke and Church. But the immediate situation was anarchic. In the lengthy process of subduing his enemies and establishing himself as effective ruler of the duchy, Duke William was able in many ways to convert his Viking principality into a Norman state; to bring it into line with French feudal fashions. The Normans were to prove themselves at this period the most adaptable people in Europe, as well as the most energetic. But the rapidity of their expansion and adaptation was partly made necessary by the social changes taking place in Normandy itself.

Already before the Conqueror's accession, Norman bands had begun to seek land and adventure in southern Italy. Many of the great states of northern France were expanding and developing at this time—Flanders, Blois, Champagne, and Normandy's great rival, Anjou. But in the late eleventh century the Normans outstripped them all and founded great states in England and the south of Italy, and also wandered far and wide in the Mediterranean world and the Near East. Norman population was growing fast, and the Normans had somehow acquired or inherited a vigour which made these immense enterprises possible. But there must have been special reasons why they were, notoriously, the most land-hungry people in Europe.

One at least of these reasons is the development of an orderly feudal hierarchy in the Conqueror's early years. This is of special interest to us, because the same men proceeded later to plant feudal institutions in England. This was their dress rehearsal; and it gives us an opportunity to inquire into the nature of feudalism.

If we wish to understand what Anglo-Norman feudalism was and how it worked, we must first have a clear understanding of two notions which are foreign to us; the attitude of our medieval ancestors to property and their attitude to inheritance. They are the threads by which one may find one's way about what is so unhappily called the feudal system, which I prefer to think of as the feudal labyrinth. Property is a simple idea until one comes to analyse it. A piece of land either is mine or it is not; it may be let to a tenant; it may be requisitioned; but it is mine. Our feudal ancestors had no such simple conception. Property they had—clothes and weapons and jewellery and pots and pans and, sometimes, slaves—but not property in land. In land everyone was a tenant save the king. That did not make even the king owner of the land in our sense of the word; and there was land here and there which did not belong even in theory to the king.

Indeed, it is best to avoid using the word 'ownership' in connection with land at all. Land could be held or possessed; the key words are tenure and possession. The difference between them is quite simple. Possession is a matter of fact; whoever has hold on the land and is actually exploiting it is in possession of it. Tenure is a matter of right; the holder of a piece of land must have acquired a right to it from someone else, must hold it *of* someone. The possessor may simply have moved in.

Tenure is the distinctive feature of feudalism. A feudal society was a military society in which land was the basis of the military organisation: by granting out plots of land in exchange for service the king ensured an adequate supply of heavily armed cavalry troopers; and these knights, as we call them, were the backbone of his army. It was the specific and permanent association of the knights with plots of land which made feudal tenure different from the less organised military society which preceded it; and it was the close association of land with military service which distinguished feudal tenancies from tenancies such as we are used to. In every plot of land a number of people had an interest, and its produce was divided between them. The share of the peasant, such as it was, and the services he performed, will concern us in the next chapter. The peasant served his lord by working and not by fighting, and so we draw a distinction between the feudal labyrinth which involved the upper classes, 'those who fought', and, in a slightly odd way, 'those who prayed', and the manorial labyrinth, which involved 'those who worked' and subjected them to the needs of the ruling *élite*.

Feudal society was a hierarchy, with the king at the summit and the humble knights, the lowest class of the truly professional soldiers, at its foot. At the time of Domesday Book, most of the land in England was held by the king, by ecclesiastical landlords—bishops, cathedrals, abbeys, minsters—and by about

180 barons. These men, barons and ecclesiastics, were called tenants-in-chief, because they held their land directly of the king. William himself seems to have advanced the theory, early in his reign, that England ought to be able to provide him with about 6,000 knights, and he distributed the land on condition that each baron provided him with what was reckoned a reasonable share of this number; the greater churches and monasteries were also required to produce their share. Barons and churches were expected to sub-let portions of their estate in return for the service of these knights. Each knight's estate was called a knight's fee. The king had the right, if he wished, to call out the whole feudal host for sixty (later forty) days a year.

So far, the picture is tidy enough; far tidier than in any other European country. But even in England it was never so simple as this. There never were anything like 6,000 plots of land held by 6,000 knights; and the ladder of tenure always contained more than three rungs.

Before 1290 the law normally expected a man who held a piece of land to hold it, 'for himself and his heirs', for ever. Thus if the king granted a piece of land to A, and A re-granted it to B, and B to C, C would continue to hold of B who would hold it of A who would hold it of the king. It was possible for B to contract out of the hierarchy, but it very frequently happened that he stayed in. In time B might grant another manor to A, so that each was tenant (or 'vassal') of the other. By the late twelfth century the lawyers had discovered that every possible complication could arise.

Land-tenure, moreover, was only one aspect of a complex relationship. The baron did homage and swore fealty to the king for the land he held, for his 'fee' or 'fief' or (if it was especially large) his 'honour'. In a ceremony of the greatest solemnity, he knelt before the king, placed his hands between the king's and said, 'I become your man', promising good faith in all his dealings. This constituted homage; the vassal then rose, laid his hands on a copy of the Gospels, and swore fealty, faithfulness. The baron's own vassals did homage and swore fealty to him in the same way—and so on, to the foot of the ladder. Homage and fealty were expressions of a very tight, very personal bond; the bond which held the feudal hierarchy together. It was very difficult for B to be A's vassal for one manor and A to be the vassal of B for another; at least they had to sort out the relationship in some way, and this was

108

usually done by taking the major tenancy as the key to the situation. A man did liege homage, as it was sometimes called, to the lord from whom he held most of his land, or to the lord who had first given him a fief. But this was never a full answer to the problem, which arose at every level of the feudal hierarchy, even at the summit, where the King of England, as Duke of Normandy, had to do homage to the King of France.

The king's oath to the King of France occasionally influenced his actions. On the whole, most English kings were at enmity with the French king, and paid little heed to their act of homage. But this does not mean that we can take it lightly. It was a solemn matter, and on occasion could be taken very seriously indeed. King John forfeited a great part of his domains in France for taking his oath lightly. The feudal bond, however, was more powerful and more significant when combined with more intimacy than could possibly exist between two rival kings. The structure of law surrounding land-tenure derived mainly from the law of the late Roman Empire, as adapted and modified in the Frankish kingdoms in the eighth and ninth centuries. The origin and atmosphere of the feudal oath is to be sought in the *comitatus*, the following, which we met in the England of King Alfred and, very vividly expressed, in the poem on the battle of Maldon. Loyalty between leader and follower, confirmed by oath, was the deepest obligation a man could have in a feudal society; just as treachery was its greatest crime. Robbery and murder could be more lightly treated, and they were certainly common; but no-one took treachery lightly. The vassal swore fealty, faithfulness, obedience, good service, to his lord; the lord in return undertook protection, justice, and good lordship.

The feudal bond was sacred, but not indissoluble. As we should say, it was a contract; and if either party broke the contract, the other was freed from normal obligations—was obliged, indeed, to try to restore the contract by force. This game, like all medieval games, had its rules. The vassals of an unfaithful lord were expected to pronounce the breach of faith —the *diffidatio*—in solemn form, as did the barons before Magna Carta. The feudal bond provided a loose cement in a lawless society. Feudal society was in its essence military and violent; the bond was often broken on a slight excuse, and the complexities of feudal tenure gave plenty of occasion for perplexity, and also for fraud.

The feudal bond, however, was never the only bond in society, the only basis for law and order, least of all in England. It is for this reason that I have insisted on the narrow, legal, tenurial definition of feudalism. The word, indeed, has been very variously used. 'Feudal society' can be taken to cover all the social arrangements of a society in which feudalism flourished; that is reasonable enough. It has sometimes been taken by economic historians as a synonym for manorialism, the structure of peasant society, which is merely confusing. It has commonly in modern times been a term of nostalgia or a term of abuse.

Of all the other definitions of feudalism, the most interesting is the military definition. Whatever feudalism was, it was inseparable from a military upper class. It was always looked on as a means of providing a lord with a troop of well-armed, well-trained cavalry. But closer inspection reveals that feudalism did not inevitably accompany a particular type of military tactics. The core of any feudal army was the company of heavily armed knights; and in a feudal society the majority of these knights was normally provided by feudal military service. But no great military leader of the eleventh, twelfth, or thirteenth centuries reckoned to recruit an army entirely in this way; all leaders used mercenaries, even among the cavalry. Most of the archers and foot-soldiers in the English army, at least in the twelfth and thirteenth centuries, were paid men.

We still know far too little about military tactics in this period. The English fought on foot at Hastings, and so have usually been supposed to have had no cavalry. They fought with axes, like the Danes. But the Normans could also fight on foot when circumstances dictated, as many did in the battle of Tinchebrai in 1106, when Henry I of England won the duchy of Normandy. Furthermore, the basic equipment of both armies was the same: chain mail, helmet, shield—and the English used sword and spear as well as axe. It has recently been suggested, indeed, that the English housecarles and thegns normally fought on horseback. The question whether English society was profoundly different from Norman is one to which we must shortly turn; we can say at once that it is doubtful how different they were in military tactics. More certain was the difference in fortification, and this was fundamental, since the defences of a strong castle were the most formidable weapon in eleventh- and twelfth-century warfare. There were few castles in England before the Conquest, and the English fortresses were usually *burhs,* i.e. walled towns. Even so, we know too little about the English methods of defence to be sure that this simple distinction is wholly true; the early Norman castles were mostly very primitive; and the significant development was the stone keep—an extreme rarity even in Normandy before 1066.

The heavily armed knight had formed the core of Frankish armies before there was any trace of feudal institutions in the sense in which I have defined them. Feudal institutions in some form survived the great changes in tactics which took place in the twelfth and thirteenth centuries. Vital as were the archers at Hastings, the Norman army more commonly depended for its success on the charge of the heavy phalanx of knights, who might hope to carry all before them by the weight of horse, armour, knight, lance, and shield. In the twelfth century more complex tactics came to be adopted. The knight remained a heavy-weight; in fact, he became heavier and more expensive. Henry II in the late twelfth century hired him for eightpence a day; he cost King John early in the thirteenth century two or three shillings. The number of knights expected from each tenant-in-chief had to be scaled down. From being a heavy cavalry trooper, the knight was becoming a kind of primitive tank, a change consummated by the arrival of the far heavier plate armour in the fourteenth century. In the end this development, allied to a social change which subdivided knights' fees and made knights more difficult to mobilise, heralded a major alteration in feudal structure. But it is clear that the history of military tactics is too loosely connected with feudal history for the military definition to be helpful.

Feudalism, then, meant the holding of land in exchange for military service; respect, obedience, in return for protection. It seems a settled arrangement, if we compare it with the circumstances under which barbaric warriors had lived in earlier centuries. But we shall see how artificial and uncivilised it was when we look at the impact of growing civilisation on it in the twelfth and thirteenth centuries.

One aspect of its artificiality strikes us at once, for it was a grave restriction on changes in land-ownership. The plot of land which was intended to support a particular knight had been granted by the king to a baron and by the baron to his knight for the specific purpose of providing baron and king with a

111

military retainer. King and baron would do everything they could to ensure that this plot of land continued to provide them with a knight, and this made them very resistant to any suggestion that the land should be divided or any part of it sold. If the knight held it, he could be expected to be reasonably efficient in performance of his service. If it became divided, endless trouble might be involved in deciding who should do the service, or how the various tenants should divide it between them. Many people in twelfth- and thirteenth-century England had possession of one-half, one-quarter, or one-tenth of a knight's fee; and these fractions can hardly have been convenient to the lord.

In strict theory a feudal holding, a fee or fief as it was called, was not hereditary. When a baron or a knight died, his heir had to pay a large fine, or 'relief', to have possession of his predecessor's land—a relic of the theory that an entirely new contract was being made. But in course of time a fairly strict custom of inheritance by primogeniture—by the eldest son or the nearest blood relation—was established in the upper strata of English feudal society. This partly reflected ancient social traditions; partly, too, a simple compromise between lord and tenant. The lord wanted his vassal to be succeeded by another able-bodied warrior, and he could reasonably expect his vassal's eldest son to have been trained for the job—the eldest, in addition, was the most likely to be of full age and ready for action when his father died. The vassal would naturally wish to pass on his holding to his family. The normal play of human affection might make him wish to divide it among all his children, or at least to provide portions for his daughters and some kind of support for his younger sons out of the inheritance. From the tenant's point of view a strict rule of primogeniture for the whole holding was better than nothing; but such a rule was rigid and artificial; he would undermine it if he could. The efforts of tenants to undermine the unity of holdings in favour of family provision—and the partition of some estates between heiresses—is the explanation of the fractions of knights' fees which one encounters in the late twelfth century and later; and this partitioning made it more difficult to fasten the duty of knight service on any single tenant.

The history of inheritance was somewhat different on the Continent. No continental monarchy was powerful enough to prevent the partition of many feudal inheritances. The law of Normandy was stricter than most continental laws: it forbade

112

the division of a military holding, while allowing that the elder brother had the moral obligation to provide for his kin as best he might. 'Not upon the Normans as Normans,' wrote Maitland, 'can we throw the burden of our amazing law of inheritance.'[1]

Primogeniture was artificial because it disinherited all a man's heirs save one. From this fact stems a great deal of English social history. In particular, it set the problem of how younger sons were to be employed. There is a story of how an impoverished Norman knight had twelve sons, and scarcely anything with which to endow even the eldest of them; and of how he sent them to a distant land to earn their bread. The story is pathetic; but its consequences were far from trivial. One of the younger sons of Tancred de Hauteville was Robert Guiscard, founder of the Norman principalities of south Italy; another was Roger, the first Norman lord of Sicily. His grandchildren included Roger the Great, the first King of Norman Sicily, and Bohemund, the most accomplished leader of the first Crusade, the admiration and terror of the Byzantine Empire. In this tale the fearful problem of younger sons in a feudal society and Norman resourcefulness in facing it are both remarkably illustrated.

The barons and knights who came from Normandy with the Conqueror came from a country in which many elements of feudalism had recently become established. In certain respects the feudalism of the Norman settlement in England was more highly organised than the feudalism of Normandy. When William enfeoffed one of his barons with lands in England, he specified the service due from that fee: the number of knights which the baron was expected to settle on his land, the number of 'knights' fees' he was expected to establish. It might take a number of years for the new tenant-in-chief to distribute the land among so many knights. For the time being he would have to lodge them in his household, as did the first Norman abbot of Peterborough, to the consternation of his monks; and the word 'knight', *cniht*, originally a servant or household retainer, is an interesting reminder of this stage in the Norman settlement. But once he had placed his knights on the land he was expected to find no less and no more than the number of knights' fees on which the king had decided. If he enfeoffed more knights than the 'service due', his service was increased; and there were investigations from time to time to see that this was done. In Normandy the duke had no safe check on the number of knights his vassals enfeoffed. The vassal might well find that his private interests and his private feuds made desirable a larger force than he was bound to produce in the duke's service. Nor could the duke summon the whole of his entitlement on every occasion. The whole host could be summoned for the defence of the duchy; for lesser occasions or for service with the duke's own lord, the French king, only a fraction could be summoned. Finally, private warfare was forbidden in England, whereas it could only be held in check in Normandy. The difference in practice was not so great: even in England only the strongest of kings could hope to prevent it.

The Anglo-Norman hierarchy consisted, very roughly, of barons, lesser barons, and knights. The barons formed a remarkably homogeneous class of about 180 men. A few of them stood out: in particular, the Conqueror's brothers, Odo Bishop of Bayeux and Earl of Kent, and Robert, Count of Mortain, both English landholders on a colossal scale. The barons of the Welsh frontier—the 'march' of Wales—were given property sufficient for them to have the power to resist attack and even to carry out offensive operations on their own. Hence the large endowments of the Earl of Hereford, William FitzOsbern (forfeited by his son for rebellion in 1075); of the Earl of Chester, who had large estates in Cheshire and special rights there, as well as immense estates in other parts of England; and of the Montgomery earls of Shrewsbury. But even these were never so eminent among their fellows as the leading earls of Cnut and Edward the Confessor. And all these earldoms save Chester had left the families of their founders before the death of Henry I.

The word 'thegn' had included every stratum of the Anglo-Saxon hierarchy, from men as well-to-do as the greatest Norman barons down to men poorer than most Norman knights. It originally meant a servant or follower, a member of a *comitatus*. The Anglo-Saxon upper class was differently constituted from the Norman; it was more loosely knit. Before 1066 several thousand thegns, of every variety of standing, held their tenancies directly of the king. For the most part, only the great held of the king in Norman times; lesser men were tenants or sub-tenants of the barons. On the whole, too, the Norman military class could be divided fairly easily into two, into barons and knights. There was no fixed line, and it was comparatively easy for a knight who won royal favour to become a baron or for the younger sons of barons to sink swiftly to the level of the poorest knights. But the baronial class was comparatively homogeneous. In Anglo-Saxon society the leading earls had powers and privileges and estates which set them apart from their successors. We have already seen how their power had unbalanced English politics. In wealth and influence a considerable number of middling thegns came immediately below them, most of whom were comparable in standing to the lesser barons of the Norman period; below the middling thegns came the large body of lesser thegns, predecessors of the Norman knights.

(2) THE NORMAN SETTLEMENT IN ENGLAND

The question is often asked, was feudalism introduced by William the Conqueror? What traces were there of feudalism in the time of King Edward? To these questions very various answers have been given, partly because historians have differed about the facts, partly because the question itself is ambiguous. Medieval men thought in concrete terms, of fees and fiefs; the idea of feudalism is a rationalisation invented by modern lawyers and accepted by historians as a matter of convenience. 'Were an examiner to ask who introduced the feudal system into England? one very good answer, if properly explained,' wrote Maitland, 'would be Henry Spelman [a distinguished seventeenth-century lawyer and antiquary], and if there followed the question, what was the feudal system? a good answer to that would be, an early essay in comparative jurisprudence.' [2] Feudalism, as we have seen, was anything but systematic. It is easy to prove that there was no feudal system under the Confessor; equally easy to prove that William's feudalism was as near systematic as any in Europe. If we must answer the question, then let us say: under William English feudalism was on the way to becoming the least unsystematic in Europe; under Edward it had been present only in fragments.

The Normans were extremely adaptable. They could destroy, but they could also pick out from the ruins valuable materials, and make with them buildings more elaborate than those they had destroyed. The Norman Conquest was a catastrophe; the Anglo-Saxon upper class was almost exterminated in twenty years. But it left behind it strong traces. In an earlier chapter we talked about hides and hundreds. The hide was an ancient unit of assessment; in origin, it was the land which could support one family—and also, we may now add, one fully equipped soldier. But as time passed, equipment became more elaborate and more expensive. St Oswald in the tenth century still reckoned that he could endow a warrior with two or three hides; but he sometimes increased this number, and on the whole kings and great landowners of that period were tending to think of five hides as suitable support for a fully armed warrior. Needless to say, this was only a rough approximation; the 'hide' was a very variable measure. But here and there about England, and most notably in the diocese of Worcester, we find traces of a 'five-hide unit', which supplied a fully armed warrior for the royal army.[3] Five hides provided Bishop Wulfstan of Worcester with a warrior and general factotum in 1062, when he became bishop; the same five hides gave him a knight in 1095, when he died. What we shall never know is how widespread this type of continuity was. We may be sure that the 'five-hide unit' was in the Conqueror's mind when he set about fixing the quotas of knight service; we may be sure that it did not always solve his problem; we may be fairly sure that the situation in the diocese of Worcester was more coherent than was common before the Conquest; and we may reasonably guess that a policy of gradualness would be more successful in the rare cases, as at Worcester, where the pre-Conquest lord survived until after Domesday. The Anglo-Saxon state had collected the materials; the Normans knocked them into a rough building.

How was it done? The feudal map of England is infinitely complicated. The holdings of most great barons were scattered about in many parts of the kingdom. The Earl of Chester held a reasonably compact estate in Cheshire, but his broad acres in other parts of the kingdom were widely scattered. Ingenious historians of a former age deduced from this that the Conqueror had cunningly spread his followers' estates, so that they should not have compact domains to form a basis for independent action. It is clear that the motive alleged had little or nothing to do with the method of distribution: it is doubtful if such a scheme would have commended itself to the Conqueror, and certain that he could not have accomplished it if he had tried. As it was, in Sir Frank Stenton's words, 'the combination of several thousand small estates into less than two hundred major lordships must have been an administrative achievement comparable with the Domesday Inquest itself.' [4]

No doubt the Conqueror and his followers began with the idea of distributing the immense estates of the house of Godwin fairly widely, but of keeping the lands of lesser men intact. But the process of piecemeal distribution, piecemeal forfeiture, and constant dispute between new tenants about their rights made the pattern increasingly complex. Some of these disputes became *causes célèbres*. For three days the shire court of Kent sat patiently on Pennenden Heath while the Earl of Kent (Bishop Odo) and Archbishop Lanfranc disputed large portions of land. One of the great purposes, or at least achievements, of Domesday Book, was to sort out many outstanding claims.

For the most part, the only estates which passed without serious alteration through the Conquest were those of the greater churches. There were a few exceptions to this; but to see the sort of thing which happened, let us take four examples from the single county of Wiltshire. Alfred of Marlborough held over 142 hides in the county in 1086, of which $112\frac{3}{4}$ had been held by Karl, an English thegn, probably of Danish origin, in 1066. William d'Eu held $86\frac{1}{4}$, of which 77 had been Aelfstan of Boscombe's—Aelfstan had also held most of the land in other shires which William acquired. The largest tenant-in-chief in the shire, Edward of Salisbury, was one of the unusual cases of an Anglo-Saxon thegn who had survived—he lived to found a great family, and his grandson became an earl. But Edward evidently owed his fortune to the Conquest. His holdings in 1086 contained remnants of 32 different estates, his own probably included. Milo Crispin, another large landowner, held much land in Wiltshire once Earl Harold's, much land once held by a middling thegn called Leofnoth, and the estates of five smaller men.[5]

Duke William's reign both in England and in Normandy provided many opportunities for social promotion. Many of the families in English history—Warennes, Montgomerys, Montforts, and the rest—who formed the backbone of the baronial class after the Conquest, had made their fortune in Normandy either in the service of William or of one of his immediate predecessors. Few of them can be traced before 1010 or 1020. And the opportunities for promotion did not cease to grow as the Norman dukes established themselves in Normandy and England, and Norman adventurers built kingdoms and principalities in Italy and Syria. Many new baronies were formed in the twelfth century. One of Henry I's new barons married Milo Crispin's heiress. William d'Eu's estate was forfeited for rebellion under Rufus, and so passed back into royal hands, to strengthen the royal demesne and free other lands to endow new baronies under Henry I. Of the estates I have listed, only Alfred of Marlborough's survived as a barony in the later Middle Ages. Social change continued, carrying with it the chance of promotion and aggrandisement.

(3) NORMAN GOVERNMENT

Another question which is often asked is: did feudalism conduce to strong government or to anarchy? Such a question is not nonsensical. A governing class for whom warfare is a normal kind of exercise is not easy to control: a feudal society was never wholly peaceful. The country feudalised most early, what we call France, was the most anarchic in Europe in its day. Even in England, feudal anarchy flourished in the reign of Stephen (1135–54). But the question itself can never be answered. No king ever ruled by feudalism alone; most of the problems of government cannot be answered in these terms. Anyone who wishes to understand the politics of this period must study feudalism in all its aspects; but he must study other things as well. The Anglo-Saxon monarchy survived, developed and strengthened by the Norman kings. The Norman kings, notably Henry I and Henry II, have sometimes been described as anti-feudal. This they could not be; they were feudal kings in a feudal age, accepting the whole range of values and aspirations of their class. But they were also the heirs of Alfred, Athelstan, Edgar, and Cnut.

This meant, first of all, a close liaison with the Church. William and Lanfranc were as close as Edgar and Dunstan. The partnership was not reproduced by their successors, owing to changes which we shall inspect later on. But the king remained king *Dei gratia*, as was emphasised by Henry II in his later years, when these words became a regular part of the royal style in all official documents. The Normans inherited the beginnings of literacy in government. They had been used to more primitive methods in the duchy. But they accepted what they found, and developed it. The writ was translated into Latin, since English was no longer the common language of the country. But it gained rather than lost in practical use. It rapidly became a normal instead of an occasional instrument of government. Its terseness was admirably suited to the Norman temper. 'Henry king of the English to Ranulph Meschin, Osbert the sheriff, Picot son of Colswein and Wigot of Lincoln, greeting. Go and view the boundaries between my manor of Torksey and my manor of Stow, and have the boundaries vouched for by approved men of the shire; and if you do not believe them, let them confirm what they say by oath. For my will is that the bishop [of Lincoln] shall truly hold what his predecessors held there. Witnessed by Wigot of Lincoln, at Winchester.' Or even more succinctly: 'Henry king of the English to Almod the archdeacon, greeting. Give back to the abbot of Thorney his manor of Sawbridge [Warwickshire] in the condition in which you received it—and do not let me hear any complaint of injustice. Witnessed by Geoffrey son of Wimund. If you do not do what I say, Ralph Basset will. Witnessed by the same at Westminster.'

These writs were sent to individuals. But most writs were still addressed to sheriffs and shire courts, and there read out and interpreted to the people. The smaller hundred court lost something of its importance, but the Norman kings took stern measures to preserve the shire court as the essential point of contact between the king and the people. In the early days after the Conquest it had been necessary to appoint as sheriffs men of power, capable of handling a dissident population, capable of standing up to the most ruthless of their own colleagues and helping to organise the great redistribution of land. It is small wonder that some of them became ·bywords for force and greed. Sometimes the king had to intervene to curb their oppressions. But they were the only instruments capable of doing the job. They alone could manage the immense tasks which fell to royal officers and public courts.

In time their strength and their capacity became a serious danger to royal control. They wished their office to be hereditary; they hoped to absorb more and more royal functions and perquisites into their family rights and inheritance. The Norman kings were slow to intervene. A few of the more unruly were removed, but the problem was not seriously taken in hand before the reign of Henry I. Henry himself tried various experiments. A cleric closely involved in royal administration, called Hugh of Buckland—a man with neither the family ties of a baron, nor the landed wealth which could make him independent, became sheriff of eight of the home counties early in the reign. Sheriffs were more often removed than hitherto. Finally, in the late eleven-twenties Henry felt strong enough to remove a large number of the sheriffs in one stroke. He appointed two trusted lay officers, Aubrey de Vere and Richard Basset, with a kind of roving commission as sheriffs of a large number of counties, whose administration they tidied up. After this the sheriffs were more tightly controlled; but their opportunities for oppression were still great, and Henry II had to take similar measures in 1170, when he set up a commission to inquire into their doings, and removed most of them. In the long run, other royal officials were to weaken the hold of the sheriffs over the counties.

Henry I began the experiment which was to be enormously developed by Henry II and his successors, of sending itinerant justices on tour, on 'eyre', to try cases in the shires. The court they sat in bore many superficial resemblances to the shire court; but when the royal justice was present, the shire court became for a space the king's court, *curia regis*, and acted with royal authority. Thus were born the modern assize courts, and with them a closer liaison between king and shire.

Justices and sheriffs were the principal links between local and central government. The itinerant justice visited the shire, the sheriff reported at the royal court. These reports continued and increased in significance under the Norman kings. The audit of the royal Treasury became a more elaborate and literate affair, conducted in a new office called the Exchequer, set up at the turn of the eleventh and twelfth centuries, and developed under the guidance of Henry I's most distinguished administrator, Roger, Bishop of Salisbury, whose family held the royal treasurership on and off until the early thirteenth century.

The Exchequer took its name from the system of auditing, on a table resembling a chess-board or 'chequer' (*scaccarium*). The table was divided into columns representing sums of money, and the accounts of each sheriff, and so the whole royal revenue, were worked out by moving counters about in these columns. The audit took place in the Exchequer chamber at Westminster twice a year, at Easter and Michaelmas. The new system of addition, brought in from the Arabs at about this time, not only speeded the arithmetic, but made it possible even for illiterate officials to follow what was being done by observing the movements of the counters. The clerks of the Treasury worked out the accounts meanwhile on great rolls, called Pipe Rolls, and the leading royal officers were present to settle disputes which might arise, to act as judges. The Public Records still contain a Pipe Roll from the year 1130, and something like a continuous set from 1156 until the early nineteenth century.

Treasury and Exchequer were the first more or less fixed departments of government—sometimes at Winchester, sometimes at Westminster. They were the only departments too cumbersome and regular in their activities to move with the king, as did the rest of the court. A description of all the court officials and their perquisites was drawn up just after Henry I's death in 1135, and shows us that the household was still quite a simple organisation. Sixty different types of official are named, from the Chancellor, Treasurer, and chamberlains down to the larderers, fruiterers, ushers, tent-keepers, and wolf-hunters ('20d. a day for horses, men and hounds; and they should have twenty-four running hounds and eight greyhounds, and £6 a year to buy horses; but *they* say £8'). Great men and small jostle each other in the list, and it has a homely look. Chancery and chapel are still one department though their head has the new style of 'Chancellor', introduced by the Conqueror. Finance is kept within the province of the Chamber, which originally meant quite literally the king's bedchamber—even if royal treasure for centuries had been kept in separate treasuries. But some of this homeliness is deceptive. The dispensers, butlers, and sewers were great officers of state, leading barons; so were the constables and marshals. From the larder to a bishop's throne might be only one step, as one of Henry I's clerks discovered. The household, furthermore, was often the scene of great ceremonies, the essential pageantry of medieval government. 'He kept a great state,' says the chronicler of William I. 'He wore his royal crown three times a year as often as he was in England: at Easter at Winchester, at Whitsuntide at Westminster, at Christmas at Gloucester. On these occasions all the great men of England were assembled about him: archbishops, bishops, abbots, earls, thanes, and knights.' In this way the Conqueror had attempted to prove to all his subjects, English as well as Norman, that he was king. The state he kept also emphasised the continuity of English government. He claimed to rule as Edward's rightful heir, and the Normans were very glib in their references to the laws and customs of King Edward, to which they claimed to adhere.

In course of time the Norman kings discovered another great predecessor to whom they could point. Alfred and his supporters had been inspired by lays of their heroic predecessors. In the late eleventh and twelfth centuries, the favourite entertainments in the royal and baronial courts of Europe were the *Chansons de Geste*, epics of feudal warriors and feudal heroes, centring in the court of Charlemagne. A version of the most famous of these, the *Song of Roland*, gave the Norman army heart as it went into action at Hastings. The court of Charlemagne became a direct political inspiration for his successors, the kings of Germany and France; and it must have given great pleasure to the English kings when Charlemagne found a rival in the British King Arthur. The Arthurian legend only became really active in the second half of the twelfth century, but already in the eleven-thirties Geoffrey of Monmouth had put Arthur on the map in his fabulous history. Arthur appears here in the improbable guise of a twelfth-century Anglo-Norman king. In the central scene of his book Geoffrey makes Arthur wear his crown at a Whitsun festivity. He describes the solemn ceremonial, the music, the festivities, the tournaments, and the business which occupied the court. If one subdues his exuberant detail and knocks a nought or two off his figures for the numbers present, one can accept Geoffrey's account as a picture of the crown-wearing ceremony in the Anglo-Norman court.

1. *History of English Law*, II, p. 266.

2. *Constitutional History of England* (1908), p. 142.

3. The services of the Worcester tenants were miscellaneous, often including riding on the king's errands, helping in the repair of *burhs* and bridges, and so forth. Some of the more particular services—helping in the lord's hunting expeditions, for instance—formed the basis for a special form of feudal tenure, known in Norman times as serjeanty. This literally meant 'service': the tenant held his land in exchange for a specific service to the lord, such as looking after his hounds, acting as his steward, or the like.

4. *Anglo-Saxon England*, pp. 618–19.

5. See *Victoria County History of Wiltshire*, II, pp. 98–112 (R. R. Darlington).

CHAPTER SEVEN

MANOR, VILLAGE, AND TOWN

(1) THE MANOR

In the last chapter we studied the king, barons, and knights, who comprised the ruling class. In all they numbered not much more than 5,000; in the next chapter we shall add to this the higher clergy. The English upper classes fill the pages of this book, because they controlled the country's destinies, and because 'those who worked' have left little memorial. But it is well to remember that the enormous majority of the million to a million and a half of eleventh- and twelfth-century Englishmen was peasants, farm labourers, or artisans.

Corresponding to the feudal organisation of the upper class was the manorial organisation of the peasantry, of the villages and 'manors'. England in the Middle Ages was a country of small and isolated farming communities. The unit was the village—and a much more self-contained unit it was than anything to which we are accustomed. But within many villages there was a legal, social, and economic institution which historians have reckoned typical of medieval England, and to which they have given the name 'the manor'. The manor was an organisation by which the English villages were fitted to the social structure of medieval England and its economic needs; and it can be viewed in its social setting—its relation to the feudal hierarchy—and as an economic thing, the source of England's food. But the term itself is odd, and a word about its origin is necessary to make plain what follows. The manor in all essentials is ancient; but the word itself came over with the Conqueror, and came of age, so to speak, in Domesday Book. The Domesday commissioners collected their description of England shire by shire, hundred by hundred, and village by village. Then their clerks set to work to rearrange the material within each shire into the holdings of each tenant-in-chief; that is to say, by feudal holdings instead of geographically. All statisticians need units; the men of Domesday Book expected lists and inventories to consist of concrete things—men and beasts and ploughs and pennies—not of abstract values or theoretical notions. But the ploughs and the stock had been recorded precisely because the commissioners wished to be able to compare the value of one holding with another; and for this purpose not all ploughs and not all oxen are equal. And so the clerks and commissioners set to work to make their concrete terms just a little abstract. They boldly assumed, for example, that eight oxen made a plough-team, and bullied their statistics to fit the equation.[1] They failed to introduce real uniformity, but for their day they did an impressive task. Some of the results are confusing, some weird. At Stanford in Bedfordshire Alric held a tiny farm directly from the king. 'There is land for half an ox; and half an ox is there: *ibi est semi-bos.*'

When the clerks rearranged the returns, which had been collected under hundreds of villages, into their feudal segments, a fundamental problem immediately arose. Many villages were wholly the property of one lord; but many more were not. Villages were thus too variable to be treated as units, and the village had to be replaced by something which might be its equivalent in size, might be smaller, might even, in a few cases, be larger. This difficulty made the fortune of the Latin word *manerium*, which is a version of the French *manoir*. *Manerium* meets us on every page of Domesday Book.

From what we have just seen of the methods of the makers of Domesday, we should expect *manerium* to be at once concrete and abstract. Abstract it was, in that it represented the unit of feudal lordship within a village. But to the men who used the term it conjured up a definite image. *Manoir* in French probably represented *heall* in English—a hall, a strong building of wood or stone in which the lord might or might not reside, but which would at least contain offices, a bailiff, cellars, and storehouses; a symbol of the lord's authority over the men of the village, or at least of his holding in it. Nor were the clerks disturbed by the fact that in many villages there was no hall. The manor was a concrete and an abstract notion at the same time. This is how we came by the word: the French call it *seigneurie*, that which pertains to a *seigneur*, a lord—a lordship, as we might say.

In the feudal societies of medieval Europe, the manor or *seigneurie* was the irreducible unit of lordship. A feudal society was a society organised for war; a society whose landed resources were mobilised for the support of knights. The knights,

124

being professional soldiers, had to be supported by the labour of peasants. The manor is the basis of the hierarchical society geared for war; the sinews of the feudal army. Feudalism could not have existed without manorial or seignorial institutions; and these in their turn existed at their most developed in just those parts of Europe where feudalism was most developed, that is, in northern France and in England. Nevertheless, the farming unit, the manor or *seigneurie,* was older than the military unit, the 'fief'. In England it was the word and not the substance of the manor which the Normans introduced. The villages of Anglo-Saxon England contained social arrangements and systems of tenure of an infinite variety; and their history is exceedingly obscure. But so far as one can tell, something like manorial institutions may well have existed in many places as long as the Anglo-Saxons had been settled in the island, certainly as long as the period covered in this book. In many places, but not in all: throughout the Middle Ages there was great diversity in different parts of England.

Medieval villages were small and isolated communities; their horizon was very limited. We should expect to find great variety among them—variety of methods of cultivation, of social customs, and of economic organisation. In the modern world, diversity is the product of economic specialisation; our work and jobs, by medieval standards, are highly specialised; but you meet much the same range in London as in Liverpool or Edinburgh. There was far more regional divergence then than now. One sometimes hears talk of 'the medieval village' or 'the medieval peasant' or 'the typical manor', as if they were types. Eileen Power once said that 'the manor' was a term about as descriptive as 'the mammal'. We now know that the 'classical' manor described in the older textbooks was by no means so common or so characteristic of medieval England as was once supposed. But it still provides the best starting-point from which to pursue the history of the manor.

One meets it in many parts of the Midlands and the northeast, where the land is rich and fertile, where the population was always fairly large, and especially on monastic estates, where the administration was fairly continuous.

In the centre of the village lay church and manor house; and near them the little streets of peasant houses; the crofts and tofts —small gardens and fields attached to the houses. The inhabitants of Burston were evicted in 1488, and the shape of the

125

village, still visible in the turf, remains clear. In the centre lie the vestiges of streets and houses, with tofts and crofts clearly marked; outside these lay the fields. The rest of the village would be divided between open fields, on which the main crops were grown, meadow for sheep and cattle, and waste land, including woods and forests, which provided timber and game, and acorns and beechmast for the pigs of the lord and of the village community. The villagers lived by growing corn for bread and beer (ale, not milk or water, was their staple drink); sheep provided wool, cattle produced hides for clothing, both provided meat for the table. Thus the basic necessities were grown within the village, or at least a major part of them.

Before the days of modern scientific agriculture, the great difficulty was to prevent arable land from becoming stale, to ensure, that is, a reasonable harvest. Against occasional disaster —bad weather, floods, and war—the medieval farmer had little defence. But he developed a certain knowledge of methods of tillage. He knew the value of manure; and he knew that land benefits from a change and a rest. Where the soil was reasonably fertile and the village population large, the arable fields had to be cultivated as intensively as possible, and so the whole area came to be divided either into two or into three fields. One of these in rotation was always 'fallow'—i.e. it had no crop; it had a rest for one year in two or three. The other field in a two-field village bore all the year's crops—wheat, oats, barley, peas (such vegetables as they had, like leeks and onions, were grown with the herbs in the toft). In a three-field village, the rotation was slightly more elaborate. Each field was fallow one year; bore 'winter' corn (i.e. wheat or rye, sown in autumn) the next; and spring corn (barley, oats, or peas) the third. The large open fields were elaborately sub-divided; first into smaller irregular areas called furlongs, then into long narrow strips. The layout of a medieval village may still be vividly reconstructed in places like Laxton in Nottinghamshire, where something of its life still exists, or like Burston, where its outline is still clear in the turf. Outside the village proper one commonly sees the outline of long strips and furlongs in what was once its open fields. The corrugated turf, 'ridge and furrow' as it is technically called, which marks the site of old strips, often shows us the plan of the open field. Not all corrugations are ancient: the raised ridge between furrows dug for drainage was a common way of ploughing enclosed fields in

126

many places down to the nineteenth century. But quite often, when strips continue across a more recent hedge or road, or when their layout can be compared with an early map, it is possible to prove that they represent ancient open fields. The fields in Padbury, for instance, can be compared with a map of 1591, which shows that the ridge and furrow exactly represent the open fields of Elizabethan times; and there is no reason to doubt that they are in all essentials medieval.

The twelfth and thirteenth centuries saw more elaborate techniques in the administration of big estates, growing literacy in this as in other types of government. We have treaties on *Husbandry* by Walter of Henley (*c.* 1270) and others; and we have, for the first time, large-scale, elaborate, and detailed surveys and descriptions of village fields. At this date we find that the strips in the open fields were minutely sub-divided between the various members of the village community. A number may have been held by the lord, though in some cases the land which the lord kept in his own hands, the lord's demesne as it was called, was concentrated; in other cases there was no demesne. Each peasant's holding was widely scattered, sometimes according to a regular pattern, sometimes quite irregularly. The regular patterns, by which each peasant received a share of many different parts of the open fields, suggest that in an early distribution the land of the village was divided so that every peasant had his share of good and bad land; or (on occasions) that each new furlong brought under civilisation was divided among the community. The strips originally allocated to each peasant seem often to have amounted approximately to thirty acres (a 'virgate') or some fraction of this area. It has been suggested that in early days the strips were allocated in proportion to each peasant's contribution to the plough-team.

In many villages all over the country, however, the land was divided in a manner which seems to us wholly chaotic. We find this chaos in the Midlands, in villages which may well have been originally divided into regular virgate holdings. It was the fruit of that constant debate between common and private interest which is the stuff of life in every moderately primitive agricultural company. The disorder seems often to have been due to prolonged small-scale transferences of land. In various parts of the country at various times the law was theoretically very strict in limiting the extent to which peasant lands could

127

be divided or sold by the peasants of their own free will. How these laws operated is imperfectly known. What is certain is that innumerable minute transactions—gifts, sales, divided inheritances, marriage portions, and so forth—must lie behind the chaos we meet in many thirteenth-century surveys.

Every acre of land was held by a hierarchy of tenants, each of whom expected some return for it. To king, baron, and knight it was part of a knight's fee. To the knight himself, or to whoever was lord of the manor, it was also the source of money dues and labour services; to the peasant who did the work it meant bread. All this helps to explain the very complex relations between lord and peasants in the manor. Peasant tenure varied as much as other forms of tenure; but there was one broad distinction, that a peasant was either free or unfree. The freeholders were the aristocracy of the small farmers, and where they were plentiful, as in Lincolnshire or East Anglia, manorial institutions had a less tight control over individuals. The unfree were not slaves. Slaves existed in the time of Domesday, but they were rapidly disappearing, and their work came to be divided between peasant tenants and wage-labourers. The unfreedom of the villeins lay mainly in their being tied to their plots of land; they were not free to move. Their money, cattle, implements, and other property, furthermore, were technically chattels of their lord. The villeins were usually burdened with very heavy obligations—they had to work on the lord's demesne two or three days a week, and additional days at times of special stress, at ploughing time and harvest time especially. When we hear about villein tenure in detail in the thirteenth century, we are told of all manner of payments and restrictions. But the villeins had not always been so restricted, and some of the burdensome conditions of their tenure existed more on paper than in fact. We even hear tell of villeins who engaged in trade, and used their villein status as an excuse for not paying their debts. Since they had no property of their own, the argument ran, their goods coulds not be distrained.

The labour force which worked the lord's demesne was organised by the reeve, usually one of the peasants, under the lord's bailiff. The bailiff had at his disposal the labour force provided by peasant labour services, and on almost all manors a team of hired labourers, which might be small or large according to circumstances. This labour force was organised to do all the work of the lord's demesne, which was run as a large farm. Specialised jobs would tend to be done by hired labourers, the more exalted ones by those village aristocrats, the smith, carpenter, and miller; but in the really big tasks, ploughing, harvesting, and carting, almost the whole village would do its share, The lord was a man of power, and the capacity of the villagers to stand up to him, to enforce their rights against him, was a very variable thing. Many factors of law, social organisation, and personality played their part; but the most general factor was economic. When land was plentiful and labour scarce, the labourer and the peasant fared better at the lord's hands; when there were more men requiring land and work—when land was scarce and labour plentiful—the lord had it more his own way.

The lord's demesne was a large farm run by communal enterprise; and it was part of a larger communal farm, which comprised the whole village. When the peasants' strips were scattered broadcast over the fields and the lord's mingled among them, the farm work could not be done on an individual basis. Only a very prosperous peasant would own all the apparatus needed, or even plough and oxen. They were often shared; hence the 'half-ox'. It is clear that the land was often cultivated in a fashion more reasonable than its tenurial divisions imply. Groups of strips, even whole furlongs, might be ploughed or reaped together. Thus a strong element of communal organisation combined with the strongly individual system of possession to make the ungainly manorial economy work.

One fact about the strips remained constant: they were always long and narrow. The reason for this seems to have been that the plough which tilled them was heavy and cumbersome —it was pulled by three or four oxen—and difficult to turn. The strip was designed to give the ploughman as few turns as possible in his day's work. Thus the heavy plough was designed to deal with heavy soils; and we are immediately reminded that the kind of economy we have been describing was characteristic only of a certain part of England, where the country is open and reasonably flat, and the soil heavy; in particular, of the claylands of the Midlands and of the vale of York. The layout of the fields in the thirteenth century, furthermore, was the result of centuries of change. The complex distribution of strips is a palimpsest of partition, re-partition, of piecemeal expansion, of a multitude of sales, leases, or exchanges. We return to where we started: in different parts of England there were different patterns, and some of these were profoundly altered by the passage of time. Place and time affected manor and village; we must take their effects in order.

Open fields gathered round a large village centre were characteristic of the Midlands where the large village is still very common. Isolated farmsteads have always existed in every part of the country, but scattered farms and hamlets, with more compact holdings and small rectangular fields, have always been especially characteristic of Wales and Cornwall and the Lake District. In Wales in particular, this also reflected a radically different social system, but everywhere geography played its part. Hilly country and poor soil did not support large populations. The lighter soils were suitable for rough pasture for sheep and cattle. When crops were to be grown, there was no need for a heavy plough; and a light plough could conveniently be manoeuvred round a rectangular field. The boundaries of these fields, sometimes great mounds of earth or stone walls, provided (and often still provide today) essential shelter for cattle or crops in the bleaker climate of the highland zone. Earth and stone walls have served the same purposes for many centuries—several millennia perhaps—and some are of immense antiquity.

In a similar way the poorer soils of many parts of England favoured less intensive types of agriculture; and special conditions have favoured the growth of specialised tillage. Kent, for instance, has always been the orchard of England. These local peculiarities have often been enhanced by local customs and traditions, and historians have sometimes emphasised the identity of geographical and racial frontiers. The country of hamlets and scattered farmsteads is the country from which the Saxon never ousted the Celt. Kent was the home of a whole world of social and legal custom as eccentric as its economy.

When manor and village were coterminous, when the village was a large nucleated settlement, with the houses grouped together, when the bulk of the tenants were villeins, when the lord had the right to call on most of his tenants for labour services; then the lord's control of his manor was strong, the manorial structure tightly riveted. Such manors were common in the thirteenth century, especially in the Midlands. In no county did they form a majority. On most manors, at least in practice, the lords drew more from rent than from labour. But in most villages of

130

this area the rights of the lord were manifold and carefully maintained.

In strong contrast stand some manors in Devon and East Anglia. Heath Barton and West Town in Devon were two small manors in Domesday Book, but they were never villages. They were the centres of about ten isolated farmsteads. In such cases communal organisation, and the hold of the lord over the village economy, was slight. Similarly, two villages in Cambridgeshire contained between them no less than twenty-two manors. In these cases the manor had lost most of its significance; it was merely a unit of lordship in a very divided village. Between the extremes of the closely organised and the loosely organised manor lay many varieties. Even in the manorialised Midlands, on the one hand, there lay villages of free peasants, like the village described in Dr Hoskins's *Midland Peasant*. Even in Devon and Cornwall, on the other hand, the lord was no cipher. West Town was held in 1086 by the formidable sheriff, Baldwin, one of the leading barons of the south-west. Personality and circumstance sometimes counted as much as geography and social tradition.

The simplest way to grasp the main outline of manorial chronology—to see the effect of time on the manor's organisation—is to watch the activities of the lord. It was the lord, by and large, who controlled the relations of the manor with the outside world; and so he was the key to many changes, though not the only key. As soon as we ask, when did lordship start? we are faced with the first of many insoluble problems, the problem of the origin of the manor. In the past, two fundamental answers were given to this question: either that we inherited the manor from the Roman villa, or that it came much later, because the early Saxon settlements were settlements of free men. Dependent tenure, on the second theory, was the product of time and depression. Both views still have their defenders; most scholars would say that both were wrong. The first is wrong because Anglo-Saxon village settlements, with very few exceptions, are not on the sites of Roman villas; they are new creations. The second is wrong because so far as we know there never was a time when most English peasants were free or independent of a lord. Hastings and Woking are well-known examples of a type of place-name which probably originated very soon after the Saxon conquest: they mean 'the settlement of Haesta and Wocca's folk'. Haesta, Wocca, and

131

their like impressed their name on villages, most probably because they were lords of these villages.

To say this is virtually to say that the manor is as old as the Saxon settlement; it is not to say that the sixth-century manor was identical in form with the manor of the later Middle Ages, nor that it was ubiquitous as the manor of Domesday Book. We do not know how widespread the manor was in Saxon times. There were villages of free peasants in every century. We know very little about the early manor, save its existence, before the Norman Conquest. That little includes some inkling of the forces of change which were at work. First of all, we know that men were slowly changing and improving agricultural techniques through the centuries—especially by devising ways of increasing the acreage regularly under the plough in many villages, and so supporting a larger population, and in particular by experimenting with elementary methods of crop rotation. The three-field village of the thirteenth century is the product of long centuries of evolution, speeded up by a rapid growth in population between Domesday Book and the end of our period. The years between 1086 and 1272 witnessed a great expansion of the area under cultivation, the 'colonisation' of much land previously waste.

With the progress in technique went progress in other aspects of manorial economy. We sometimes think of our medieval ancestors as if they were in a state of subsistence agriculture— as if a village produced enough for its own support and no more, and was entirely dependent on its own resources. A medieval village was far more self-supporting than a modern one. But we must be careful not to overestimate this self-sufficiency in the Middle Ages; and the lord's demesne is a reminder of this. The demesne produce might be used in one of two ways: it might be carted direct to the lord's house and there consumed by the lord, his family and followers, his retinue, his servants, and hired labourers; or it might be sold for money in a market. The produce of the medieval manor was used in both these ways; predominantly in the first way, by direct consumption, in the early Middle Ages, predominantly in the second way, by conversion into money, in the later centuries. In very early days the king let out his manors in return for 'a farm'—the produce sufficient to support the royal court for one day, the 'farm of one night'; and other lords did the same. Some part of this system survived for centuries. The

132

manors of St Paul's Cathedral each had so many days or weeks in the year when their produce was supposed to be brought to the brewery and bakehouse of the cathedral to be converted into ale and bread for the support of the canons. The monks of Durham divided their broad acres into two groups; the produce of those lying near at hand supplied the monastery and its many mouths; the produce of more distant manors was sold in local markets.

England was on the silver standard from the eighth to the thirteenth century; its currency was based on the silver penny. There were halfpennies, farthings, and even for a time thirds of a penny; it was only in the thirteenth century that rising prosperity and rising prices began to make possible a gold coinage. Thus there was coin throughout our period; but its use changed considerably. Only gradually did coined money become a regular and essential part of the economy of every village and of every peasant. Only gradually were even the royal food farms converted into money; by the twelfth century the process was complete.

Throughout the period of this book the change was taking place. More and more the economy of the manor came to depend on sale of its surplus, whether corn from the fields or wool from its flocks or meat from its herds. The permanent markets were in the towns. There were fairs, too, occasional large markets, held here and there for a few days each year. On the whole the buying of more permanent stores—spices and other lasting goods, and to some extent cloth and clothing, took place at fairs; but the regular buying and selling of goods took place in the permanent town markets of the neighbourhood. The growth of towns and the changes in manorial economy are thus intimately connected. The surplus corn of the manor went to feed the specialised population of the town, engaged in trade or elementary industry—or, from the eleventh century onwards, went to feed the large industrial population of the cloth-making towns of the Low Countries, along with the wool which provided much of the raw material of this industry. In return, the money provided by these commodities provided lord and tenants with their incomes. The lord could earn money in one of two ways. He could lease the land to a farmer, and so receive the profit indirectly, in the form of rent; or he could farm it himself and market the produce. When the profits of agriculture were high, there was more money to be made by

133

taking the produce to market oneself. But this was always difficult to organise, particularly on large estates; and when profits were uncertain, or prices were falling, a steadier return could be ensured by letting the land out to a farmer and living on the rent.

What was involved in the lord's living on rent? First, money and markets, where the tenants could earn the money to pay the rent. Nor was it only the produce of the manor which had to be translated into cash. The lord's wealth in a highly manorialised village included the labour services of his villeins, an important part of his capital. When the lord ceased direct exploitation through his bailiffs and reeves, he might dispose of labour either by passing it on to the farmer, or, more commonly, by turning it into money like the harvest itself—by demanding more rent instead of labour. Whichever was done, the lord would lose interest in his labour services, and they would tend to become merged into the general structure of rents. But if the lord wished to resume his demesne and to set up as a great farmer on his own account once more, he would need to revive the old labour force which he had allowed to disappear; many an ancient claim to labour services would be unearthed and claimed once more; and every effort made to enforce the lord's rights by legal and economic pressure. And this is precisely what happened in the thirteenth century. The population grew; there were many mouths to feed, more men wanting land; the price of corn and the value of land went up. For the landlord it meant a boom in demesne farming—a golden opportunity to revive every source of income and of labour to work his demesne. That is why the records of the thirteenth century are so full of references to the enforcement or re-enforcement of labour services. But even at the height of demesne farming, it was not solely by labour services that the demesne was worked—there was need for hired labourers, too, in almost every manor, and money was needed to pay them. All this means that the market played a crucial part in the history of the manor. Produce for market was only a small proportion of the whole produce of the manor, but sufficient to alter the manor's nature fundamentally—just as the sale of cocoa and ground-nuts by peasant-farmers very little removed from the subsistence level is fundamentally altering the economy of large parts of Nigeria today.

In detail, the chronology of the manor is very imperfectly

known. Money and markets began to play a decisive part in the tenth and eleventh centuries. In the later twelfth century, when we first have records on any scale, many lords were living on rents, even though labour services were far from forgotten. In the thirteenth century, rising population made land and its produce increasingly valuable, and both market prices and rents rose. Where improved methods of administration made it possible, landlords, especially monastic landlords farmed much of their land themselves. The manorial economy, in harness with local markets, was at its height.

(2) TOWNS AND COMMERCE

The intimate connection between town and manorial profits can still be seen in places like the port of Alnmouth, built some time in the twelfth century by the Vescy family, to provide a harbour for ships carrying goods to and from their head-quarters at Alnwick; or in the way the great lords of the East Riding of the late twelfth and thirteenth centuries founded ports round the Humber estuary to capture its trade and serve their manors—Hedon (now a village), Ravenserod (now sub-merged), and the king's town, Kingston-upon-Hull.

The borough in 1086, and even in the thirteenth century, was by our standards a very small affair; a cluster of little houses often surrounded by imposing walls, perhaps dating originally from the time of Alfred or Edward the Elder, dominated by a great castle built by the Normans. A town of 2,000 souls was a large town in 1086; only London, Norwich, and Winchester had substantially more than 5,000; only London was a town by modern standards. All the boroughs of Domesday Book had fields and farms attached; some were in fact small villages. But thirty or forty of the larger boroughs have an interest for us, and had a significance in their day greater than their size would suggest. They had permanent markets, which gave them the essential character of towns; they had professional merchants, and some professional craftsmen; they had walls to protect the market; many of them contained the administrative headquarters of a shire; they had from the first greater freedom from the close control of a lord than a purely rural manor could hope to have. The liberty of a borough be-gan as a matter of circumstance, and acquired legal status only in the twelfth century. Circumstance usually took the form

135

either of royal lordship, which was often generous to trading communities, or of so great a multiplicity of lordships that no single lord could acquire sufficient control to hamper the town's growth. In the twelfth century, growing pressure from lords and growing wealth in the towns led often to disputes; in the end many towns acquired charters which guaranteed them the right to farm their own taxes, the right to a share in their own government and the right to manage their own market. The body which managed taxes and government ultimately grew into the town council; the body which managed the market grew into a market gild, or 'gild merchant' as it has been called.

The market gave the town its essential character; walls and liberties were only aids to the market's growth. But now and then the walls came first. Alfred and Edward's *burhs* were sometimes placed where markets existed; many of them for obvious reasons later became market towns. Every town has its own individual story. In some it even happened that market and traders came after the whole edifice of defence and government had been planned. King Richard I (1189–99) built a new town at Portsmouth; and in the late thirteenth century Edward I laid out a series of new towns, and then enticed merchants and artisans to occupy them. Not all these new towns succeeded; some faded away into insignificance. But most grew and flourished; and the kings did not engage in town-building on this scale before it had become clear that towns were to play a large and growing part in national life.

Long before Domesday Book was compiled London had been the largest and most famous of English towns. At first sight it seems strange that a city which has played so dominant a part in English history should lie so near the south-coast corner of the island. It owes its importance to the fact that it has been for long stretches of time the commercial and political capital of England. It first sprang to prominence when Britain was a distant province of the Roman Empire. Its position on the Thames made it a convenient port for visitors from the Continent; as such it was an ideal base for military conquest, and the Romans made it the centre of their great network of military roads. After the Romans left, London fell into decay, but it was known at least as early as the eighth century as the foremost port in Britain. Though always important in later Saxon times, and always the main centre of commerce in the country, it was never the political capital of the country again until the twelfth century. Indeed, there was no capital, in the modern sense, before then; the court moved with the king; only the treasury remained stable, usually in Winchester. But as more offices of state became static, a headquarters had to be found which would suit a king constantly travelling between England and France, and at the same time be a suitable centre on which travellers from all over England could converge. Thus in the days of the Angevin kings some of the conditions of Roman times were re-established: London became once more the political as well as the commercial capital; the greatest of the royal palaces was the palace of Westminster, a favourite residence since Edward the Confessor had built his great abbey there, conveniently sited only two miles upstream from the city. Even as early as the eleventh century the leading citizens had claimed to have a say in the election of a king.

'Among the noble cities of the world,' wrote William Fitz-Stephen in the eleven-seventies, 'the city of London, seat of the English kingdom, is one which has scattered its fame as widely, carried its wealth and commerce as far, raised its head as high as any. It is happy in its climate, in its Christian observance, in the strength of its fortifications, in the nature of its site, in the honour of its citizens, in the modesty of its matrons; happy too in its sports and fertile in noble men '—and he proceeds to enlarge on all these aspects of London's greatness, concluding his account of eminent persons born in London with a description of Thomas Becket, in whose honour the author had written his account of the city. He speaks of the churches and schools, of the sports of the citizens, and of many other fascinating aspects of London life. Most striking of all to the historian is the evidence of how much the royal court and mercantile prosperity already meant to the city. FitzStephen describes the royal castles, including the Tower of London in the city itself, and the palace of Westminster. 'Almost all the bishops, abbots and great men of England are, as it were, citizens of London; they have their own fine houses there, where they stay, where they live expensively, when they are called by king or archbishop to councils, or come to transact their own business.' London, in the author's eyes was almost perfect, save that there was 'too much drunkenness, and frequent fires' owing to the compactness with which a great number of wood and wattle houses were crowded within its walls.

Two features of London which particularly impressed Fitz-

137

Stephen were the large public kitchen by the river (with supplies of fish ready to hand) and the weekly horse market just outside one of the gates. To this market came barons and knights in search of good mounts for war, for travel, and for the chase. There were horses there to suit every need, 'for ploughs, for sledges, for carts'; and this reminded him of the city's commerce. 'Merchants from every nation under heaven are happy to bring goods by ship to the city.'

The merchants who visited London in the first half of the twelfth century included an Englishman from Lincolnshire called Godric. No doubt he had visited London before, when plying his trade; on the occasion of which we have information he came *en route* for Rome, where he was making the pilgrimage which was to be one of the early stages of his conversion to the religious life: he later became a monk at Durham and a hermit by the river Wear at Finchale. As a hermit he became famous. Another monk of Durham wrote his life; and to this we owe one of the few surviving accounts of how an English merchant made his fortune in the early twelfth century.[2] Starting as a scavenger looking for wreckage on the seashore, he acquired enough money to become a pedlar for four years in Lincolnshire. Then he ventured farther afield, to Scotland and Italy; and soon entered into a partnership, under which he owned a share in a boat, of which he himself acted as captain. Godric was evidently a fine sailor, and his pursuit of gold took him to Denmark and Flanders on many occasions, as well as to Scotland; and his fondness for travel and the first stirrings of piety took him also to the great centres of pilgrimage, to Jerusalem, to the tomb of St James the Apostle at Compostella in north Spain, and to Rome.

Long-distance trade, from being a rare and occasional thing, was becoming a normal part of the European scene; and with the growth of trade went a development of many other aspects of mercantile life. Godric and his associates were partners in their ship; and more elaborate forms of joint-stock enterprise were beginning to be common. A wealthy financier would provide money for an enterprise and draw his share of the profits. Increasing use of money meant that money-lending and moneylenders became more common. The profession was particularly associated with the Jews, and Jewish merchants and moneylenders had settled in England under the protection of William I and William II. But not all money-lenders were Jews: if the

138

most famous of twelfth-century money-lenders was Aaron the Jew of Lincoln (whose wealth passed into the royal exchequer at his death *c.* 1185 and whose affairs needed a special department to deal with them), a close competitor was William Cade, a Fleming, who died about 1166. Cade's loans helped the young Henry II to rebuild the shattered royal administration in the years following his accession in 1154.

Cade was a Christian, and therefore (nominally at least) subject to the strict rules of the Church concerning interest and usury. The Church had always set its face against avarice, against the pursuit of wealth for its own sake, and viewed with deep suspicion the progress in economic techniques which took place in the eleventh, twelfth, and thirteenth centuries. Money was the just reward of labour; but this could not justify a man for letting out his money at interest and so enjoying the profits of a venture in which he had taken no active share. Money, it was felt, ought not to breed money. The effect of this view was partly to limit the financial activities of Christians—and so at first to leave much of the money-lending business in the hands of the Jews—and partly to encourage ingenious evasions. William Cade seems to have used two chief means of evading the rules against usury. Sometimes he pretended to have lent more money than he had parted with so that when the sum was repaid it was enlarged without the facts being recorded in his bond; sometimes the loan was secured by a pledge of a piece of land, whose profits Cade drew until the loan was repaid. These remained for centuries the favourite techniques of the Christian usurer; though others—including various forms of partnership—were also devised. The Church meanwhile gradually realised that money-lending was not always vicious, and that the lender, even if engaged in no physical activity, was involved in the venture to which he lent his aid, and might well suffer if his money was not returned. Subtle distinctions came to be developed between lending upon usury and receiving some payment for the risk involved in lending. The Church ramified its teaching; but the central doctrine of the wickedness of usury remained unaltered. Down to the eve of the third Crusade in 1189 the Jews were the chief money-lenders in England. In that year England was afflicted for the first time by a wave of anti-Semitism such as had commonly accompanied the preparations for a Crusade on the Continent, and widespread massacres started the decline of the English Jewish community.

The Norman kings had brought Jews with them, and also increased the number of Flemings in the country. Many of the merchants carrying English trade in the twelfth century were Flemings, though Scandinavians and Germans were also common. It was at this time that the close liaison between the Flemish and English economies which played so large a part in English history in the later Middle Ages was finally formed. There were large flocks of sheep in many parts of the country already in 1086; by the mid-twelfth century a large share of the wool of English sheep was going to Flanders to be woven into cloth. The export of wool was not new; but the scale of it was far greater than in earlier centuries. English wool was already made into cloth in England itself, and the cloth industry grew in the twelfth and thirteenth centuries. But in the period covered by this book English prosperity depended above all on raw wool. The finer grades of English wool were the most sought-after in Europe.

In the twelfth century exports consisted mostly of wool, foodstuffs, and other raw materials; and the towns, though growing, were not centres of large-scale industry. Even the cloth industry, centred in York, Beverley, Lincoln, Louth, Stamford, and Northampton, was to a great extent to move out of the towns in the thirteenth century and later, when the invention of the fulling mill [3] drove the fullers out into country districts where fast-flowing streams would turn their millwheels. Apart from cloth, the most notable English industries were iron, tin, lead, and salt. The twelfth and thirteenth centuries saw rapid development of the resources of the iron-mines in Sussex, Gloucestershire, and Yorkshire. At St Briavels in the Forest of Dean in Gloucestershire all manner of iron implements were made; they included 50,000 horseshoes ordered by Richard I for the third Crusade. Cornwall and parts of Devon throve on their tin-mines; from the Yorkshire moors, from Derbyshire, and from the Mendip Hills in Somerset came lead; and from the lead-mines of Devon the king also extracted much of the silver used by the royal mint. Already in the time of Domesday carts came from far and wide to collect salt from the salt towns in east Cheshire—Northwich, Middlewich, and Nantwich.

The activity of the merchants of the eleventh and twelfth centuries was an important part of the growing economic specialisation of the later Middle Ages. In earlier centuries the large majority of the population had lived near the subsistence

140

level; they could cease to do so only if they could market a perceptible proportion of their crops, especially of their crops in corn and wool. The corn and other food, and to a large extent the wool, too, went to market to provide for the feeding and clothing of men and women who did not grow what they needed: kings and their courtiers and retainers; barons and knights and their large households of domestic servants; bishops, monks, nuns, and all the higher clergy; merchants and artisans—weavers, fullers, dyers, miners, smelters, moneyers, stonemasons, carpenters, and the rest; shipbuilders and seamen. Royal and baronial courts were growing larger at this time; and all the classes listed here were increasing. This was only possible because surpluses were being produced for sale in the market; and because the elaborate machinery of commerce existed, or could be developed, to organise the distribution of these surpluses.

1. It is unlikely that eight oxen were yoked to a plough at one time: perhaps four was a normal team, and eight allowed for two relays. But there was much variety.

2. Reginald, monk of Durham's *De vita et miraculis S. Godrici de Finchale* (Surtees Society, 1847).

3. Fulling was the process by which the woven cloth was beaten and compressed in water, and in the process shrunk and given a felt-like surface to make it more durable, with a smoother finish, and also cleaned. The way in which fulling was mechanised by the discovery of the fulling mill is described by E. M. Carus-Wilson in 'An Industrial Revolution of the Thirteenth Century', *Medieval Merchant Venturers* (London, 1954), pp. 183–210.

141

CHAPTER EIGHT

THE ANGLO-NORMAN CHURCH

(1) LANFRANC AND PAPAL REFORM

The Normans invaded England under a banner blessed by the pope. One reason for papal favour was the contumacy of Archbishop Stigand, who was finally removed in 1070 and replaced by Lanfranc. There could not be a more remarkable contrast: Stigand was the very image of old corruption, Lanfranc one of the foremost monks and scholars of his day. Lanfranc and William set to work to reform the English Church.

The contrast between the two archbishops has sometimes been taken as a symbol of the effect of the Norman Conquest on the English Church. The Normans, it is said, reformed a corrupt, backward, isolated English Church. But it is now realised that the truth is more complex, more interesting, and less flattering to the Normans. The court of Edward the Confessor had been one of the most cosmopolitan in Europe; it had contacts with France and Lorraine and Scandinavia, and even with the Mediterranean world and with Hungary. The English upper clergy were certainly not isolated before the Conquest. Nor were they corrupt by the standards of the first half of the eleventh century—Stigand is no fair reflection of the general state of the Church. The monastic reformation of Dunstan's day had not entirely lost its force; here and there— as at Worcester under the saintly Wulfstan II (1062-95)— monastic reform was in full swing in 1066. The English Church was still strongly under monastic influence; and even the secular cathedral chapters had all been reformed so that their canons should follow some kind of organised rule. English architecture was mean by Norman standards; but in religious art, in painting, and probably in sculpture, England had the mastery in western Europe. The history of manuscript illumination is continuous from the age of Dunstan to the twelfth century. Even before the Conquest English styles were penetrating Normandy; after the Conquest the Norman monks in

England adopted the superior techniques of the English; in course of time a subtle blend of native traditions and new themes produced the Anglo-Norman schools of the twelfth century. In some fields of art the Norman Conquest was a disaster, as in sculpture; in some it was the reverse of a conquest, as in illumination; only in architecture did the Conquest bring real development.

The Normans profoundly altered the English Church. In some ways they may have made it better, in some ways worse; they certainly made it different. If we look at Normandy and England together, and at the whole of the reign of William the Conqueror on both sides of the Channel, we immediately see that in church affairs, as in feudal organisation, the Normans changed themselves as much as they changed the English. There is a sense in which the Normans brought the English Church into line with continental fashions. It might have happened anyway in the late eleventh century, because the changes reflected two great movements which dominate the history of the Church at this time: the reform of the papacy, commonly known after its most dramatic figure, Pope Gregory VII (1073-85), as the Gregorian Reform, and the intellectual revival, which started in Italy and France in the eleventh century, and blossomed all over Europe into the Renaissance of the twelfth century. The papal reform was in part a general attack on clerical standards and clerical immorality. The reformers tried to enforce the rule against simony (the sale of church offices) and against the marriage of the clergy. There had been for centuries laws forbidding the clergy to marry, but they had never been strictly enforced over most of Europe. The papacy could claim that it was simply telling people to obey the law (a modest proposal); but in practice, in many places, it was putting into effect a social revolution. To make matters more difficult, the law was still very complicated. The case of Héloïse and Abelard in Paris at the turn of the eleventh and twelfth centuries helps to bring this home to us. After their baby had been born Abelard offered to marry Héloïse. But Abelard was in clerical orders. Héloïse realised that if he married he would be barred from promotion; she was prepared to remain his mistress for the sake of his career. For once Abelard's affection and sense of honour got the better of his vanity; he insisted and they were married. That should have destroyed his career in the Church, but there was a loop-hole. Such a marriage could be dissolved if both parties entered religious communities—and in the end, Héloïse became a nun and an abbess, Abelard a monk and (for a time) an abbot. Their story shows something of the tangle of the celibacy laws. It also gives us an insight into what they meant in terms of human suffering. Their passion and tragedy make Héloïse and Abelard unique, but their circumstances cannot have been so unusual. They, and others like them, were victims of the forces of change. Their story illustrates one aspect of the change in discipline for which the reformers were fighting.

Equally important was the attempt to establish papal supremacy on a new footing. It was not that the popes made new claims, so much as that they found new ways of putting their claims into effect. They created what we call the papal monarchy. The princes and bishops of France first felt the force of the new movement of reform at the dramatic synod of Rheims in 1049, presided over by Pope Leo IX in person. At this assembly, conducted in the presence of the relics of St Rémi, patron saint of the city, the pope ordered any of those present who had committed simony—that is, paid money for his office—to confess. Leo was committing a social gaffe, because his host, the Archbishop of Rheims, had won his preferment in this way; so had a number of other bishops, including Geoffrey, Bishop of Coutances. But Leo got his way: most of the bishops confessed. And though most of them were reinstated, European society suffered a shock from which the popes did not want it to recover.

Simony had been part of the normal process by which kings and princes appointed bishops, and behind the attack on simony lay the threat of an attack on royal control. Apart from their ecclesiastical duties the bishops were officials of the lay power—royal councillors, providers of contingents for the royal army. In countless ways bishops and abbots had always been pillars of royal authority. Many kings and princes had been extremely generous to the Church, and they expected a return—in two ways. They expected the Church to provide knights and they expected prayers. It suited them to have saintly monks and worldly bishops. But in the papal view bishops were spiritual leaders, pastors, shepherds of their flock—they must be spiritual men; the Church must be free from lay control. In the last analysis, when pope and king fell out, their divergent views on the function of bishops nearly always

145

lay at the heart of the quarrel. Was the bishop a royal official or a father in God? The question was never answered: he had to be both.

The papacy claimed to be a spiritual monarchy; and it claimed in particular to be the fount of justice in spiritual matters. In the twelfth century appeals in all sorts of important and trivial cases affecting ordinary people went to Rome. This was possible because of the development of canon law—the law of the Church—and the intensive activity in the law schools of Europe. Practising lawyers were being taught and textbooks compiled; research was flourishing. This intellectual activity was affecting all sorts of subjects. Scholars were taking books on law, philosophy, theology, on the spiritual life, on history, and even on science from library shelves, blowing the dust off them and finding a world of new ideas in their pages. Schools sprang up; students flocked to well-known teachers. A renaissance had begun. Some of this new learning raised difficulties for the Church; from time to time teachers like Abelard were accused of heresy. But on the whole papal reform and the rise of learning were allies. At least we can say that the papal monarchy of the later Middle Ages is unthinkable without the sensational development in the study of law in this period.

At the time of the Council of Rheims in 1049, the Norman Conquest was only seventeen years away; a vital coincidence. Even in that time Duke William and his churches felt and absorbed something of the new spirit. It is one thing to preach a reform; another thing to have it enforced. William the Conqueror won golden opinions from contemporaries and has often been complimented since on his sincerity in the pursuit of church reform. There are many things in his career which make us believe in the reputation; but there are also passages which lead another way. He looked to the great churches of his duchy (and later of his kingdom) for prayers and for knights; and he sometimes appointed an abbot or a bishop notable for producing the one, sometimes for the other—sometimes for both. It is perhaps unfair to judge him by the two great warrior bishops, Geoffrey of Coutances and Odo of Bayeux, who fought at the battle of Hastings, since Geoffrey, a scion of the great house of Montbray or Mowbray and later founder of their fortunes in England, had bought his bishopric before the Council of Rheims, and Odo was William's brother. A more characteristic example perhaps was Gilbert Maminot, Bishop of Lisieux. He was the son of a baron and had been chaplain, head physician, and astrologer to the Conqueror. This is how Orderic Vitalis describes him: 'He was very skilled in the art of medicine, learned and eloquent, flowing in riches and good living, beyond measure inclined to have his will and pamper the flesh. He took his ease, and often indulged in gaming and dicing. In Divine Service he was idle and negligent, and always ready and eager—too eager—to hunt and hawk.' Then he passes to his better qualities—his generosity to the poor, his justice and rectitude, his kindness, and his good advice to the penitent; and his close and friendly relations with his subordinates in the chapter. 'He instructed them in arithmetic, astronomy and physic, and other profound matters, and made them the confidants of his salon and boon companions in his revels.'

From the point of view of an ardent reformer, Bishop Gilbert was an untidy mixture of old corruption and the new learning. From our point of view he seems not a bad example of the material that the Church had to use throughout this period. But the churchman on whom the Conqueror most relied was of a very different stamp.

Lanfranc of Pavia had established his reputation as a master of dialectic and theology before he left Italy as a comparatively young man and settled in the newly founded abbey of Bec in Normandy. He soon gathered a school round him, so that Bec became one of the famous centres of learning north of the Alps. It was often in this sort of way—by students gathering quite informally round a great teacher—that important schools were formed. The organised university grew up only in the twelfth and thirteenth centuries.

As Archbishop of Canterbury Lanfranc found himself abbot of a leading English community of monks, leader of the English Church and first councillor to one of Europe's most powerful monarchs. He entered into all three tasks with great intelligence, energy, and persistence. We must not underestimate him as monk and theologian, nor yet as politician; but he showed above all in his later years the qualities of a great administrator, and what interests us now is his work as head of the English Church.

Lanfranc's career is an epitome of the story of the Church in the eleventh century. He was born in Italy when new thoughts and new principles of reform were stirring; as a monk he lived the life from which the inspiration for church reform ultimately sprang; in Normandy and England he observed the dissemination of, and himself disseminated, the principles to which he had been brought up. He had belonged to a generation in Italy which was alive with new ideas; but he had grown up none the less before the special direction of the papal reform could be discerned. He accepted the primacy of the Roman see, but not in the active, aggresive form in which it was proclaimed by Gregory VII. In this one respect, Lanfranc was conservative; and that made him the ideal colleague for the masterful William the Conqueror. Lanfranc's successor, Anselm, had had a very similar career, and had been his pupil at Bec; but he was a generation younger, and was more sensitive to the possible dangers of too close links between Church and state. The result was that, though far from being cantankerous by disposition, he found it as difficult to collaborate with the Conqueror's sons as Lanfranc had found it easy to co-operate with the father.

Lanfranc came to England, not as a Norman reforming the decadent English by Norman standards, but as an Italian representing a new outlook in the Church, which had to struggle for a hearing on both sides of the Channel. In the long run, Lanfranc seems to have found the pulse of the Old English Church; when he first arrived, he was far from sensitive to its special needs and special glories. He reformed the calendar, showing little respect for English saints. To replace the *Regularis Concordia,* he produced a new code of monastic customs and regulations aimed to bring English observance more into line with modern French customs. He did not try to enforce it outside his own community in Canterbury, but he clearly expected it to be widely used. Lanfranc was interested in making church law and its operation more efficient. He brought his own law-book with him from Bec, and had it circulated. In earlier times there had been no separate law-courts for the Church, and bishop and sheriff had both presided in the shire court. At one of his councils Lanfranc passed a decree establishing church courts separate from the shire—a decree made effective by a celebrated instruction from the king. This combination of conciliar decree and royal writ is characteristic of the close co-operation of king and archbishop. But in some respects Lanfranc's mastery in the Church was storing up trouble for future kings. His frequent ecclesiastical councils, in

148

which the details of reform were planned, gave the leaders of the English Church a sense of community.

Lanfranc himself was only Archbishop of Canterbury; but he compelled the Archbishop of York to admit an entirely novel claim that Canterbury had primacy over York—a primacy of age and distinction it may have had before, but not the primacy Lanfranc claimed. A united Church under Lanfranc's guidance suited the king; and it may be that he found advantage, too, in Lanfranc's wider ambition. Lanfranc pursued his claim to be 'primate of all Britain' further than William pursued his efforts to assert suzerainty in Wales and Scotland. The Norman infiltration in Scotland and Wales was hardly under way in 1087, and Ireland was untouched. But Lanfranc asserted his leadership in parts of Scotland and in Dublin, though the conquest of the Welsh Church did not effectively begin before the early twelfth century; King William made a 'pilgrimage' to St David's over thirty years before a Norman was established there as bishop.

Lanfranc resisted papal intervention except in technical matters like the conferment of the 'pallium', the archbishop's scarf of office, and normal diplomatic exchanges. Simony and clerical marriages he attacked. In his handling of marriage, he was cautious and tactful; and it used to be said that this was owing to the special circumstances of the English Church. But it was the Norman clergy, not the English, who had the reputation of being among the most uxorious in Europe: two reformers of the period who preached celibacy to the Norman clergy were nearly lynched—one by the clergy, the other by their wives. One of Lanfranc's councils decreed that married priests could retain their wives; but no married men were to be ordained to higher orders in the future—and this decree seems to have been made to suit Norman as well as English churchmen. In the event it was a couple of generations before this was at all generally enforced among the upper clergy, much longer before it was enforced among the lower.

Lanfranc and his Norman associates, the archbishops of Rouen, with much help and some hindrance from their colleagues on the episcopal bench, and much cautious encouragement and some obstruction from their king and duke, were engaged in the common task of introducing the new European fashions of ecclesiastical life and thought both to the English and the Norman Churches.

The Normans altered the complexion of the English Church in two particularly obvious ways: they replaced most of the upper clergy with themselves, and they converted the bishoprics and larger abbeys into feudal baronies. Bishops and abbots always had been leading royal councillors; now they became the suppliers—sometimes even the leaders—of feudal contingents. Some of them were appointed for their capacity to manage knights and plant them on the estates of suffering abbeys. Not many perhaps: William was too conscientious and Lanfranc too powerful for many cynical appointments to be allowed. But the feudal contingents were often extremely large—several abbeys had to produce forty or even sixty knights.

By the Conqueror's death most of the abbots, and all the bishops save St Wulfstan of Worcester (1062–95), were newcomers. So were a large proportion of the cathedral clergy. The cathedral chapters, indeed, were often completely remodelled. The English cathedrals had been peculiar in being served by two quite different kinds of community. Many were served by chapters of canons; a few by monks, with the bishop as titular abbot, and a prior occupying the stall of the dean. Monastic chapters were an insular peculiarity, and some of the Normans looked askance at them. But the monastic chapters soon won Lanfranc's patronage, and more were founded not long after the Conquest. The chapters of canons were mostly in a weak state at the time of the Conqueror's accession; such as they were, they were all under some form of a rule, binding them, in theory at least, to a communal, celibate life. They were not chapters of 'secular' canons, living independent lives in houses in the cathedral close, such as those to which the Normans were accustomed.

The English cathedrals—Durham, Norwich, Winchester, and several others—are the greatest surviving monument to Norman energy. For their day the Norman cathedrals were immense structures, heavy and usually, before the time of Henry I, crude in construction; but extremely impressive. They were in marked contrast to their Saxon predecessors. The Saxon cathedral at North Elmham in Norfolk was less than 140 feet long. A Norman cathedral was rarely less than twice this length. The size of North Elmham corresponded with that of churches built on the Continent two centuries before; recent continental movements had increased the scale of church building tremendously. Sometimes the Normans rebuilt, as at Winchester or Canterbury. Often they moved the cathedral to a larger centre of population, and started afresh, as at Old Salisbury, Chichester, Norwich, and Bath. The last two were monastic chapters, the first two secular; and at Salisbury Bishop Osmund (1078–99) founded the chapter which was to be the model for most English secular cathedrals, with a dean and dignitaries and a large body of canons, each with a separate income. The close link of bishop and chapter was emphasised by the presence of the bishop's chief officers, the archdeacons, among the canons. The secular chapter, the dignitaries, the archdeacons, were all Norman innovations—not based on any single Norman model, but an adapted version of what was normal in the north of France. In this respect their institutions and their architecture were of a piece. The Salisbury model is derivative, but not purely derivative; Norman architecture was based on Norman and continental models, but new ideas and new techniques were added to the Norman or Romanesque style in buildings like Durham Cathedral.

Why did the Normans build so large? The new continental fashions included a love of processions, growing ceremonial of every kind; demanded, too, a supreme effort to build a stately home for the saint who lived in it. Winchester Cathedral was the highest effort of Norman building; and it is a symptom of the rapidity with which Norman and English settled down together that it was built to house the shrine of a native English saint, St Swithun.

(3) THE MONASTERIES

Monasteries and monks played a very conspicuous part in the Norman Church; not quite so conspicuous at court as in the days of Dunstan, but among the people at large, considerably more so. Between 1066 and 1154 the number of monastic houses in England rose from 48 to nearly 300; the number of monks from about 850 to well over 5,000—at a time when the total population was perhaps one-thirtieth of what it is today. Counting heads is a crude way of measuring changes in monastic life, but it tells us something. It reminds us that this was the golden age of medieval monasticism. The great

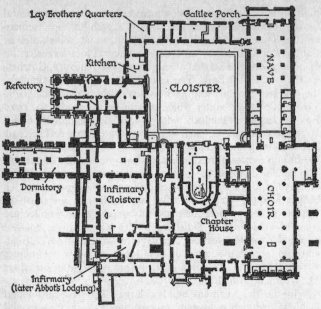

Plan of Rievaulx Abbey

religious movement of the eleventh century started in monasteries in different parts of Europe. From 1050 to 1150 a great number of the Church's leaders were monks; many of the best minds of the day were being recruited into monasteries; and this was so in England as on the Continent.

The housing of increasing numbers of monks is among the reasons why Norman monasteries and Norman cathedrals were built so large. To understand the kind of changes which were taking place, let us move forward to the middle of the twelfth century, and inspect the life in one of the great Cistercian monasteries being founded and built at that time. Then we can return to compare the Cistercians with the other leading Orders of the day.

The ruins of the abbey of Rievaulx, whose plan we reproduce, still dominate an almost unspoiled stretch of country near Helmsley in Yorkshire. They have been much altered since the twelfth century, but the plan is essentially what it always was—that is, what all Cistercian plans were supposed to be. It lay isolated, surrounded by its own fields and sheep pastures a large complex of buildings served within and without by its own community. The choir monks maintained divine service and formed the core of the monastic body; a large number of illiterate or semi-literate lay brothers tilled the fields and maintained the flocks. The buildings, like many Norman monasteries, were far larger than Saxon monasteries had usually been; but in the eleven-sixties they had to house 140 choir monks and 500 lay brothers. This was quite exceptional, even among the Cistercians, even at Rievaulx. But the church always had to be large, not only to house the monks, but also to provide chapels in which those choir monks who were priests—as most were—could celebrate daily mass. Next to the church, usually on the south side (as at Rievaulx) to catch the sun, lay the open square of the cloister, surrounded by a covered walk, at this date unprotected against the wind, where the monks could work or walk—an extraordinary and singularly unsuitable survival of the open courtyard of Mediterranean lands, where monastic customs had first been established in the West. Round the cloister lay the main offices and public rooms of the abbey. Above the east walk was the dormitory, where all the monks slept. About two o'clock every morning the community went down a staircase from the dormitory into the church for the first office of the day; and then after a brief rest, there followed for them the main body of daily offices and masses lasting until about half past eight. Beside the church, beyond the sacristy, under the dormitory, and with its main door in the east walk of the cloister, lay the chapter house. To this room the monks came next, for the daily chapter, where matters of business and discipline and the like were discussed. Then followed a short period for reading in cloister, and a longer period of work in the fields. In the south walk of the cloister lay the door to the most imposing of the conventual buildings, the refectory, the monks' dining room. They visited it only twice a day at most. After the midday meal (and in summer a siesta) they worked again and read; then went to church for the evening offices of vespers and compline, and so to bed. Communal prayer, private prayer, spiritual reading, and work in the fields had each their share of the monks' waking hours.

In many respects the Cistercian life differed from that lived in other communities. It was based, like that of most monas-

153

tic Orders, on the rule of St Benedict, which had grown steadily in prestige since the sixth century when it was written. In the early eighth century a centralising movement in the Frankish Empire had made St Benedict's rule, coupled with additional customs compiled by St Benedict of Aniane, the official rule of all Frankish monasteries. Although this movement rapidly lost its force, the reformers of the tenth century, whether of Cluny, Gorze, or Glastonbury, all looked to the combined works of the two Benedicts as the source of their way of life. This meant a very elaborate ritual filling an ever increasing part of the day; it meant here and there a flourishing school within the monastery; it meant that the monks did no manual work. One of the effects of the intellectual revival of the eleventh and twelfth centuries was that monastic leaders came to know more and more thoroughly the ancient books on the spiritual life, and above all, to read them freshly, without the accretions of tradition laid over them, as though they had just been discovered for the first time. The eleventh century saw many groups of hermits, or monks leading something like the life of hermits, formed in Italy and France, under the inspiration of the lives of the desert fathers, and of their great interpreter to the West, John Cassian (of the early fifth century). Some of these developed into real hermit Orders, like the Carthusians. The Carthusian Order has altered least of all religious Orders in the 850 years of its existence. The monks still live in their cells a life of total silence, only meeting occasionally in the church and for conferences. Some of the hermits, however, came to form more normal Benedictine communities. In their way of life the influence of both Benedict and Cassian is very evident. The English Carthusians were few in number, but they included St Hugh, especially famous for combining, in later life, the austerity of his Order with the office of Bishop of Lincoln (1186–1200).

The Cistercians, who first sought their vocation at Cîteaux in 1098, came to be the most famous of these new Orders. They owed their exceptional fame to the groundwork, both spiritual and constitutional, of the third abbot, the English Stephen Harding, and to the dynamic inspiration of St Bernard (died 1153), abbot of the daughter abbey of Clairvaux. Several of the most distinguished of the English houses, including Rievaulx and Fountains, were daughters of Clairvaux, founded under Bernard's own instruction.

154

It may well have been the founders of Rievaulx, passing through York early in 1132, who fired a number of the leading spirits in the Benedictine house of St Mary's, York, with a desire to follow the Cistercians into uninhabited places. St Mary's lay near the heart of a busy city; the Cistercians looked for the silence and solitude of a deserted spot away from the cities. They looked for solitude for the community, and for space for fields which their own lay brothers could till. The Benedictine abbeys were often in cities, and they had no lay brothers, so that it did not matter to them if their estates were not compact and close. So vital, indeed, was solitude to the Cistercians, that on occasion they created it by moving villages, almost like an eighteenth-century landowner laying out a park.

The insurgent group in St Mary's, York, prepared to leave the abbey late in 1132. The abbot refused his permission—he did not wish to lose so many of his best monks. The monks appealed to the Archbishop of York, Thurstan, who was sympathetic. The archbishop visited St Mary's, but was mobbed by the abbot's party, and had to take refuge, with the monks who had appealed to him, in the abbey church. In the end he and they escaped, and the group of monks, now in touch with St Bernard, were established in a remote and wild spot near Ripon, given to them by Thurstan. To the modern visitor the ruins of Fountains, made more romantic by the skill of an eighteenth-century landscape gardener, have a unique enchantment. But they are the memorial of a very exacting life; and before the great stone buildings went up, when the first community lived in temporary huts round the great elm which gave them their first shelter, life there must have been exceedingly austere.

The most distinguished of the English Cistercians was St Ailred, the third abbot of Rievaulx. We can get quite an intimate picture of this attractive, patriarchal abbot from the contemporary life written by his disciple, Walter Daniel. Ailred was a kindly, friendly superior—he gave his monks more opportunity for discussion, more spiritual conferences, than can have been common. One has the impression that human relations were more intimate and life less severe than in some communities; but physical conditions were certainly austere, and Ailred himself gave a stern example of asceticism. His biographer, however, quotes him as saying that 'it is the singular and supreme glory of the house of Rievaulx that above all else it teaches tolerance of the infirm and compassion with others in their necessities.' This is a very attractive quality, and helps us to understand Walter's famous remark that on feast days you might see the church crowded with the brethren like bees in a hive, 'unable to move forward because of the multitude, clustered together, rather, and compacted into one angelical body'. Rievaulx was a haven of peace for the many rather than a home of strict vocation; and this is a striking fact, because one of St Bernard's most telling charges against Cluny was that it let monks in without a strict noviciate. The Cistercians recruited over 1,400 choir monks and founded over fifty houses in their first twenty-five years in England, and this sensational growth can be paralleled in many parts of western Europe. It shows that they were never very strict in accepting candidates. To use the monastic vocation seems a very special one, suitable only for the few. In their first enthusiasm the Cistercians, like many other religious Orders and movements, felt themselves to have found the best path to heaven, and found it difficult to deny access to any man. In their early days they attracted a wide variety of character and talent, including many of the best minds of the age. They were in the forefront of several movements, and contemporaries felt them to be so. In one of his letters, St Bernard compared the spiritual life to Jacob's ladder, on which the angels went up and down but did not stand still. So, he argues, in the spiritual life, 'you mount—or you fall: you cannot stay still'. There were bad monks and evil influences even then; but down to the third quarter of the twelfth century many communities seemed to be mounting.

(4) THE SCHOOLS

One of the movements in which monks played a leading part in the late eleventh and early twelfth centuries was the revival of intellectual life. North of the Alps monastic libraries played a part only second to cathedral libraries in supplying the material for revival. It is significant that three of the greatest names in Italian learning in the eleventh century, Peter Damian, Lanfranc, and Anselm, became monks. Two of these men became Archbishops of Canterbury. The upper clergy formed a thoroughly cosmopolitan society. The clergy had an international language, Latin; they came and went freely in the schools of western Europe, especially in France and Italy. There was still much freedom in the organisation of these schools: the reputation of a great teacher could make a school, his disappearance mar it. It was only as the twelfth century went on that university organisation began to crystallise; but already at the opening of the century Bologna had achieved the pre-eminence for the study of law which it was to hold for centuries; and Paris in Abelard's day was winning a special fame for philosophy and theology. England had her higher schools, mostly cathedral schools; but it is not until the end of the twelfth century that Oxford begins to be in any sense eminent, and not until the thirteenth that Oxford and Cambridge grew into universities.

Anselm was the dominant figure in English learning at the turn of the eleventh and twelfth centuries. But in spite of his immense prestige, and although he gathered pupils and disciples round him at Canterbury, his intellectual influence was limited to a small circle, and confined by the circumstances of his office, and by his frequent absences from England. None the less, his distinction serves to remind us that monks still played an important role in English learning well into the middle of the twelfth century. This is especially true in theology, hagiography, and the writing of history, in which English monks, led by William of Malmesbury, excelled. But to get an impression of the scope of learning and the ways in which it spread at this time, and of the life of scholars, one must look at the careers of a few individuals. Here are three examples.

The chief studies of the higher schools were theology and law; the foundation for these was broad, including almost every discipline known at the time (with special emphasis on Latin grammar—rhetoric and dialectic—or logic), but the summit of recognised sciences was comparatively narrow. This makes the exceptional career of Adelard of Bath all the more interesting. He was born before the eleventh century was out, and lived well into the middle of the twelfth. He studied at Tours and Laon—two French cathedral schools; he travelled in Greece, Asia Minor, Sicily, south Italy, and probably Spain. He formed an extraordinary link between Moslem and Christian learning; between the two great Norman states of England and Sicily; between literacy and statecraft. He was probably one of the men learned in Arabic and Greek mathematics who had a hand in developing the accounting techniques in the English Ex-

157

chequer. His main work lay in more academic fields, in translating Greek and Arab philosophical and scientific treaties—it was Adelard who first introduced Euclid to the West. But he was sufficient of a courtier to write a treatise of falconry for Henry II when Henry was a boy.

A contemporary of Adelard's, meanwhile, was making a more conventional career for himself as a theologian in the schools of Paris. What makes Robert Pullen's career remarkable is that, when already one of the foremost theologians in the French schools, he elected to teach in England—at Exeter and Oxford—in his middle years. In the eleven-forties he returned briefly to Paris, and was then swept into the papal curia, made a cardinal and papal chancellor; he died in 1146.

One of the students who sat at Pullen's feet in Paris in the eleven-forties was a young Englishman called John of Salisbury. John had already heard most of the lecturers who were making the humanist studies of Chartres and the philosophical and theological studies of Paris celebrated at this time. At Chartres he acquired his immense classical learning, his love of *belles lettres,* his elegant Latin. At Paris he saw many of the great teachers of the day, starting with Abelard himself. He was twelve years a student, gathering one of the most substantial educations a man has ever had; and then he had to search for employment. His time in France brought him in contact with two distinguished abbots, Peter of Celle, who gave him temporary employment and became his closest friend, and St Bernard of Clairvaux. To his friendship with Peter we owe one of the few really intimate correspondences which survive from the Middle Ages. But it was Bernard who helped him to employment in the household of Theobald, Archbishop of Canterbury. Canterbury was his headquarters from 1147 to Theobald's death in 1161. There he met many of the leading ecclesiastical administrators of his generation, and made friends with his patron's successor-to-be, Thomas Becket. Much of John's first years under Theobald were spent in journeys to the papal curia; his fascinating book of reminiscences, the *Memoirs of the Papal Court (Historia Pontificalis),* is based on his experiences during these visits. It was also in this period that he made, or renewed, his friendship with an English cardinal, Nicholas Breakspear, later to be pope as Adrian IV (1154-9)—the only Englishman to have held the office; a man who, as pope, began what was to prove a long and bitter conflict with the Emperor Frederick Barbarossa. In doing so Adrian worked out in his life principles of ecclesiastical liberty which were also strongly held by John. Unfortunately that part of the *Memoirs* which dealt with Adrian IV has been lost—if it was ever written. But what survives reveals John's skill in portraying his contemporaries in witty, though not usually malicious fashion. In Theobald's last years John was his personal secretary, writing many of his letters; but John also had leisure to bring out his most substantial books, the *Policraticus* and the *Metalogicon*. The former is a vast rambling encyclopedia of learning and lore on political theory and related (often remotely related) themes; it was dedicated to Thomas Becket, now royal Chancellor, and covered every topic in which John thought his friend ought to be concerned in his new office. At the same time he wrote a shorter book on contemporary logical theories and their sources, the *Metalogicon*, also dedicated to Thomas, to which we owe our knowledge of John's early career, and his famous description of the great teachers of his day. After Theobald's death and Becket's succession, John joined the latter's household, and he was mainly engaged in defending his friend's case and vindicating his memory until fortune brought him back, at the very end of his life, to the cathedral in whose shadow he had received the main intellectual inspiration of his life; he was Bishop of Chartres from 1176 until his death in 1180.

In John of Salisbury several of the finest traditions of twelfth-century learning were represented. He is best remembered as one of the most learned scholars of his day, at least in the pagan classics; and as a distinguished humanist. Humanism is an ambiguous and confusing word; but whether we look in it for devotion to the classics or for a deep sense of human values, both are present in John—the latter perhaps not so powerfully as the former. In many respects he and a few others like him foreshadowed the humanism of the later Renaissance. He knew no Greek; his passion for the great figures of the past was diffuse. Perhaps he differs most from scholars of the fifteenth century in the way he saw the classics through the spectacles of post-classical writers, especially of the pagan and Christian writers of the later Empire. John's outlook was entirely Christian.

Though not endowed with a high measure of physical courage, John held clear convictions and expressed them forcibly

159

in his writings. Like many men who passed through the schools at this time, and came in contact with current theological and legal doctrine, he held clearly fixed in his mind the supremacy of the papacy in spiritual affairs and the ultimate supremacy of the spiritual over the temporal. Thus conviction as well as loyalty to friend and patron made him support Thomas Becket. It would be wrong to think of John as typical in this respect. It came as a great surprise to most contemporaries that Becket, after a normal clerical career in the schools, in the service of the archbishop and of the king, emerged when archbishop as a strong exponent of these views. The leading churchmen of the day were brought up in two worlds: in the world of lay custom of their parents and secular relations, and of the king whom most of the bishops had at one time served; and also in the clerical world of the schools, in which they learned the theory of papal and clerical supremacy. In the minds of most of them custom held a stronger place than in John of Salisbury's or Thomas Becket's. But the conflict in which they became in-volved can be understood only as part of the story of English politics in the century after the Conqueror's death; and to this we must now return.

CHAPTER NINE

WILLIAM II, HENRY I, AND STEPHEN

(1) WILLIAM II, 1087–1100

In the last three chapters we have tried to give a broad sketch of Norman England. We have seen continuity in some parts of English life, rapid and catastrophic change in others. The Normans who settled in England were comparatively few in number; they came as war-lords, royal servants, bishops, abbots, archdeacons, canons, and clerks. They did not come as peasants. Naturally they altered the feudal structure more fundamentally than the manorial, the cathedral more than the parish. By the Conqueror's death the main lines of change were clear. English and Norman were still distinct—the story of assimilation will come later. But there was no longer an English aristocracy to engineer an English restoration. Not that the English were negligible or their royalty extinct; St Margaret, the Queen of Scotland, was descended from Alfred, Edgar, and Ethelred; and her brother, Edgar Aetheling, had nearly become king for an hour in 1066. Henry I found it prudent to marry Queen Margaret's daughter immediately after his accession. But Henry I lacked even a clear Norman title at that stage. His queen was much loved by the English and helped her husband in many ways; but we must not attribute too much political significance to the match.

The Conqueror had done his work thoroughly. Deep scars in the landscape of England still reminded men what it meant to resist the Norman will; none of his children needed to be so ruthless in devastation as he had been. After his death his sons quarrelled and fought for his inheritance; but when Henry, the youngest, finally won Normandy as well as England in 1106, he was able to build a state to all appearances even stronger than William's.

The quarrels began at the father's deathbed. The eldest son, Robert, was in rebellion, and his father knew his incapacity. The old king reckoned that he could not pass his whole inheritance to William, his second surviving son, known as Rufus, and so gave his voice for Robert as Duke of Normandy, for William as King of England. William left his father's side even before his death, and within a little over a fortnight he had presented his credentials to Archbishop Lanfranc and been crowned in Westminster Abbey. It was the final act of the great partnership of Lanfranc and William I; the crucial importance of having the old king's voice, and of taking rapid possession of throne and crown were never so clearly expressed. The Norman barons had never given their formal consent to the Conqueror's arrangements; to many of them, with their estates divided between the two lands, a divided allegiance must have seemed exceedingly inconvenient. A party of them, headed by the new King's uncle, Odo of Bayeux, were more inclined to Robert than to William.

Early in 1088 William II faced the most dangerous rebellion of his reign. Most of his father's closest followers, the archbishop excepted, were against him. If Robert had acted with the same energy as William, he would probably have won the throne. But William kept a few great men on his side, a large number of lesser folk, and the bulk of the English who still counted—to whom Norman politics meant nothing. In the course of this campaign William's subjects were forcibly reminded that their King was a great warrior and a remarkable personality, and that the English king, whoever he might be, still counted for more in the country at large than any of the barons. In a few months the rebellion was crushed and only the Bishop of Durham still resisted. Under safe conduct he appeared before the King and claimed exemption, as a bishop, from trial in a royal court. He appealed to Rome. Already the force of the new canon law was a weapon which could be turned against the King. The bishop, however, had little support from his own colleagues. In 1082 Odo of Bayeux had been imprisoned, not as a bishop, but as Earl of Kent, as the Conqueror had neatly explained; and Lanfranc and the English bishops seem to have accepted this view of the Bishop of Durham, too—it was as a baron, for his lay fiefs, that he was tried. The end of the case was a compromise; nor was the bishop again to be found defending ultramontane principles.

William II's government was strict and severe, and in 1095 he again provoked some of the barons to rebel. With the suppression of the second rebellion—a more stringent suppression than had been possible in 1088–9—he was secure, as secure as ever his father had been, in his English kingdom, and could turn his attention to the conquest of Normandy.

By 1095 King William was thoroughly established in his reputation as king, Duke Robert thoroughly discredited in his reputation as duke. Both were fine soldiers. But in William the knightly qualities were only one aspect of a complex personality; Robert was strong in nothing else. Robert enjoyed a battle too much to worry about its consequences; he always forgave an enemy as soon as the enemy was beaten. He was incapable of controlling the Norman barons. But he was, though not a moral man, a pious one, and other events of the year 1095 gave him the opportunity for a far more promising adventure than petty war in Normandy provided. The pope was preaching the first Crusade, and found a ready listener in Duke Robert. Robert's only difficulty was money; and this he found by the happy expedient of pawning his duchy to William. To the Crusade went Robert, and made a good name for himself, so to speak, as a brigade commander; nor did he return until after William's death.

William was a splendid knight by the standard of the day, but no crusader. To his own knights he was lavish; and he was never happier than when on campaign or in the hunting field. As a soldier he was loyal to his subordinates, in the way that he himself had been loyal to his father. He was a strict upholder of the soldier's code as he understood it. It was the only code he knew or cared for. He had nothing of chivalry in the modern sense; cared not a rap for religion or the Church; and knew no restraints save those of the camp. And so he was remembered in knightly circles as the greatest leader of his day; by churchmen as a depraved tyrant. Granted the standards of the two communities, there is little to quarrel with in their judgments.

In fairness to Rufus, it must be acknowledged that his worst fault in the eyes of the Church was material: his rapacity. His boundless generosity to his followers, and the expensive adventures of his last years, made money a constant and urgent need. Since he cared nothing for the Church he did what he could to mulct it. He left abbeys and bishoprics vacant, including the see of Canterbury itself, and took a substantial share of their revenues. He was thus provided with a plentiful store of silver, and was spared for the time the unwanted advice of another Lanfranc.

163

None the less, the chroniclers' portrait of Rufus is not inhuman. They hated him for his oppression, but they enjoyed telling stories about him; he was an engaging ruffian. He lacked his father's dignity and presence; he stammered and blustered when in difficulties. But he had a sharp sense of humour and a gay abandon in blasphemy which several chroniclers recorded. The London Jews brought him a present one day, and asked leave to hold a disputation with Christians in his presence. 'God's face,' said the King, with great delight, and announced that if they had the better of it, he would change his faith. A more serious tale was told against him by the historian Eadmer, that Rufus was once bribed by a Jew to compel his son, who had been converted, to abjure his Christianity, which the King —to his own intense annoyance—failed to do. These stories have given rise to a theory that Rufus was a thoroughgoing sceptic, but this is doubtful. He was what the Elizabethans called an atheist: not an unbeliever, but a blasphemer. When secure from fear of death he scoffed at the Church and ignored it: he was also a wit, who kept no control of his tongue.

It is a strange irony that Rufus, of all English kings, should have invited one of the most attractive, distinguished, and saintly of possible candidates to occupy the see of Canterbury. In 1092–3 many of the leaders in Church and state were in a conspiracy to fill the see, vacant since Lanfranc's death in 1089. They were attracted by the immense prestige of the abbot of Bec, Anselm of Aosta, and he was invited to visit England. Anselm suspected what was afoot, and refused to come, although his abbey's possessions in England required his presence. Eventually the importunity of the savage old Earl of Chester, who swore he was on his deathbed, compelled Anselm to come. A sudden and violent illness made Rufus a party to the plot, and Anselm found himself, very much against his will, constrained to accept the archbishopric. 'You would yoke a weak old sheep to an untamed bull,' he said. Small wonder that he resisted: he was already an old man, and it needed no deep prescience to foresee that he would have to dedicate his last years to a fearful task. In the event he lived sixteen years, and spent them in resisting two of the most strong-willed and unscrupulous monarchs in the Europe of his day.

One cannot read either of Eadmer's books about him, or any contemporary description, or his own writings, without feeling the impact of Anselm's charm. The division of clerical and lay was never more sharply exemplified than in the contrast of Anselm and Rufus. Yet Anselm was no sheep. He did not fancy himself as a politician; and he gives the impression of always striving to find some way out of the endless battles in which he was involved. But it was not for nothing that he was the finest philosopher whom Europe had seen for many centuries. He saw vital points of principle with extreme clarity and precision, and never wavered in defending what he regarded as essential. As a monk, spiritual director, thinker, and theologian, Anselm held and deserved an immense reputation. There seems at first sight something wasteful in the way he was pulled from his cloister and set in the militant theatre in which his last years were passed. But if we wish to understand the Middle Ages, Anselm's career is worth careful reflection. The Earl of Chester was not given to basing essential choices on sentiment. Nor were he and his like driven by fear alone, as was Rufus. It may be that Earl Hugh's chief wish was to stand before God's judgment seat and claim to have won for the English Church a saintly head. But in addition to this the story of Anselm shows that, however sharp the contrast between the two worlds of clergy and laity, men like Anselm and Earl Hugh could communicate.

The immediate result was a violent reaction by Rufus, who felt that he had been tricked into appointing Anselm, and used every trick he knew to be rid of him. There was trouble about the way Anselm should receive his pallium of office. There were two rival popes at the time, and the King claimed the right to choose which one should have the English allegiance. Anselm, however, had already accepted Urban II while abbot of Bec, as had the whole Norman Church. This dispute was followed by other difficulties, until a number of bishops and a few barons reckoned that there would be no peace till Anselm had withdrawn from the archbishopric. In the end Anselm found his position untenable, and went abroad in 1097 to consult the pope. King and archbishop agreed to part; Rufus was saved from excommunication by Anselm; but it must have appeared that the English Church would be without an archbishop until either Rufus or Anselm died; and since Rufus was barely forty and Anselm about sixty-five, the outcome seemed clearly predictable.

Rufus was himself so anti-clerical that historians for long ignored the evidence that his clerical supporters were extremely active in developing some of the literate aspects of government. It may even have been in his time that the new system of accounting came in at the Exchequer. What is certain is that it was in response to his urgent need for money that his notorious chaplain, Ranulph Flambard, developed and enforced the machinery for levying and manipulating taxes. Ranulph was as hardly treated by the chroniclers as was his master, and he was evidently unscrupulous; but his long period of office in Chancery and Treasury marked an important stage in the development of royal government. What is uncertain is how much part the King played in these activities. Clearly his real interests lay elsewhere.

While Duke Robert was on Crusade, William set to work to restore order and expand the frontiers of his new principality in Normandy. He had only temporary possession of the duchy, but evidently intended to retain it altogether if he could. A series of campaigns against the heir to the French throne, the future Louis VI (1108–37) brought him the exercise that he and his followers loved, but no decisive advantage. Normandy became secure, however, and he was successful in reducing Maine to submission. England was secure as never before: in 1099 King Edgar of Scotland bore William's sword before him at the crown-wearing at Westminster, and the faithful Ranulph Flambard was rewarded with the frontier bishopric of Durham. There was talk of the Duke of Aquitaine following Duke Robert's example, and pawning his duchy to Rufus. In the summer of 1100 Rufus boasted that he would spend Christmas in Poitiers. But on 2nd August he was shot by an arrow while hunting in the New Forest, and instantly died.

Contemporaries ascribed the event to an accident, but they saw in it God's judgment on his blasphemies and oppression. Some recent historians have suspected conspiracy. William and Robert had made each the other's heir, to the exclusion of their youngest brother Henry. Henry had no hope of William's nomination; his only chance of the throne was to seize it by force when Robert was in no position to intervene. At the time of Rufus's death Robert's return from the Crusade was imminent, and he brought with him a bride who might bear him a son. Henry was a member of the fatal hunting party; they were only a short distance from the royal treasure house at Winchester. The arrow was discharged by Walter Tirel, whose relations were treated by Henry with great favour. All the circumstances were singularly fortunate for Henry, and a suspicion attaches to him of conspiring to have his brother cut off. Of this we may probably acquit him. We might believe him capable of murdering to win the crown; but to murder one's brother and liege lord was an act of treachery, the suspicion of which would have blasted his reputation. The stigma of quite a remote acquiescence in his brother's murder never left Ethelred II; it is hard to believe that Henry could have been in a conspiracy and no wind of it reach us from contemporaries. If conspiracy there was, it was extraordinarily well concealed.

(2) HENRY I, 1100–35

Henry succeeded only just in time. Rufus died on the afternoon of 2nd August. By 5th August Henry had seized the Treasury at Winchester and had had himself elected and crowned at Westminster. Within a few weeks Robert was back in Normandy, and preparing to punish his upstart brother. Henry had still much to do to win sufficient support to face the threat. He made a bid for the barons and the Church by issuing an elaborate charter repudiating the notorious abuses of Rufus's régime; like Rufus he made more promises than he had any hope or intention of keeping. He pursued his advantage with the Church by speeding the return of Anselm. He conciliated his English subjects by marrying Edith (alias Matilda), daughter of St Margaret of Scotland and niece of Edgar Aetheling. He won recognition from Louis of France, who was not sorry to see the Anglo-Norman Empire divided. But his position remained very insecure. Some of the great barons, with estates in both England and Normandy, feared that civil war between the two brothers would not be in their interest, and hoped that Robert would quickly unite kingdom and duchy again; others saw advantage in civil war, and encouraged Robert to invade for a different reason; others again felt that a crusader's rights should have been better respected.

At first the peacemakers had the better of the argument. Robert came, and at Alton peace was arranged between the brothers before the situation had come to a fight. Robert was to have Normandy and a large pension, Henry England and a Norman castle; both were to forgive their rebels. Whether this was regarded as a lasting settlement is not clear. In any case Henry rapidly set to work to undermine it. Robert's fame as a crusader gave him a momentary return of prestige, which his incompetence soon dissipated. Henry meanwhile was proving himself a strong, capable, and just ruler. After his death he was known as the lion of justice. The title implies the nostalgia of men oppressed by the chaos of Stephen's reign which followed, and is in part a formal symbol. But the lion is not a kindly beast, and Henry succeeded, like his father, because he rapidly inspired fear and respect. He was capable, thorough, and ruthless. Like his father, he was also pious; he liked to be on good terms with the Church—if the Church would respect and obey him in turn—and he took a real interest in endowing religious houses, a taste he shared with Queen Matilda. But his piety did not affect his morals; though less systematic in destruction than his father, Henry was not a merciful man; unlike his father, he was not a good husband. He acknowledged upward of twenty illegitimate children. Henry I was a constructive monarch in his way; but as a person he is unattractive. It must be remembered to his credit that he kept men's allegiance; after 1102 there were no more rebellions in England until his death. Partly this was because, unlike King Stephen, he was feared and respected, but partly too, because, unlike King John, he was trusted.

Duke Robert was no match for his brother. Henry quietly wove a fabric of alliances round Normandy, so as to ensure that his conquest of the duchy should be uninterrupted; he also used every opportunity to prepare Normandy to accept him as duke. Rufus's old minister, Ranulph Flambard, was engaged in clerical intrigue on his own account and political intrigue on Henry's in Normandy in these years; Henry's most distinguished lay supporter, Robert of Meulan, was sent to help Robert suppress disorder. In 1105, Henry openly invaded the duchy, and again in 1106. At the end of September Henry and Robert met at Tinchebrai, and the battle ended in Robert's capture and Henry's conquest of Normandy. Robert ended his days a prisoner in Britain; Henry became Duke of Normandy; the Anglo-Norman barons were freed from their divided allegiance; and Ranulph Flambard returned to Durham to enjoy the novelty of being a respectable bishop. The nave of Durham Cathedral is a striking monument to the artistic unity of the Norman dominions, to the prosperity of Henry's kingdom, and to the ability and munificence of Bishop Ranulph.

Like his father in 1066, or William of Orange in 1688, Henry had achieved his conquest because of the temporary quiescence of neighbouring powers. Like them, he found himself in his triumph suddenly ringed with enemies. Some of his further schemes came to nothing, and he made no headway on the frontier between Normandy and the royal domain of France against the rising star of Louis VI. But he held his own in Maine, and continued to practise his diplomacy against the other powers of northern and central France. His diplomacy in Anjou was later to spoil his plans for the succession to his throne.

Meanwhile in England, Henry had made his peace with the Church. Anselm's return at the beginning of the reign had revealed a fundamental difference of principle between king and primate, which soon led the latter into exile again. Papal councils of the last decade of the eleventh century had been condemning with ever growing urgency the practice of lay investiture, first called in question by Gregory VII in 1075. It was the custom in most European kingdoms and many principalities for a new bishop or a new abbot to be granted his office by king or prince in a symbolic ceremony in which ring and pastoral staff were presented to the elect. Symbol and reality were felt in the Middle Ages to inhere in one another to a degree we find difficult to comprehend; and staff and ring were the essential symbols of pastoral office. For those churchmen who were concerned to emphasise the distinction of lay and clerical, to free the Church (as they saw it) from lay control, this symbol was in every way offensive. Anselm had been present at two of the councils of the ten-nineties and could not ignore the problem. He refused to consecrate bishops who had been invested by the King. On the other side, many royal supporters thought the symbol as precious as the reality, and there was stout resistance to Anselm's demands. Many churchmen thought any kind of royal influence as offensive as its symbol, and the declared papal policy was to make the offices of bishop and abbot purely spiritual—to cut off the lay power from any say in the making of spiritual officials. To the King this was intolerable. He relied on the bishops for counsel and for knights as well as for prayers; they were among his leading barons, usually his most faithful barons. It was essential to his government that he should choose them.

The impasse was solved by the desire of Anselm and Henry

for peace. Anselm was weary of exile, anxious to return to his flock and perform his proper function as archbishop. Henry preferred to be on good terms with the Church, and needed all the support he could get for his attack on Normandy. And so in 1105 the basis for agreement was found. It was suggested to Henry that he give up investiture but retain the essential custom of receiving homage and fealty from the bishops. Anselm, after some hesitation, agreed to submit the proposal to the Pope, who accepted the condition, so long as it remained a personal grant to Henry alone. In 1107 Anselm was finally able to return to England, to consecrate the many bishops elected in his absence, to hold a last council and pass stringent decrees on clerical discipline (1108), before he died in 1109.

The compromise between Henry and Anselm later provided a pattern for the compromise between the Pope and Henry's son-in-law, the Emperor Henry V, in 1122. In both a formal renunciation of investiture was made in exchange for a personal grant of the right of a symbol devoid of spiritual significance. In both cases the right survived, because the King's successors regarded it as the immemorial custom of their realms. Their actual influence on elections depended on political circumstances; by and large the English kings had no difficulty in managing elections before the fourteenth century. But it rarely happened in the Middle Ages that a symbol was surrendered without cost. A profound movement was in progress; clerical education was bringing men more and more to assume a measure of clerical independence. These new assumptions rarely came into the open except at times of conflict. But men about the English court must have noticed the disappearance of this well-known ceremony. It marked a stage in the process by which the king ceased to be undisputed master in the English Church. Henry I still got his way in later years; but papal envoys—or legates, as they were called—and church councils became commoner.

Henry governed England by the fullest use of every traditional instrument. Like all the English kings of the twelfth century, he was a feudal king in a feudal age. His tastes lay in hunting, and preparing for war, like those of all his line. His natural associates were barons: Robert of Meulan and his family, and other like them, were constantly about him. Rebels he treated severely after his first two years; he even broke the great house of Bellême-Montgomery, who had held semi-independent sway in the marches of Normandy and Wales under his father and brother. He broke them because they were rebels, not out of an 'anti-feudal' policy. If the greater baronage was weaker in 1135 than in 1100, the explanation lies in the fullness with which Henry used all the other instruments of government, not in any conscious effort to weaken his fellow feudatories.

The feudal aristocracy was certainly not caste. Henry himself was accused by Orderic of promoting men from the dust. But in practice his new barons were not yeomen or peasants; they had all, by definition, to be trained to knightly pursuits, to be brought up in the traditions of the feudal classes. Henry undoubtedly added to the numbers of the barons, endowing them when possible by marrying them to heiresses; when heiresses were lacking, he gave them portions of royal demesne. This was partly the fruit of necessity, partly of choice. The prestige of a usurper or of a newcomer to the throne was always liable to be weak if the great luminaries of the court in no way reflected his glory. It no doubt gave Henry strength in his own and other men's eyes that not all the great men of his court owed their place to his father or brother.

Henry's most important creations were able royal servants. The English royal council, be it Alfred's Witan or the Tudor Privy Council, has always contained an element freely chosen by the king and an element with something like an inherited claim to be invited. In a measure the English king always retained the right to consult and be counselled by whom he would. One of the most notable features of Henry I's court was the distinction of his councillors, both clerical and lay. We have already glanced at the achievement of Bishop Roger of Salisbury and his family in the Exchequer and elsewhere. Most English bishops of this time were recruited from the royal Chancery or some other office of state—with the singular exception of Canterbury, which always had a monk or canon regular before 1162. Greatest among Henry's lay officials were Aubrey de Vere and Richard Basset, who were given a roving commission in the late eleven-twenties to reform the sheriffdoms of much of England. Richard was a royal justice and perhaps for a time Chief Justiciar—a new office, carrying with it supremacy in judicial and administrative affairs in the king's absence; Aubrey was made Master Chamberlain, that is, chief financial officer of the royal household, in 1133. In the next reign Aubrey's son acquired an earldom, and the Veres were earls of Oxford until 1604. The origins of Vere and Basset are an interesting commentary on Orderic's sneers. Aubrey's barony was not of Henry's creation. The founder of the family came from Ver near Coutances in western Normandy, and doubtless owed his promotion to the Bishop of Coutances; by 1086 the first Aubrey was already established as a tenant-in-chief in his own right as well as tenant of the bishop in two counties. The Bassets held a small fee in southern Normandy, and Richard's father had already attracted William II's notice before Henry came to the throne. Their sensational rise and wide English possessions (with one very valuable marriage to an English heiress), they owed to Henry I. Henry did not choose his subordinates haphazardly; he selected men who had already proved themselves in a lower capacity. The man who owed most to him was his nephew Stephen, who can only be described as a favourite. Stephen was the son of Adela, Henry's sister, and Stephen, Count of Blois; his elder brother, Count Theobald, was a constant ally of Henry against the French king. Two large English fiefs and two of the richest fiefs of Normandy came Stephen's way before 1118; and in 1125 he married the heiress of Boulogne, Matilda, niece of Henry's first queen, and so sprung from the Old English and the Scottish kings. Count Stephen was a magnate after the order of Earl Godwin or Earl Harold.

As Henry's nephew, Stephen, had a place in the queue for his succession. It was not at first a very lofty place, since Stephen had an elder brother and Henry had children. But circumstances favoured him. In 1120 a boat carrying Henry's only legitimate son, William the Aetheling, and many leading men of his court, struck a rock in the Channel and sank. The wreck of the White Ship made a deep impression on contemporaries, and was a fearful shock to Henry. He married again, but had no children by his second wife; it was the pitiful irony of his later years that he should be surrounded by bastard sons, whom neither the customs of the land nor the Church would allow to succeed him. In spite of his evident affection for Stephen, he was very slow to think of him as a possible heir, and it is doubtful if Stephen took his own claims seriously before the very end of the reign.

There remained Matilda, Henry's only legitimate daughter. Matilda, at the tender age of eleven, had had a taste of a higher office than any other member of the family; she was married to the Emperor Henry V. The marriage was childless, and on her husband's death in 1125 the Empress returned to her father's court, to be prepared for the English succession. On 1st January 1127 the English barons, including Stephen, swore to recognise her as Lady of England if Henry died without male heirs. Later in the year Henry betrothed her to Geoffrey, Count of Anjou, and capped a year of triumph over enemies in France by marrying her to Count Geoffrey in June 1128.

For once Henry had overreached himself. The marriage was exceedingly unpopular. The terms allowed Geoffrey to become King of England and Duke of Normandy. To this the English barons had not given their consent. The Norman barons, many of them also English barons, reacted violently to the prospect of being ruled by their traditional enemy, the Count of Anjou. The French king naturally disapproved of an alliance between two leading powers of northern France. Finally, the Empress herself objected to an entanglement with a mere count ten years her junior. The English barons were threatening to repudiate their oath to Matilda when, in 1131, Henry found an opportunity for cajoling them to confirm it. Geoffrey repudiated his wife, and Matilda returned to England, apparently free of the Angevin yoke. The barons renewed their oath. But very shortly after, Matilda and Geoffrey were reunited, and on 5th March 1133 the future Henry II was born. The English barons had sworn to acknowledge Matilda, not her husband; the King had promised the succession to Geoffrey, and Geoffrey was at first determined to have it. It is likely that Henry was beginning to repent of his offers to Geoffrey, and he certainly refused him an immediate share in government. The result was that Henry and Geoffrey were at war when the old King died (of a surfeit of lampreys) in December 1135.

(3) STEPHEN, 1135–54

Stephen won the throne by a rapid and forceful manoeuvre, comparable to the manoeuvres of 1087 and 1100. But he was never able to assert his supremacy in England as his uncles had done. From 1139 to 1148 the Empress Matilda was in the

173

country, and never lacked supporters; after her departure her son was always plotting and executing dashing invasions. After 1144 Normandy was irrevocably lost: it had been conquered by Count Geoffrey. In England Stephen's reign was remembered, with some exaggeration, as nineteen years of chaos, anarchy, and suffering. In fact, the anarchy was intermittent and often local, and the later years of the reign were less severe than those which followed the Empress's invasion in 1139. But anarchy there was, such as England had not seen since the Conquest.

The anarchy has sometimes been viewed merely as a reflection of Stephen's weakness of character, sometimes as the inevitable outcome of the circumstances in which he took the throne, and of the disputed succession; sometimes as a natural reaction against the excessively autocratic rule of Henry I. Let us look at these aspects in turn.

'When the traitors saw that Stephen was a good-humoured, kindly, and easy-going man who inflicted no punishment,' wrote the Peterborough chronicler, 'then they committed all manner of horrible crimes. They had done him homage and sworn oaths of fealty to him, but not one of their oaths was kept. They were all forsworn and their oaths broken. For every great man built him castles and held them against the king; and they filled the whole land with these castles. They sorely burdened the unhappy people of the country with forced labour on the castles; and when the castles were built, they filled them with devils and wicked men. . . . Never did a country endure greater misery, and never did the heathen act more vilely than they did. Contrary to custom, they spared neither church nor churchyard, but seized everything of value that was in it, and afterwards burned the church and all it contained. . . . And men said openly that Christ and his saints slept. Such things and others more than we know how to relate we suffered nineteen years for our sins.'[1]

King Stephen was easy-going, though a good knight and in his way a pious man. In fact, he resembled his uncle Duke Robert, save that he had more than Robert's share of energy and determination. Indeed, he achieved more than Robert while lacking most of Robert's advantages. His right to the throne is not easily assessed. Matilda was nearer in blood to Henry than was Stephen; she had been designated by Henry and received the oaths of the barons. It is true she was a woman, and would not be expected to rule alone; and the barons had never accepted her husband as king. But Matilda and Geoffrey jointly had Henry's voice, and their children would have a far better hereditary claim than Stephen. But Stephen's claim was not negligible. It was solemnly debated before the pope in 1139, and upheld. Hereditarily it was weak, but heredity was only one of the elements in king-making, and not the most important. Some of the Norman barons were for Count Theobald, who became duke for a day; but when news came that Stephen had been crowned King of England, Theobald gave way to his younger brother, and for the time Stephen was accepted as *de facto* duke in Normandy as well as king in England.

In putting himself at the head of the English baronage in their rejection of the deep-seated plans of Henry I, Stephen stored up for himself future trouble. Henry I had been increasingly autocratic in later years; his rule had grown harsh and oppressive. He had used his rights arbitrarily to extort money from the powerful, and they had come to resent his rule. The course of Stephen's reign shows that the English aristocracy saw little advantage to themselves in strong government; and bitterly distrusted the financial organisation developed under Roger of Salisbury. Stephen was carried to success on the shoulders of a baronial reaction, and had to show the barons some return for their support, in the shape of a milder government. More important, perhaps, he had the prejudices of his class—the feudal hierarchy meant more to him than royal authority, and he had the layman's distrust of the literate clerical civil servants.

In 1138 Count Geoffrey had invaded Normandy and at the same time rebellion first showed in England, headed by Matilda's half-brother, Robert, Earl of Gloucester, and timed to coincide with an invasion by David, King of the Scots. But the two attacks were beaten off; the Scots were defeated in the famous 'battle of the Standard'; and Stephen seemed secure. Rebellion had aroused his suspicions against Roger of Salisbury and his family, and he proceeded to throw his own administration into confusion, and embroil himself with the Church by picking a quarrel with Roger himself, with Roger's son, who had been royal Chancellor, and his two episcopal nephews of Ely and Lincoln. Roger only survived his arrest four months, to die in December 1139. Meanwhile Stephen's

175

brother, Henry of Blois, Bishop of Winchester, at this time head of the English Church in virtue of his office of papal legate, had attempted unsuccessfully to rouse a Church council to condemn his brother's action; and the Empress had landed in England.

From 1139 to 1145 there was anarchy in England. Fighting took place sporadically in many parts of the country, especially in the west and west Midlands, where the Empress's following was strong, and in East Anglia, where one of the most powerful of the robber barons, Geoffrey de Mandeville, Earl of Essex, was at large. In 1141 Stephen was captured at the battle of Lincoln; for a moment the Empress was triumphant, and she marched to London to be crowned. But some of Matilda's difficulties were of her own making: by temperament she was self-willed and haughty, disinclined to make concessions to her subjects' demands or even to good manners. Within a week she was forced out of London, and a few months later, after a hazardous march, she was established once again in the western strongholds of her half-brother, Robert, Earl of Gloucester. A powerful counter-attack under forces organised by Stephen's queen led to Robert's capture late in 1141. Robert and Stephen were exchanged, and the Empress's brief triumph was at an end. But not the anarchy; it continued unabated, and rose to its height in 1144. In that year Geoffrey de Mandeville died. He had played one side off against the other, exacting bribes and favours from each in turn, and so had won large estates, royal offices, and an earldom. The same game was played more subtly for even higher stakes by the Earl of Chester, who fancied himself as a king-maker. He remained a power to be reckoned with until his death in 1153, but after a brief arrest in 1146 his activities were somewhat curtailed. From 1145, indeed, the anarchy began to subside; the arrest of the Earl of Chester in 1146 and the death of the Earl of Gloucester in 1147 marked important stages in its decline; when the Empress finally abandoned the struggle in 1148 and returned to her husband, the way seemed clear for a return of peaceful government. But Stephen's difficulties were far from over.

The greater barons had tasted liberty and many of them were still disinclined for a stronger régime. They met threats to the peace of their own domains by organising pacts with their neighbours. By the end of the reign a generation was growing up which had forgotten both the peace and the oppressions of Henry I. Some were prepared to accept a stronger yoke and the security which went with it; others rejoiced in present opportunities for plunder and promotion. The anarchy was a rare interval when the strong government of Norman kings was relaxed, and some of the more violent potentialities of feudal society could come into the open. Many tendencies in twelfth-century society fought against such violence; but the great barons in whose hands lay the decision of the conflict needed to be convinced that it was not to their interests to let it continue.

As Stephen grew older he made more and more urgent efforts to settle the succession. Following a practice common on the Continent, he wished to have his elder son, Eustace, crowned in his own lifetime. To Stephen the deciding factor on this occasion was heredity and his own voice; he had decided, Eustace must be king. It was true that the nobles had tasted new opportunities for bargaining, had acquired a new sense of their own importance in king-making, as a result of the anarchy. Secret and open Angevins were now for the Empress's son, Henry, who made his existence known by raids in 1147 and 1149. But Angevins, for the moment, were few; and Stephen was able to win his barons' consent for the succession of Eustace. The only determined opposition came from the Church. The papacy had never withdrawn its acceptance of Stephen, and never agreed to reopen the case after 1139. But formal processes of king-making were not of major concern to the Church; its essential interest lay in the suitability of the candidate for his lofty office, especially suitability as the Church's protector, and the Church's own part in the business, the ceremonies of anointing and coronation. In 1152, acting on the Pope's specific prohibition, the Archbishop of Canterbury refused to crown Eustace, and fled the country.

Archbishop Theobald's refusal was the culmination of a remarkable effort to maintain a consistent front in the circumstances of the anarchy. When he first became archbishop, he was compelled to take orders from his subordinate, the Bishop of Winchester, because the Bishop was papal legate. Theobald had done homage to Stephen, and even in 1141, when Stephen was imprisoned, and the Church rallied round the Empress, Theobald refused to give up his allegiance without Stephen's

177

permission. He remained throughout the reign a reluctant supporter of the King. At the same time, he attempted to maintain the unity of his province in a divided country and against the encroachments of rebellious bishops. After 1143 Henry of Blois was no longer legate, but he continued to strive for independence from Canterbury; so did the Bishop of St David's. To maintain his position, Theobald had to enter into correspondence with the Empress's supporters. Presumably for this reason, he became the object of violent suspicion to the King, and was forced into temporary exile two or three times and once took refuge in Angevin territory. Stephen's attempts to resume control of the Church became increasingly ineffective; even episcopal elections took place behind his back. Meanwhile the Angevin cause, though weak in England, had prospered in Normandy, which was conquered by Count Geoffrey in the early eleven-forties. Prolonged war between Stephen and Geoffrey would in effect be civil war, since the leading barons held fiefs on both sides of the Channel. It is clear that at some date in the eleven-forties Theobald and his circle made up their minds to work for an Angevin succession. It can only have been at their instance that the pope forbade Eustace's coronation.

The factors which told against Eustace helped his rival in other ways as well. Henry returned to England in 1153 under very different circumstances from those of his earlier visits. He was now Duke of Normandy in his own right, and since his father's death in 1151, Count of Anjou; he had recently married the ex-Queen of France, Eleanor, heiress of Aquitaine, whose marriage to King Louis VII had been annulled. Henry was lord of half France, and a mature warrior of nineteen. For those who wished for lasting peace, he offered some prospect of a return to the days of his grandfather. For those barons with extensive Norman domains, he held out a threat of blackmail. The solution was either the immediate defeat of Stephen or a compromise by which Henry should be recognised as Stephen's heir. But Stephen was not easy to defeat, and Eustace's ambition prevented a compromise. The impasse was solved by Eustace's sudden death. Stephen's younger son, like his father, was a great feudal baron at heart, and was satisfied with the many lordships which Henry I had granted to his father. Great trouble-makers like the Earl of Chester trembled for their Norman lands, and joined the Archbishop in negotiating peace. Stephen was to be king until his death, and Henry was then to succeed. Stephen died in the next year, and on 19th December 1154 Archbishop Theobald had the satisfaction of crowning Henry king.

1. *Peterborough Chronicle*, under the year 1137 (*Anglo-Saxon Chronicle*, trans. G. N. Garmonsway, pp. 263–5).

CHAPTER TEN

HENRY II, 1154–89

(1) HENRY II AND THOMAS BECKET

Henry II was one of the most remarkable characters in English history. We know a great deal about him. He lived in an age when it was fashionable to comment on the activities of kings, when history and especially contemporary history was popular; and Henry impressed his contemporaries so strongly that they could not refrain from saying what they thought of him. Most of them disliked him. His enemies found him too brilliant and mercurial, too overwhelming to be forgiven; those close to him feared both his charm and his occasional outbursts of wild anger, and were exasperated by his unpredictable activity. But they all admired him. He was a great figure in European society, comparable in prestige to the Emperor Frederick Barbarossa. He married his daughters to kings of Sicily and Castile and to Henry the Lion, Duke of Saxony; the Duke was father to the Emperor Otto IV, the King of Sicily cousin to Otto's famous rival and supplanter, the Emperor Frederick II. Henry's wife was Eleanor of Aquitaine, 'divorced' wife of the King of France—Eleanor's children and grandchildren became kings or queens of most countries between England and the Holy Land.

Henry had been named after his grandfather, and in many ways resembled him. Both were ruthless and cunning, yet both were fundamentally trusted as well as feared by their followers. Both had an exceptional capacity for choosing men to serve them; both had a ferocious eagerness to see justice done. Few men have done more for the peace and security of the English kingdom. The resemblance is in part increased by the younger Henry's admiration for his grandfather, whose reign provided a model for his own. Henry II had many friends, and some intimates. But he was not an easy man to live with. Like Henry I, he was unfaithful to his wife; nevertheless, he had seven children by her before they finally quarrelled. Eleanor was probably as difficult as Henry, but when the breach came the

181

sons, on the whole, followed Eleanor. For ordinary courtiers Henry's behaviour could be a nightmare. Peter of Blois has left a vivid account of the horrors of living in a court always on the move—the constant uncertainty, the stale food, difficulties with the billeting officers, 'and if the king promises to spend the day anywhere, especially if a herald has published the royal will, you may be sure that the king will leave the place bright and early, and upset everyone's calculations in his haste. It frequently happens, that those who are having bloodletting, or receiving treatment, leave their cure and follow the prince, and chance their life, as it were, on the throw of a dice, risking to lose themselves rather than lose what they haven't got and are not going to get. You many see men rushing madly about, urging on the pack-horses, fitting the teams to their wagons; everyone in utter confusion—a perfect portrait of hell. But if the prince has announced that he is setting off early to reach a particular place, beyond doubt he will change his mind and sleep till noon. You will see the pack-horses waiting loaded, the wagons silent, the runners asleep, the court merchants in a pother, everyone grumbling.' He goes on to describe the throng of camp followers waiting for news of the king's movements. Then word came [1] that the next night would be spent in such a place, and hopes rose, because shelter and food were to be found there. But as the day drew in, the King changed his mind, and 'turned aside to another place, where there was maybe a single house, and no food for anyone else. And I believe our plight added to the king's pleasure.' Peter had seen enough of court life: 'I shall dedicate the remainder of my days to study and peace.' But the King's perversity and sudden changes of plan were not the only qualities which had impressed Peter of Blois. Elsewhere he fills out the picture. The physical description is famous: the hair once reddish, now turning to grey, of middle height, round-headed, his eyes brilliant as lightning when roused, his face lion-like, surmounted by a fine mane, his deep chest, strong arms and bow legs. The legs were constantly sore because he was so often in the saddle, yet he never sat down, not even at mass or in council—he was tirelessly active. Peter attributes this partly to his many interests, partly to his desire not to grow fat—which also explained his comparatively simple and frugal manner of life. Peter then goes on to give a conventional, though doubtlessly sincere account of Henry's remarkable qualities as a leader and ruler, and of his special interests. 'He is an ardent lover of the woods: when he is not at war, he amuses himself with hawks and hounds. . . . As often as he has free time he occupies himself in private reading or expounds some knotty problem to his clerks.'

Henry I had been called 'Beauclerc', because he could almost sign his name. Henry II was the first English king after the Conquest to be fully literate. He had been well tutored as a young man, and showed something of Alfred's mixture of kingliness and culture: he liked to have learned men about him, was passionately curious about history and literature as well as about war and hunting. There is a certain integration in his intellectual apparatus. His idea of history was a French epic on his forefathers and their great deeds—the *Roman de Rou*, which he commissioned; his idea of science was a treatise on falconry. Many other treatises were dedicated to him; a sign that his patronage was generously given. Thus he emerges a brilliant figure, fascinating, dangerous and yet somehow intensely human.

The King's energy, the size of his dominions, and the complexity of his tasks make it very difficult for us to get a comprehensive view of his reign. We must limit our vision drastically. Wales, Scotland, and Ireland belong to the next chapter; leaving them aside, we may crudely divide Henry's reign into three segments—his attempt to reconstruct the England of his grandfather, which culminated in his quarrel with Thomas Becket; his attempt to develop the legal machinery of his grandfather and lay new foundations for English government; and his attempt to resolve the problem of governing an unwieldy empire and an unruly family by setting the family to rule the empire. Between each of the three there is a rough logical and chronological division, but they often overlap.

Henry had won the throne because many Englishmen wished to see a return to more settled government, and a few great ones saw specific advantage in supporting him. His first task was to convince the former that good government was to be restored, and to prevent the latter from repenting their choice. The great barons presented him with many tricky problems, but good fortune aided him to solve them. The Earl of Chester died late in 1153; the Earl of Hereford retired to a monastery to die in 1155. Henry did not try to abolish the earldoms granted under Stephen, but it was still necessary for him to destroy the new castles which were the most formidable weapon in twelfth-century warfare. In 1155 he seized the Bishop of Winchester's castles, his first overt attack on Stephen's family; in 1157 he treated the castles of Stephen's son, Earl William, in the same fashion—and relations between Henry and William stayed uneasy until William's death in 1159. Castles fell; faithful subjects found the new King prepared within limits to respect the *status quo*; would-be rebels found him a terrible enemy. The financial machinery of the Exchequer, the old mechanism of local government, and the royal courts very rapidly returned to the efficiency of Henry I's day. Henry II was fortunate to succeed before the memory of the exercise of crown rights by his grandfather had died away. It was a number of years before Henry tried any striking innovations: what his grandfather had done was at first sufficient.

The most powerful man in England after the king was the old Archbishop of Canterbury, to whom Henry owed much. Relations between them were outwardly cordial, and Henry rarely refused an urgent request from Theobald. Most striking evidence of Theobald's influence was the presence of his favourite clerk and archdeacon, Thomas Becket, in the office of royal Chancellor and in the most intimate counsels of the king. But it is clear that Henry felt that the Church had acquired the habit of acting more independently than was fitting: and that he found the old man too assiduous a counsellor. Under these conditions was born the most disastrous of all Henry's schemes. When Theobald died he was to be replaced by a man who would fall in with Henry's plans, who would assist him to rule the Church as his grandfather had done, and would be a constant and welcome ornament of his court. In Thomas Becket Henry pictured a right-hand man after the pattern of Rainald of Dassel, Archbishop of Cologne, Archchancellor of Italy and confidant of the Emperor Frederick Barbarossa.

Becket as chancellor had revealed just that mixture of efficiency and glamour which made him a perfect servant for Henry; someone who could maintain the pageantry, organise the detail of a great court, and yet be wholly subservient and wholly congenial to the King. His life was moral, but extremely worldly. There was nothing to indicate that he would not play the same role when he became archbishop in 1162. But in fact from that date he changed his way of life and tried to find an entirely new relation to the King. He became the ascetic monk; the prophetic spiritual leader; the King's father in God. Henry was bewildered and irritated. He had looked for secure co-operation from Becket; the more Becket acted out of his character (as Henry knew it) the more insecure Henry felt. A series of minor disputes, which would normally have been settled by compromise, swiftly developed into a major quarrel. At last, in 1164, Henry determined to break him. In January, at Clarendon, he tried to secure the consent of the Archbishop and bishops to a catalogue of essential customs governing the relations of Church and state. The Constitutions of Clarendon describe themselves as 'this record or recognition of a certain part of the customs, privileges, and dignities of the king's predecessors—to wit of his grandfather King Henry—and other things which ought to be observed in the kingdom'. They were no statement of new law, but a solemn affirmation of ancient practice, and Henry browbeat Thomas and his colleagues into assenting to them.

The constitutions covered many disputed points where the jurisdiction of Church and state overlapped. To take two crucial examples, they laid down the procedure by which clergy convicted of crime ('criminous clerks') should be punished, and they affirmed that no appeal should go to Rome without royal assent—clearly implying that this was to be something exceptional. The constitutions were for the most part a fair statement of practice under Henry I; many clauses indeed were not controversial. But the essential clauses, including these two, were far from being fair statements of practice in Stephen's later years, and were inconsistent with the Church's law. By publishing the constitutions, Henry made it certain that the area of conflict should become known to the pope, and so invited condemnation. Had the customs never been forced on the pope's attention in so lucid a form, the King might have been able to continue quietly to enforce them.

At Clarendon Becket submitted; then repented of his submission, and put himself at the mercy of the Pope. In October the Archbishop went to Northampton, where he had been summoned to face trial before the king on several of the points at issue between them. But whatever the ostensible grounds of the Archbishop's trial, everyone knew that the real question was whether the Constitutions of Clarendon were binding and whether Becket was to continue in office. At Northampton Becket refused to submit to trial. He claimed as clerk and bishop total exemption from the jurisdiction of lay courts; and his final answer to the King's persistent threats was to fly the country and appeal to the Pope. By this act Becket symbolically breached two of the most critical of the Constitutions.

The rights and wrongs of this quarrel will be disputed to the end of time. In the point of law each side was right on its own assumptions. Henry was upholding royal custom; Becket the law of the Church. Beyond question the two were incompatible, though it was no easy matter to decide how far. Clerks accused of anything, say the Constitutions, shall go to the royal court to answer what pertains to its jurisdiction, to the Church court for what belongs there. So far Lanfranc at least would have agreed. Nor need the rider that a royal justice should go to the Church court to keep an eye on proceedings be taken too seriously. More dangerous was the vague final sentence: 'If a clerk has confessed or been convicted, the Church shall protect him no further.' In practice this meant that a clerk would be unfrocked by a Church court for some crime, then punished in the lay courts as a layman for the same crime; nor was it clear that this was contrary to canon law. But Becket maintained—and in the end the Pope settled the matter (for the time being) by accepting his interpretation—that no man could be punished twice for the same offence. On this issue there was no question of right or wrong: the law of the Church was obscure.

Behind the law lay a whole world of ideas and assumptions in which the lay and the clerical view diverged. It affected most critically the office of a bishop or archbishop. He was a leading figure in the Church's hierarchy, a lord spiritual; but he was also a leading figure in the hierarchy of the kingdom of which he was a member, a leading subject, and counsellor of his king. The dichotomy and the dilemma it created were neatly summarised by Becket himself when writing to King Henry: 'You are my lord, you are my king, you are my spiritual son.' Good order in the Church depended on good appointments to bishoprics, on the spirituality, strength of character, and independence of the bishops; good order in the state depended only to a slightly lesser extent on the king's controlling his bishops, on their being sound, reliable statesmen, with a strong sense of loyalty to him. At every point the issues between Church and state touched deep convictions of the medieval mind: the theology of the Church, the sacred nature of kingship, the sacredness of the feudal bond tying bishops to their king, the inherited tradition of social prejudice which accompanied the deep cleavage between clergy and laity.

Beyond all this lay the personal clash between Thomas and Henry, and the tragedy of an intimate friendship translated into a bitter quarrel. Henry's view of the matter was comparatively straightforward. He had trusted Becket implicitly, and Becket had let him down; the Archbishop had sworn fealty to the King, and broken his oath. He was 'the traitor'. But why had Becket changed? What strange compulsion accounts for the new mode of life of 1162–3, for the alternating submission and resistance of 1164? How was the man who had dedicated his life to the service of the King from 1154 to 1162 able to spend his remaining years in resisting him—able to face exile from 1164 to 1170, and death in 1170? It is unlikely that these questions will ever be answered satisfactorily, because their answers must depend on reconstructing the logic of a world which is irrecoverable, and on fathoming the mysteries of a deep and complex character, one who puzzled his contemporaries as much as he puzzles us. Becket was only too well aware that, at the time when the King forced the monks of Canterbury to elect him archbishop, he was widely regarded as a time-serving royal minister, who would continue his old way of life even as Archbishop of Canterbury. Above all, he knew that the older bishops, led by Gilbert Foliot of London, one-time monk of Cluny, and Roger of York, a colleague of Becket in the circle of Archbishop Theobald, regarded him as a caricature of an archbishop, a royal toy. Circumstances counselled him to make some effort to convince the world that he was going to try to be a real archbishop, not too unworthy a successor of Lanfranc or Anselm, or his old master Theobald; above all, he needed to dispel the illusions of the King. But it was not only circumstances, powerful as they were, which compelled Becket to act as he did; in some way he was compelled by his own nature. Can we go further, and say that he felt the necessity to convince not only kings, bishops and old associates, but also himself? No set of events in the twelfth century is better recorded than the dispute of Henry II and Thomas Becket; we have twelve or so

Lives and some 800 letters from which to reconstruct the story. But the central character remains an enigma.

At the end of 1164 the Archbishop laid his case before the Pope, Alexander III (1159–81), then in exile at Sens. Alexander was a fine theologian and canon lawyer and a diplomat of great distinction. Becket was a fearful embarrassment to him, since he already had an anti-pope and a war with the emperor on his hands. The Pope never let Becket down, yet managed to restrain the Archbishop's occasional outbursts of violence until 1170, when a much more favourable international situation enabled Alexander to take sterner measures. Behind the scenes the old rivalry of York and Canterbury played a significant part in embittering the struggle. By custom Canterbury alone might anoint and crown a new king; and custom was supported by a papal mandate to protect Canterbury's rights while Thomas was in exile. But Henry II was impatient to have his eldest surviving son, another Henry, crowned king in his own lifetime—he wished to prevent his own path to the throne setting any precedents detrimental to royal authority or hereditary succession. Impatiently he ordered York and his colleagues to crown the young Henry; and York complacently agreed. In June the son was crowned; Archbishop Thomas (supported by the Pope) instantly threatened an interdict—an order closing all the churches in the kingdom. The grave effects of an interdict on a medieval kingdom made this a threat too strong even for Henry II, who immediately patched up a reconciliation. Shortly afterwards Becket received authority from the Pope to excommunicate the bishops who had assisted at the coronation. At first Becket hesitated; then he decided to publish the anathemas, and the next day (1st December) he returned to England in an atmosphere no less charged than at the time of his departure six years before. The King was violently angry; and a host of difficulties awaited Thomas, made worse by the King's renewed hostility. But his troubles were soon over. On the evening of Tuesday, 29th December, four knights, incited by the furious anger of the King, broke into Canterbury Cathedral, and deliberately and brutally murdered the Archbishop before a crowd of witnesses.

Few events in medieval history shocked the conscience of Europe so profoundly or so immediately. Becket's death was followed by a whisper that miracles had been performed at his tomb; soon the reports became insistent and widespread,

188

and in a very short time the Pope was moved to canonise the murdered Archbishop. Then even his enemies had to submit, and King Henry was compelled as an act of penance to walk barefoot through the streets of Canterbury and submit to a thorough flogging from a number of bishops and from the monks of Canterbury Cathedral. In due course churches were dedicated to Thomas's name in many remote corners of Europe.

The practical effects of the murder in the cathedral were less dramatic. The Constitutions of Clarendon were abrogated; but most of their clauses remained quietly in effect. On all crucial issues new compromises were found. The King could not stop appeals to Rome; but that had been a forlorn hope in 1164. Criminous clerks were saved from the gallows, but not long guaranteed from secular penalties. 'The Church holds the felonious clerk,' writes Professor Cheney, 'but the sheriff holds on to his chattels.' It was a long time before another English bishop came so near to secular condemnation as Becket in 1164. But the character of the episcopate was not altered. The long quarrel had left many sees vacant; when they were filled in 1173–4, one, Canterbury itself, went to a monk, most of the remainder went to royal servants—including one or two of Becket's particular enemies. As a young man Henry II had seen the affairs of the Church too exclusively in terms of his grandfather's customs. In his later years he learned to accept so much of the new canon law as had won general acceptance, while retaining in substance much of the influence held by his predecessors.

(2) LEGAL REFORM

Violent though this quarrel with Thomas Becket was, it did not hinder the steady reconstruction of royal government in England. Frequent outbreaks of crime and, in particular, the frequent usurpation of property by force or guile, remained as the heritage of the anarchy. It was against these two evils that royal justice was most powerfully mobilised under Henry II; and in the process of mobilising it he developed the structure of royal jurisdiction and laid the foundations for that co-operation between royal and local officials which was to be the hall-mark of English government.

The detection of crime was a rough and ready process; all

that Henry could hope to do was to make life difficult for the notorious criminal. In the Assize[2] of Clarendon of 1166, elaborated by the Assize of Northampton ten years later, a procedure was laid down by which a committee, or jury, of twelve men from each hundred and four men from each township, should periodically denounce to sheriff or royal justice any notorious criminals of the neighbourhood, or harbourers of criminals—who should then be put to the ordeal. The procedure was crude, but at least it was a procedure; and it was supported by the strongest power in the land. 'Liberties' and 'franchises'—areas normally exempt from royal jurisdiction —were ignored; the sudden rounding-up of criminals became a regular event in the countryside.

This procedure was probably not new: like so many of Henry's expedients, it had been tried out by his grandfather. But it was enforced with a new energy, and from being a very occasional instrument to deal with a crime-wave it became a normal police measure. Similarly Henry's even more important measures for improving land-law were based on earlier precedents, but made effective in a new way.

Cases dealing with land-tenure had hitherto been dealt with in feudal courts—that is, in the courts of barons, not the royal courts; land-tenure provided the most important business of the barons' courts. But disputes between tenants-in-chief, or disputes of unusual complexity between lesser men might come to the King's court. The power of the royal courts had been greatly enhanced by the Norman Conquest and the great prestige of the Domesday Inquest. Henry II began a process whereby more and more quite trivial disputes on tenure came to the King's court—once again, he was developing and making regular what his grandfather had done as an occasional act of power.

The procedure even of the royal court, however, was inclined to be slow. A case was started by the purchase of a writ from the royal Chancery. The plaintiff might have to pursue the King to a distant corner of his empire for writs and judgment; procedural difficulties could delay a case for months. All this was an invitation to a strong man to seize his neighbour's land, and enjoy the fruits of it for many a long day until his neighbour could prove and enforce his right. Such acts had been common under Stephen, and were difficult to prevent even under Henry. What was needed was a swift and effective procedure for restoring possession to someone dispossessed without due process of law. To provide this, a number of 'possessory' actions or 'assizes', as they were called, were established. The most important of these actions was that of 'Novel Disseisin', established at the same time as the criminal jury in 1166. A holder of free land who had been dispossessed could buy a writ of Novel Disseisin, which instructed the sheriff to summon a jury and ask the members whether in fact the plaintiff had been recently put out of possession. If they said yes, the sheriff had to restore him. Once again, a rough and ready measure; but it was of unique importance in strengthening the idea that the royal court was the fount of justice *par excellence*, and a normal place in which to settle even quite minor disputes.

'Novel Disseissin' had two sister writs. 'Mort d'Ancestor' bade the sheriff ask the question whether the plaintiff's father was in possession when last a tenant died and an heir succeeded. If so, and if the plaintiff was the true heir, he was to be put in possession. 'Darrein Presentment' dealt with a different kind of property—the right to present to a rectory or vicarage—and was intended to support the 'possession' of the man who had presented on the last occasion. Some perquisites still attached to the right to present; but its value lay mainly in the opportunity it gave a man to find employment for a relation, friend, or dependant.

Behind the question of possession or 'seisin' lay the deeper question of right—not merely who *did* possess the land, but who *ought* to hold it; who had the sounder title to it. Nor did Henry II leave this question undisturbed. Towards the end of his reign he introduced the 'Grand Assize'. A baron or knight in possession, if sued for his right to a piece of land, had hitherto usually had to defend it in the ordeal by battle— that is by fighting for it. Under the Grand Assize he had the option of laying his case before a jury of twelve local knights. These 'assizes' for cases in land-tenure were of even greater importance than Henry's criminal assizes. They were popular and widely used; they accustomed men to pleading in the King's court as a normal event; they brought in much revenue and enhanced the court's importance.

The issuing of writs added to the work of the royal Chancery. In every sphere of administration and justice the second half of the twelfth century saw rapid growth. The over-

191

powerful sheriff found himself more and more subject to checks and controls. In 1170 a swift investigation of all the sheriffs was undertaken, and the majority were relieved of their posts. Furthermore, the audit at the Exchequer became more effective; more and more jurisdiction was taken over by specially appointed royal justices, who toured the country. The justices were not as yet trained lawyers, nor did they work to a system. Henry was forever trying new expedients—now a larger number of itinerant justices who could travel farther or more swiftly; now a small bench of more expert men who could work in Westminster for a longer period. Some of his judges were clerics, to whom no doubt he owed some ideas imported from canon law; some were laymen, including the Chief Justice or Justiciar of his later years, Ranulph Glanville. It was under the aegis of Glanville that the first systematic treatise on English law was compiled. It is no very elaborate treatise —essentially it is a commentary on the writs which can be bought in the royal Chancery and the way they can be used; a practical manual of procedure and of the law administered in the royal court. But its appearance was a portent. In a wholly new sense, the royal court was the centre of English litigation and justice; and there was shortly going to be a new profession for educated men—the profession of trained lawyers —who would need a manual and a textbook for their guidance.

Justices had posted into the counties and met juries long before the accession of Henry II. But from now on such meetings were regular events; and it was in the meetings of juries of local knights with royal justices that the idea of local responsibility—of the crucial link between royal government and the natural representatives of local society—was born.

(3) THE ANGEVIN EMPIRE

Henry II opened the last act of his quarrel with Thomas Becket by having his son Henry crowned king in Westminster Abbey on 14th June 1170. His family were growing up; he had already quarrelled with his wife, and for the rest of his life he was seldom free for long from quarrels with one or other of his children. These quarrels neutralised the great potential strength of his empire. Under a harmonious family, the Angevin power would have been irresistible.[3] But Henry and his sons, heirs of two of the most violent dynasties in

192

western Europe—Anjou and Normandy—were not made for peace or co-operation.

Of Henry's family it could be said that war was their pleasure, but marriage their business. It is true that Henry owed England, *de facto*, to the Norman Conquest; but he was also one of the few known descendants of the Anglo-Saxon royal line, through his grandmother, Matilda. His father had been hereditary Count of Anjou, and his mother heiress of England and Normandy and of claims in Maine and Brittany. It is doubtful if Geoffrey had envisaged the permanent union of the traditional rivals, Normandy and Anjou; but Henry was too ambitious to share his heritage with anyone else. His own marriage brought Aquitaine, and he constantly schemed and plotted for equally good matches for his children. At one moment it even seemed that he might marry his son, Henry, to the heiress of the kingdom of France. But in the end Louis had a son, and when Henry II died in 1189, he was already being outmatched by the most successful political intriguer of the day, the young King Philip II of France. Philip's speciality was to breed dissension among the Angevins; and in the end he destroyed the Angevin Empire by guile and by force.

Henry based his rule in the various parts of his empire on different claims and titles, and only slowly gave the various sections anything resembling a unified administration. In fact he was never equally secure in every part of the domains. In England, Normandy, and Anjou he was heir to a long tradition of strong government in which Stephen's reign was just an interlude; in Aquitaine he was heir to a tradition of anarchy. In a measure he and his wife and his son Richard overcame the separatism of parts of Aquitaine, but their government there was never wholly secure outside Poitou, the old centre of power of Eleanor's forbears. In the south-east of the duchy their control was utterly precarious. Henry tried unsuccessfully to subdue Toulouse in 1159, and only in 1173 acquired suzerainty over its count.

The events of the tenth and eleventh centuries had decided that England was to be henceforth a united kingdom; but they had set no firm boundaries to an English king's claims and ambitions. One of the great questions in English politics in the twelfth and thirteenth centuries was where the frontiers of England would be laid: in the Welsh marches, at the Irish

THE ANGEVIN EMPIRE IN 1154

The shaded areas include all territories under Henry II's direct rule at the end of 1154. (The Count of Toulouse accepted his suzerainty in 1173) For his relations with Wales, Scotland and Ireland see chap. 11, sect. 2-4.

Channel, or in Ireland; in Cumberland, on the Forth, or at John o' Groats; at the Channel, at the Channel Islands, in France, at the Pyrenees? None of these questions was finally settled by 1272.

The ambitions and the interests of the monarchs were only one group of factors in settling these questions. So great was the play of personality and circumstance in medieval politics that it is often most misleading to talk of 'deep underlying forces'. It is for the most part true to say that no medieval empire which could not be comfortably ruled by one man could

194

be lasting. This means that a monarch had to visit every corner of his empire and be personally known to all his leading subjects if his rule was to be effective. The empire of Henry II was made possible by the restless energy of the King; even Henry did not quite know how one man could rule it all, and he tried to take his family into partnership.

As soon as his sons were old enough to help or hinder his government, Henry began to distribute the titles of his possessions among them. Richard was enthroned Duke of Aquitaine in 1167; Henry King of England in 1170 (he was also made Duke of Normandy and Count of Anjou); Geoffrey became Duke of Brittany in 1181 by marrying the heiress; John was made Lord of Ireland in 1185. But these were not meant to be independent commands: Henry was to be kept firmly under his father's control, and the other sons were ultimately to do homage to Henry. Under this constraint they chafed, and no strong bond of family affection kept them at peace with their father: sooner or later each of them plotted rebellion. The most serious outbreak was in 1173–4, when Henry, Richard, and Geoffrey, encouraged by their mother, raised rebellions on both sides of the Channel, and were strongly supported by Louis VII and the leading powers of northern France. In the end the rebellion collapsed. Henry tried to improve his sons' humour by giving them more responsibility; but there was little trust among them. The young Henry ended his troubled career in 1183; Geoffrey died, plotting, in 1186; and only Richard and John were left to conspire with the young French King, Philip II. The final rebellion bade fair to destroy the empire; but Henry's death (1189) and Richard's rapid succession left it once more united in strong and capable hands.

1. The change of tense is Peter's; he switches from a generalised picture to a particular memory.

2. The word 'assize', *assisa*, was used in a variety of senses in the Middle Ages. Its basic meaning was the sitting or session of a court, in which the members of the court joined with the judge to settle a case or a point of law, or to make an assessment for taxation. From these usages stem the words 'assize' and 'assessment' as we use them today. The most solemn *assisae* in the Middle Ages were the sessions of the king's court, and the word 'assize' came to be applied to a law or an edict promulgated in the king's court—hence the 'Assizes' of Clarendon and Northampton; and so, by deduction, to the legal procedure laid down in an 'assize'—hence the 'possessory assizes' and the 'Grand Assize', described below.

195

3. Henry II and his successors are commonly known as the Angevin kings, because they were descended from Geoffrey, Count of Anjou, Henry's father. Count Geoffrey used as his emblem a broom flower, in French, *plante genêt*; and on this account a fifteenth-century claimant of the English throne styled himself 'Plantagenet'. This surname, often attached by modern historians to earlier members of the family, was never so used, as far as we know, by their contemporaries.

CHAPTER ELEVEN

THE BRITISH ISLES

(1) ENGLAND

In recent chapters we have been studying the effect of the Norman Conquest on many aspects of English life. We have seen England as part of a Norman and Angevin Empire; but England as a part of Britain has eluded us. The time has come to see England in its geographical context; to leave the lowland zone; to look towards the hills. Interesting as the history of these other lands is, our main theme must be the contrast between the way the Normans conquered and settled England and the way they failed to conquer Wales, Scotland, and Ireland. First, then, we must summarise the assimilation of the two peoples in England.

Eleventh-century Britain was a Babel of many tongues. In the north and west the various Celtic languages were spoken; in England itself the chief languages were the Anglo-Saxon dialects. But scattered all over the island, and especially in the English Danelaw, were people still speaking a Viking language, Danish or Norwegian; and equally scattered were the representatives of the educated clergy, who read and sang and often spoke Latin. Into this medley the Normans brought their own dialect of French, and for three centuries at least Norman French remained the language of the English courts.

This may seem complicated enough; yet it probably still gives the modern reader far too simple a picture. The Celtic languages are themselves diverse. Of the two main groups, Gaelic (Goidelic) and Brittonic (Brythonic), some version of the former was spoken throughout Ireland and northern Scotland; some version of the latter in most of Cumberland, Wales, Cornwall, and Brittany. Here and there—as in Wales—the groups intermingled; everywhere there were local dialects which might make communication with a Celt from another tribe far from easy. Although the differences between the Anglo-Saxon dialects were less profound, they might also make communication difficult between one region and another.

197

There was no 'standard English'. In these conditions many folk knew two or three languages; but interpreters were much in demand. Queen Margaret of Scotland (died 1093) had been brought up in Hungary and presumably Magyar and English were her native tongues. It is clear that she could read Latin. For Gaelic she had her husband as interpreter, as her biographer tells us when recounting how she disputed for three days to the discomfiture of a council of the Scottish clergy. The learning and ignorance of royalty have always been subject to special privileges. Monarchies, especially hereditary monarchies, tended in the past to be dynastic and international, however much they might pretend the contrary. As late as the eighteenth century England had two kings who could not speak English. The rest of the upper classes have had to accommodate themselves more promptly. It must have been normal for the Scottish nobles to talk French and Gaelic as it came to be normal for the English upper classes to talk French at court and English in the fields.

The stages by which this took place can never be precisely known; but what we do know about the development of English in the two centuries after the Norman Conquest is especially interesting, because it reveals to us, as it were in a mirror, the assimilation of the English and Norman races. One may still occasionally hear the ancient boast, that this or that person's ancestors 'came over with the Conqueror'. It has long been an idle boast. All Englishmen are descended from a number of men who fought on each side at Hastings; almost none of us can prove who our ancestors were. We are all 'Anglo-Normans' in a sense; and though the phrase had lost its meaning already before 1272, the process by which it lost it has left many vital traces in our history.

At first Norman French (or 'Anglo-Norman') was the language of the new aristocracy—and so to a large extent of the upper clergy also; English the language of the middle classes and the peasants. Both languages must have been spoken in every noble household; and from the first the mingling was enhanced by the frequency of intermarriage. Gradually, as time passed, the French language became more artificial, less and less an affair of every day. Its death lies far outside our period. But already in the twelfth and thirteenth centuries it was beginning to affect the English language which was to supplant it. Modern English may be based first and

198

foremost on Old English and Middle English (as its post-Conquest successor is called); but in structure and vocabulary it has an immense Romance element, mainly derived from French; and the bulk of this came in from Anglo-Norman in the centuries following the Norman Conquest. Romance influence may have helped to save modern English from the complex inflexions which still flourish in most other Teutonic languages, and to give it the chance to develop the freedom and variety of construction so visible in Chaucer and Shakespeare; but inflexions had already long been in decay. The fact that French was the language of the upper classes is still evident in our words tournament and jousting, lance and castle, forest and venison. But words are strange things, and if we pursue their origin too assiduously, they will play us many tricks. The Norman knight lived in his hall for many centuries; but knight and hall are English words. The greatest barons were called earls, like Thorkell the Tall and Godwin, though their wives to this day are countesses. Words give us many hints; but we must not expect too much of them.

It ought to be possible to trace the mingling of the races by observing the Christian names we meet in documents of the late eleventh and twelfth centuries. But this is particularly difficult, because the fashion soon arose for English parents to give their children French names; and because other fashions were altering the type of name favoured. Names of the great heroes of romance, Arthur and Alexander, of Old Testament figures, Adam and David, of apostles, Peter, James, and Andrew, were coming in alongside the English Edward, Edgar, and Alfred, and the Norman William, Ralph, and Robert. But it was rare for a great baron to call his children by English names. It was not until the birth of an heir apparent in 1239 —to a king who revered Edward the Confessor—that the name Edward re-entered the English royal family. The mingling of names in native English families may lead us to ante-date the assimilation of the races.

Yet the Christian names are not wholly without significance. A few great thegns survived the Conquest, married into the invaders, and founded 'Norman' baronial families. Still more Norman barons gave a shadow of legitimacy to their usurpations by marrying English heiresses. Most striking of these was Henry I of England—though he changed his wife's name from Edith to Matilda in the process. But in the middle region, below the barons but above the peasantry, intermarriage must have been common. Already at the turn of the eleventh and twelfth centuries we meet a canon of St Paul's with a French name and a French wife, but himself the son of an English father. Ralph, son of Algot, was not only a member of the upper clergy; he was also an alderman in the City. In these regions assimilation moved fastest; and since it was from canons and small knights that many bishops and new barons were later recruited, inter-marriage at this level came to have a wide significance. The Angevin Empire preserved the French contacts and French interests of the very great; a baron in the twelfth century noted in his writs that he was addressing his subjects both French and English; a chronicler, even at the end of the century, will sometimes notice that an important man is of 'English' descent. By the thirteenth century the distinction, for the most part, was beyond research.

The same story is told by the changes in English and Anglo-Norman literature. One might suppose that English literature would have gradually disappeared, to be replaced by French. In fact the two proceeded hand in hand until the point at which English conquered or assimilated French as the language of the great. It is true that the Anglo-Saxon writ died shortly after the Conquest; that the *Anglo-Saxon Chronicle* was only continued in a single copy after 1079—it came to a stop at Peterborough soon after 1154. But there is a thin stream of continuous tradi-tion in the writing of sophisticated English verse and devotional literature. In *The Owl and the Nightingale*, of the late twelfth century, asceticism and gaiety debate according to a fashion met with elsewhere, but with a skill and freshness equal to any-thing in French. The chief source book for the Arthurian ro-mances, Geoffrey of Monmouth's Latin *History*, was translated (or rather adapted, as plays and books are nowadays adapted for the cinema) both into French and English. This is a particu-larly striking example. The Arthurian legend, the 'Matter of Britain', was in a sense native to this island. But it owed its immense popularity to the way in which it was adapted to suit the tastes of courtly circles. The court of Arthur was made the centre of many cycles of courtly romances—of tales of knightly prowess performed to do honour to ladies. The chief cycles were written in Franch; the courts in which they mainly flourished were in France. Although one of these courts was the Angevin court, the romances are less associated with

England than with Eleanor of Aquitaine and her court at Poitiers, with her son Richard I, crusader and troubadour, and her daughter (by Louis VII) Marie of Champagne. None the less they flourished throughout western Europe, and it was inevitable that Arthur should be especially celebrated in England. It is significant that Arthurian romances for English audiences were written in English as well as in French; and as time went on the English versions became as widely known and as sophisticated as the French.

If we ask in the end, as we must, what was the impact on England and the English of the Norman Conquest, we ask a question to which we can expect no final or clear-cut answer. It is none the less worth asking. On numerous occasions in history we find evidence that a warrior aristocracy invaded and dominated a larger native population—it happened on more than one occasion in the earlier history of Britain. But it is very rare for us to be able to trace these settlements in detail. We know a great deal about the Norman Conquest, and it gives us a unique opportunity for studying such a movement. Furthermore, it was the central event of medieval English history, and our curiosity can never be satisfied until we have made some effort to grapple with the most fundamental problem which it invites us to face.

The Normans and their French allies came in comparatively small numbers. They settled as soldiers, knights, feudal warriors; they brought their own social organisation; their own idea of land-tenure; but they grafted them on to the highly elaborate legal arrangements of the country they had conquered. They brought no new ideas of government; they came from a duchy unprovided with elaborate administrative institutions. They took over and adapted what they found. What they brought, however, perhaps mattered more than institutions at that time: they brought a new dynasty of exceptional energy and ability, and they brought a capacity and a will to experiment and adapt. They took over the Old English institutions; but within two generations they had developed them far beyond what could have been imagined by Cnut or the Confessor.

In part this was due to the Normans themselves, in part to the fashions of the day. New ideas of statecraft were abroad. The Norman kings were more cosmopolitan than their predecessors, not because they travelled more widely—several Anglo-Saxon kings had visited Rome, and none of the Norman kings, before Richard I, travelled far outside his dominions—but because that was the fashion of the age in which they lived.

The same is true of the Norman impact on the Church. The Normans brought the English Church up to date, they brought it into line with continental models. But it had not been old-fashioned in 1050, still less had it been out of touch. It was merely that the Norman Conquest coincided with great changes in the Church at large; and that the Normans, brilliant adapters that they were, never hesitated to alter what they did not like. Many profound and ancient institutions were not affected. English spirituality seeped through to the invaders. The English taught the Normans how to paint. Meanwhile the Normans were transferring cathedrals to new sites, rebuilding cathedrals and abbeys on an immensely grandiose scale; peopling the English Church at its apex—with bishops and abbots and monks and canons—as they peopled the apex of lay society. They thought the old English dioceses disorganised, and introduced archdeacons and rural deans. Their efforts were certainly not negligible or fruitless. No group of Englishmen built on so magnificent a scale before the eighteenth-century dukes and the nineteenth-century railway contractors. Recent study has done something to soften the impact of the Norman Conquest —to show that in many directions change was not so rapid or so radical as we had once supposed. It affected the peasant far less than the thegn, the merchant, and the monk. There is very much that we do know about its effects in detail. But when all is said and done, it remains a dramatic episode, and such contemporaries felt it to be. Here, in conclusion, is the opinion of the Normans held by William of Malmesbury, one of the shrewdest observers of the second generation, and himself a man of mixed Anglo-Norman stock.

'The Normans . . . are exceedingly careful in their dress, nice beyond all conscience in their food; a race given to warfare, utterly at a loss without it; indefatigable in pursuit of an enemy, and where force is not sufficient, they use guile and money no less. They build enormous buildings as economically as possible, vie with their equals, strain to surpass their betters, carp at those beneath them while striving to protect them from everyone else. They are faithful to their lords—but swift to break faith for a slight occasion. A breath of ill-fortune and they are plotting treachery, a bag of money and their mind is changed. But they are the most friendly of races and treat

202

strangers as honourably as themselves; they intermarry with their subjects. They have raised the standard of religious observance, extinct in England at their arrival [this we need not take too seriously]. Everywhere you may see churches build'ng, and monasteries both in town and country; the land flourishes in a new way—every man of wealth thinks the day lost which he has not marked by some notable act of generosity.'

(2) WALES

For its day the English monarchy was the most centralised in Europe. This fact provides us with a great temptation to tell its story in isolation: to ignore both its intimate contacts with France and Europe, and its even more intimate contacts with Wales, Scotland, and Ireland. There is nothing more difficult in this period than to do justice to the other principalities and kingdoms of the British Isles. Their history is obscure and confused; their native traditions were immensely tenacious; yet their fate depended closely on the ambitions of the English king and the Anglo-Norman leaders. These conditions somehow created an extremely uneasy equilibrium, in which none of these lands was conquered or subdued and yet none was wholly independent of the English kings. The consequence of this is a contrast of deep importance in our history. The Normans rapidly assimilated themselves to their English subjects, and a mixed people with a mixed culture emerged. Had they conquered the Celtic lands as thoroughly as they conquered England, the British Isles might have achieved the unity which has always evaded them. But no such conquest took place. To make clear why that was so, we must first tell, in rough outline, the story of the kingdoms; then sketch the nature and extent of Norman penetration.

Alfred had had close contacts with his elder contemporary, Rhodri Mawr (the great), ruler of most of Wales, a man with a more cultivated court and apparently more stable power than a west Saxon king could expect to have had when threatened by the Danes. Welsh empires rarely survived their founder; but Rhodri's grandson, Hywel the Good, built up a power more substantial than Rhodri's, worked in close liaison with his nominal overlord, Athelstan, and left a great name as a legislator. But the sole foundation for Hywel's power was personal prestige and his relation to the English quasi-emperor. No institutions bound the Welsh principalities together and only the flimsiest of traditions supported unity. Nor could the geography of so divided a country help a ruler of all Wales; for nature has conspired to baffle and bewilder human communications.

The power of Hywel had been supported by his connection with the English court. The power of the next ruler of all Wales, Gruffydd ap Llywelyn, was won in spite of the English leaders. From this time forward princes who defied England and princes who knew how to manipulate an English alliance were often rivals for the first place among the Welsh leaders. The lords of the south, Rhys ap Tewdwr, a friend of William the Conqueror, and his grandson, Rhys ap Gruffydd ('the Lord Rhys'), owed their position partly to English favour, which helped them to retain their independence against the penetration of the English Marcher lords and their northern rivals. There were never mere satellites, nor would they have retained the respect of their subjects had they been so. The younger Rhys, indeed, had won much power at English expense early in Stephen's reign. More consistently anti-English were the leading ruler of the two northern principalities, Gwynedd and Powys. The first really distinguished ruler in the north after Harold had destroyed Gruffydd ap Llywelyn in 1063 was Gruffydd ap Cynan. Though imprisoned by the Normans from 1081 to 1093, he was able after his escape to organise a steady reconstruction of the power of Gwynedd until his death in 1137. He was succeeded by his distinguished son, Owain Gwynedd (1137–70), who started his career as leader of the northern wing of the great revolt made possible by the anarchy of Stephen's reign, and ended it in triumphant independence after twice successfully resisting a full-scale invasion by Henry II. Owain's grandson, Llywelyn the Great (died 1240), pursued a career blending the characteristics of Rhys and Owain. King John of England had had important possessions in the Welsh marches before his accession and knew something of Wales. When he came to the throne in 1199, he rapidly accepted Llywelyn, already the most powerful man in northern Wales, into his favour, and gave him his illegitimate daughter, Joan, in marriage. But Llywelyn became too powerful, and John had ambitions to annex Wales to the English crown. In the end his plans miscarried, and Llywelyn was able to take advantage of the chaos of John's last years to establish his position and clear large tracts of south Wales of English garrisons. He did homage to Henry III. In return he was allowed to live and die in undisturbed possession of his principalities. Once again it was left for a grandson of the old prince to revive his power; but Llywelyn ap Gruffydd, the first 'Prince of Wales' and the most powerful of all the Welsh princes, did not die in possession of his conquests. After a brilliant career of warfare in Wales and diplomacy in England, he was finally overthrown by Edward I in 1282, and the English ruled in his stead.

(3) SCOTLAND

The most widely known event in Scottish history before the late thirteenth century is the destruction of Macbeth and the accession of Malcolm III. These events have been wonderfully telescoped in Shakespeare's play—old Siward's victory took place in 1054, Macbeth held out until 1057, and not until 1058 was Malcolm hailed as King of Scotland. Our serious knowledge of Scottish history, the story of Norman infiltration and the effective unity of the Scottish kingdom all date from the accession of Malcolm 'Canmore' ('big head') in 1058. There had been a long preparation for this unity. By the tenth century most of northern and western Scotland was subject to the kings of the Scots and of Strathclyde. For a brief while King Edmund united the two kingdoms. More significant, in the late tenth or early eleventh century the English lands between the Forth and the Tweed, then known as Lothian, became part of the Scottish kingdom. These lands had anciently formed part of the kingdom of Northumbria, were thoroughly English, and quite distinct from the Norse and Celtic amalgams of Scotland and Strathclyde. Nor did the translation of Lothian immediately alter its character—the southern lowlands did not become fully 'Scottish' until the days of Sir Walter Scott. But the attachment of a new province, reasonably prosperous and closely allied in culture and institutions to the English kingdom, permanently shifted the centres of power in Scotland and ultimately changed the character of the kingdom. Lothian provided a base such as the Welsh princes never possessed.

Lothian finally joined Scotland in 1018, in the reign of Malcolm II, who also won Strathclyde for his grandson,

ENGLAND, WALES & SCOTLAND
in the 12th and 13th centuries

+ English and Welsh cathedrals
× Abbeys founded by King David I of Scotland

Chester, Lichfield and Coventry formed
a single diocese, as did Bath and Wells.
Some earlier names of kingdoms, etc.
mentioned in this chapter have been included.

×Kinloss

SCOTLAND

•St. Andrews

Cambuskenneth×   Firth of Forth
    Edinburgh•   •Holyrood
        •Newbattle   •Berwick
            Melrose•   Roxburgh
STRATHCLYDE   Jedburgh×   •Alnwick
        LOTHIAN   •Alnmouth

          +Carlisle   •Newcastle
  Whithorn•   Durham•

                    Rievaulx×

        Fountains×   +York
                Hull• •Hedon
                    •Ravenserod

                    +Lincoln

    +   +Chester
Bangor +St.Asaph   Norwich
GWYNEDD   +
    POWYS
    Strata•   Shrewsbury•   +Lichfield
    Marcella
WALES   •Worcester   +Coventry   +Ely
    •Strata   •Cambridge
    Florida   •Northampton
    Hereford•   •Evesham
St David's+ DEHEUBARTH   •Gloucester
        •Neath   •Oxford
Margam•   +Llandaff   LONDON+
            +Bath   Rochester+
        +Wells   Canterbury+
    Salisbury+ +Winchester   •Lewes
        Clarendon• Chichester+

    Exeter+

206

Shakespeare's Duncan, first king of all Scotland. But the dynasty and the union were both insecure before the accession of Malcolm III. Malcolm himself had the idea, then traditional among Scottish rulers, that their profession was to raid England; but the Norman Conquest of England had the effect of filling the Scottish court with distinguished English leaders, the greatest of whom was Malcolm's second wife, Margaret, sister of Edgar the Aetheling, better known as St Margaret of Scotland. This dominant lady allowed her husband to amuse himself with warlike pursuits. Meanwhile she impressed on her court, her numerous children, and the people of southern Scotland, both her Christian principles and her English culture. She was a cosmopolitan lady; though an English princess, she had been brought up in Hungary, and she found Scotland backward and cold. She brought to the north new standards of luxury in food and dress, as well as new standards in the practice of religion. But her deepest influence was felt after her death. Different as she and her husband were in every way, they were devoted to one another, and she died of grief very shortly after Malcolm's death in 1093. After an interval, three of her sons succeeded one after the other, and the reigns of Edgar, Alexander I and, above all, of David I (1124–53) witnessed a major change in the nature of Scottish government. In effect, it was David who engineered the Norman conquest of Scotland. It was not a violent conquest, and it was very far from complete; but after 1124 the history of Scotland is inseparable from the history of its relations with the Anglo-Norman kingdom. The very names of its kings—David, Alexander, William, and Malcolm—bear witness to the cosmopolitan nature of the superstructure which Margaret and her successors had built over Celtic foundations that were still deep and vital.

(4) IRELAND

Complex as it is, the history of Wales and Scotland is simplicity itself compared with the history of Ireland over these centuries. The tenth century had seen very extensive Norse settlement; in the eleventh the Norse built towns and some of them became peaceable merchants. Meanwhile the last king to enjoy suzerainty over all Ireland in the manner of the great Welsh princes was killed in battle in 1014. Nominally, all the Irish kings acknowledged the 'high-king', but his power was normally as slight as the power of the French kings in Burgundy and Aquitaine. In politics and culture the eleventh and early twelfth centuries were a bleak epoch in Irish history. There are hints that the early Norman kings had thoughts of conquering the island; and although, as in Wales, they would have had to create their own institutions, it is unlikely that they could have been very powerfully resisted. But a curious fatality attached to the few medieval Englishmen who thought seriously of settling the problems of Ireland—they included King John and Richard II.

In fact Ireland plays a small part in our story, and that in itself is a significant fact. Edward I was able in large measure to redeem the failure of the Normans to conquer Wales; the Scottish kingdom was ruled by Anglo-Norman barons throughout the later Middle Ages. These conquests only partially assimilated Angle and Celt: they came too late to give the peoples of the British Isles the sense of common domination by a Norman overlord—such as was felt by the far more diverse peoples of south Italy and Sicily—or the chance to assimilate and be assimilated together. To the Celt, the rulers of England have always been Saxons, Sassenachs. None the less, in the long run, Wales and Scotland became united to England as a part of Great Britain; so for a time did the whole of Ireland, but the contrast in its history is obvious, and is reflected already in the conditions of the twelfth century.

In the mid twelfth century, by a concatenation of circumstances, the King of Connaught was high-king of Ireland. In 1156 he died, and the kings of Ireland fought for his place. The first round was won by the King of Tyrone, aided by Dermot, King of Leinster; then Connaught's son and heir, aided by the King of Brefni, recaptured the evanescent prize. The King of Brefni had a feud against Dermot of Leinster, who had carried off his wife for a time many years before. This feud he now prosecuted with great vigour. So far the pattern was normal enough, and the story of Troy seemed about to be re-enacted. But in this crisis the King of Leinster fled to England, and Ireland entered the orbit of English politics.

(5) NORMAN INFILTRATION

Medieval kings had little sense of national frontiers. No English king would have regarded it as impossible that he should rule in Wales and Scotland; few after the Norman Conquest had any sense of incongruity in ruling much of France as well as England; several had large ambitions elsewhere. Richard I intervened in the affairs of all the kingdoms of Europe, Henry III's brother became (for a time) King of the Romans (i.e. of Germany), and his son was offered the kingdom of Sicily. But the fact that there was no strict limit to their ambitions meant that they often failed to concentrate on projects under their noses. The Norman kings were French by blood; they spent much of their time out of England; they rapidly settled their headquarters at London, which lay, not in the centre of England and Britain, but midway between the English lowlands and the Continent. This orientation is the main general reason why they were so slow to become kings of Britain.

The Norman kings inherited a tradition of uncertain supremacy throughout the island. Many Welsh and Scottish princes had sworn fealty to the leading English kings, like Athelstan and Edgar and Cnut. There are ample signs that the Normans assumed that this relation could be turned into something more definite. They settled great lords and established great lordships along the frontiers; for a time they encouraged active conquest. In 1081 William I visited St David's, 'to say his prayers'—but also to meet Rhys ap Tewdwr and establish him as prince of south-western Wales. In spite of many vicissitudes, the English frontier was pushed west; Marcher earldoms were established at Chester, Shrewsbury, and Hereford, and other lordships farther south; and Anglo-Norman barons and knights built castles throughout Glamorgan and Pembrokeshire. Gradually the area under Welsh rule contracted, so that little more than half modern Wales was included in the 'Principality' taken over by Edward I from the native princes. But even in the Marches settlement went ahead slowly, and the conquest of Wales did not take place in the period covered by this book.

The reasons for this are exceedingly interesting. In the first place, the Marcher lords, like their royal masters, had many other interests; they had lands elsewhere in England and in Normandy. The first Earl of Hereford, William FitzOsbern, was killed fighting in Flanders. The great house of Bellême-Montgomery, Marchers in Normandy as well in England, earls of Shrewsbury and conquerors (for a brief time) of much of south and central Wales, were caught up in Norman politics and broken by Henry I early in his reign. In the time of Stephen most of the Marchers followed the Earl of Gloucester in supporting the Empress, and became too deeply involved in English politics to stem the Welsh revival. These circumstances probably have more to do with the survival of Welsh independence than the power of the Welsh to resist. It is true that there were many heroic rebellions; that even the most spectacular English invasions sometimes achieved very little. The feudal host marched into Wales; the princes withdrew into the hills; no battle was fought; the English went home at the end of the season, and the Welsh were left, poorer in sheep and food, to declare an uncertain victory. This pattern was repeated many times, especially under Rufus and Henry II. But these invasions were not usually intended to be conquests; nor were the Normans foolish enough to imagine that this was the way to conquer Wales. When Edward I aimed at conquest a series of campaigns was only the prelude to building castles and towns and settling English soldiers and merchants. He was only repeating, on a very grandiose scale, what many Norman barons had done in earlier times. Political circumstances, and the chances of Welsh politics gave the Normans more time and opportunity in the hundred years following the Norman Conquest of England to build castles in south Wales than in the north and centre.

There were also deeper reasons, both for the concentration on the south, and for the slow progress of Anglo-Norman infiltration. Wales was still a country of tribes and clans; economically it was very poor, and (especially in the centre and north) utterly different from the rich agrarian lands of the nearby English Midlands. In culture, too, it was backward. We need not take seriously the taunt that Welsh and Scots were 'barbarians'; and we must not forget that the time was not so long past when Ireland and Wales had supplied teachers to England and the Continent. Nor was their learning entirely forgotten; there were a few schools still remarkably active before the Normans came. But in standard of living, in economic organisation, and in mode of life the Welsh were still comparatively primitive. They had no coinage other than cows and precious ornaments. They had not yet benefited from the economic progress of recent centuries which had made England one of the richest countries in Europe. The Normans invaded England partly because it was rich; and they were able to settle

210

because social conditions provided them with a *milieu* not wholly uncongenial. Social conditions and the whole tradition of life were more deeply alien in the Celtic lands than in England and the poverty of Wales and the combativeness of its people made it less attractive. There must often have been occasions when the Marcher earls, lords of rich land in England and Normandy, were deterred from serious efforts at conquest by the thought:

> We go to gain a little patch of ground
> That hath in it no profit but the name.

And finally, there is a sense in which the feudal warrior, bred for war, but starved of activity in a comparatively peaceful kingdom, looked on the marches as his playground. For whatever reason, Wales was the playground of English warriors for two centuries after the Norman Conquest, and suffered fearfully for it. The Normans fought and hunted over Wales; but they failed seriously to settle it or govern it.

There was, however, another Norman conquest of Wales whose story was very different, and that was the conquest of the Church. Down to 1066 the old Celtic institutions, though nominally subjected to Rome, had survived reasonably intact. Wealth and influence lay mainly with the abbots of the old *clas* or community churches, which retained a native life and tradition of their own, but resembled monasteries not at all. In later days the *clas* churches had declined, and the bishops seem comparatively more important than in other Celtic lands. But the bishops had no sees. So far as we can tell, their area of jurisdiction depended entirely on the power of the prince to whose court they were attached. The Welsh Church inevitably conformed its organisation to the secular arrangements of the Welsh principalities, cantrevs, and commotes. In the north, these arrangements were slow to change. On paper, there was an Anglo-Norman bishopric established at Bangor from 1092 and at St Asaph from 1143, and these sees corresponded roughly to the kingdoms of Gwynedd and Powys. But their tenure was uncertain and until the early thirteenth century there were long vacancies, and long periods in which the bishops, ground between Rome, Canterbury, and the Welsh princes, wandered in exile. In the south the story was very different. At first the bishops in Dyfed (west Pembrokeshire) and Glamorgan resisted Norman infiltration, and tried to

211

assert their independence of Canterbury and of one another. But as south Wales fell into Norman hands, so the Normans granted its churches and their territories away to English monasteries and appointed Anglo-Normans to the bishoprics. The diocese of St David's was created by a clerk of Henry I called Bernard, who organised it on normal lines, with archdeacons and rural deans. Superficially, he was a typical Norman organiser; but some freak in his ambitious make-up led him to accept the claims of his see to be an archbishopric independent of Canterbury, and so to win the favour of the Welsh princes. Bernard's effort to become archbishop failed of its ostensible object; but his diocese never suffered the fate of Bangor and St Asaph. His chimera, carried on heroically, and somewhat absurdly, by the famous Gerald of Wales at the end of the twelfth century, helped to make his arrangements respectable. The other southern diocese was created, so far as we know, out of nothing, by the genius of Urban, a Welsh bishop educated in England. He was consecrated at Canterbury in 1107 to serve the Church in Glamorgan, and left, like Bernard, to define his own diocese. In the end, quite logically, the diocese of Llandaff came to be roughly equivalent in size to Glamorgan, but not before Urban had attempted to include large portions of Hereford and St David's in it, had supported his case by brilliant invention and daring forgery, and spent many weary months trekking to Westminster and to Rome in its support. The result did not measure up to the effort. A Welshman created a Norman diocese in mainly Norman territory. His achievement does not compare with Bernard's, who created a Norman diocese in territory mainly Welsh. But the *Book of Llandaff*, compiled by his relations and followers shortly after his death, is a brilliant illustration of what could happen when Celtic fancy and Norman energy met and mingled.

The second stage in the Norman conquest of the Welsh Church is marked by the foundation of the Cistercian abbeys in the mid- and late twelfth century. Though never so rich or so distinguished as the leading houses of Yorkshire, Neath (1130), Margam (1147), Strata Florida (1164), Strata Marcella (1170), and the rest, played much the same role. The Cistercian monks were used to travel, had cosmopolitan connections. Not only did they bring the fervour of the new movement, the breath of Stephen Harding and Bernard of Clairvaux into the land of David and Gildas; they brought merchants, new flocks of sheep, new ideas of how to market wool, an opportunity to Wales for peaceful economic progress. Wales had always been a largely pastoral country; but it had not grown wool for export. The Cistercian settlement meant that there were men all over western Europe who had learned that Wales was more than a tilting ground.

I have dwelt at length on the fortunes of Wales, because it was the Celtic land most intimately connected with England, and because its story is repeated, with many significant differences, in Scotland and Ireland. The first and most obvious difference is that both these other countries were more remote from the centres of Norman power, and less economically dependent on England than was Wales. This affected even the Church. Archbishop Lanfranc, a figure more imperial even than his royal master, had consecrated a bishop for the Irish-Norse church in Dublin and exerted his primacy in Scotland as well as over York. But the English primacy depended largely on the strength of royal support—which normally carried little weight in Scotland, and none in Ireland. When the Irish Church came to be effectively reformed in the twelfth century it was as part of a wider movement, inspired by St Bernard and his friend, St Malachy of Armagh and Down. In the mid-twelfth century the Irish Church—which had a finer past and more undistinguished present than the Welsh—was brought into line by a great act of power exerted by a papal legate at the synod of Kells in 1152. Four provinces, with Armagh as primate, and thirty-six dioceses were created; and although for a while much of this was a paper constitution, the reform of the Irish Church went steadily on. As in Wales the Cistercian invasion gave vital impetus to spiritual revival and economic change. It was a long time, however, before reformers in the two countries ceased to grumble about the strange customs of the people—about abbots who married and passed their abbeys by hereditary succession, and about princes who practised polygamy.

Although Ireland was more remote, geographically and in every other way, from England than were Wales and Scotland, it came the nearest to a regular conquest in the late twelfth and early thirteenth centuries. Its military techniques were more primitive, and it lacked the geographical defences of Wales and the political tradition which made a single monarchy

213

possible in Scotland. Its conquest had been planned early in Henry II's reign, and the consent of the English Pope Adrian IV (1154–9) was granted in the famous bull *Laudabiliter*. But the scheme was soon abandoned. When Dermot of Leinster came to Henry II in 1166, he was allowed to recruit troops, though Henry II refused him direct support. Dermot was able to enlist a force led by Norman barons from south Wales, and in 1170 his army occupied Dublin. But it had already ceased to be an expedition for the reinstatement of Dermot, and even the pretence was dropped after Dermot's death in 1171. The small expedition held its own against great odds, and seriously disturbed both the native rulers and its own overlord. Later the same year Henry came in person, and made a swift and skilful settlement of the affairs of Church and state. The Irish princes submitted to him and were protected; the leading English invaders were settled on large estates in eastern and central Ireland. But the settlement was very temporary. The Irish hoped to recover what they had lost; the English were determined to win more. The most distinguished of the English leaders, John de Courcy, began his brilliant conquest of Ulster in 1177. He soon established himself as a semi-independent paladin in northern Ireland and married into the kingdom of Man. For a time he was made a respectable Justiciar of Ireland—that is, the king's lieutenant; he was supplanted in the time of King John. This type of career, with its dazzling promise and strange vicissitudes, was followed in a more modest fashion by many other, lesser men in this period. Meanwhile the English kings tried to maintain some semblance of control. In 1185 Henry sent John to Ireland to govern in his name. The experiment was disastrous, and he had hastily to be recalled; under John de Courcy a sounder administration was established. But Prince John had learned his lesson, and later as king he showed a special interest in his old lordship. In 1210 he visited the country again, and revealed his determination to keep and strengthen the existing system. Two-thirds of the country, 'the land of peace', was in the control of the colonists, led by William Marshal, the shrewd and loyal Earl of Pembroke; the rest still lay under its native kings, who acknowledged John's suzerainty and enjoyed his favour. Throughout the thirteenth century Ireland bade fair to become a settled sub-kingdom. The English conquest had been ruthlessly accomplished; but the Normans could be quick settlers if they wished, and they showed this inclination in parts of Ireland. In spite of this, the land of peace was not quiet long enough for a stable settlement to be made.

Scotland was the only country in which a native dynasty consistently pursued the policy of resisting English pressure by imitating English strength. After his mother's death David I had been brought up at the court of Henry I; he was endowed by Henry with the earldom of Huntingdon and one of the richest heiresses in England. When he succeeded to the Scottish throne in 1124, he came north a well-trained Anglo-Norman baron, with many like him in his following; and although Scotland remained predominantly Celtic and Norse, the extensive settlement of Norman barons, especially in Lothian, and the contact with his English fiefs, enabled David to rule more like an Anglo-Norman king than any of his predecessors. He built castles at Roxburgh and Berwick, round which collected the beginnings of flourishing towns. His Norman vassals included the first Bruce to settle in Scotland, and his steward, Walter FitzAlan—of Breton origin, as we now know, since J. H. Round laid the ghost of Banquo[1]—was ancestor of the hereditary stewards, later more widely known as Stewarts or Stuarts. Celtic land-tenure began to give way to feudal arrangements; 'mormaers' became earls; sheriffs and Norman justice made their début in Scotland.

New movements in the Church had deeply influenced Scotland in the days of St Margaret; but profound changes in organisation did not take place before the reign of David. A see more akin to an English diocese than the old Welsh sees had long existed at St Andrews, and another was founded by David at Glasgow before he became king. But before his accession the north of Scotland was still organised on traditional lines, and the formation of territorial dioceses took place gradually during his long reign. Scottish clergy came into closer contact with the Church at large; parishes were formed and parish churches built. Most important, as in Wales and Ireland, was the monastic revival. Many abbeys, including several of the most eminent in Scotland, honoured David I as their founder.

King David's household was Anglo-Norman; so were many of his leading barons. But most of the country was still only superficially Normanised, and the north remained so throughout the Middle Ages. The concentration of his power in the south of Scotland was an inevitable consequence of David's English connections. Not only were he and his son English earls, but he was constantly involved in the politics of the anarchy, from his abortive attack on Stephen in 1138, defeated in the 'battle of the Standard', to his knighting of the young Henry in 1149. For most of his reign he was Lord of Cumbria, and his son, Earl Henry, was Earl of Huntingdon (1136-52) and Northumberland (1139-52). He died at Carlisle, which lay in his possession, in May 1153, shortly before his protégé's triumph.

David's successors continued his policies: they fostered the Church, they developed Norman institutions they intervened with varying success in England. In 1173 William the Lion joined the great rebellion against Henry II, but was captured, and compelled, like many of his predecessors, to do homage to his neighbour, and to accept something like tutelage. From then on the Scottish claim to Cumbria and Northumberland and the English earldom was never seriously revived, though often discussed. But the tutelage did not survive Henry's death. Richard I restored its more humiliating symbols to William for a large price, and although John and Henry III played a crucial part in Scottish affairs, they never tried to humiliate Alexander II (1214-49) or Alexander III (1249-86) as Henry II had humiliated William the Lion.

The Norman settlement of Lothian had provided the Scottish kings with a solid foundation for their power, which grew with the passage of time, the assimilation of the peoples, and the spread of new influences over other parts of the kingdom. For long the kings were least secure in the highlands, and they frequently had to deal with rebellions there. The great achievement of the thirteenth-century kings was the subjugation of north-western Scotland and the conquest of the Western Isles. The Hebrides had hitherto lain at the meeting-point of Scottish, Irish, and Norwegian influences; and here were many indications in the thirteenth century that they might fall rather to the Norwegian than to the Scottish empire. But in 1263 the last Norwegian attempt to assert control of the islands failed, and thereafter the Hebrides were part and parcel of the Scottish kingdom.

Meanwhile the early days of Alexander III had been troubled by the first outbreak of serious faction within the ranks of the Norman-Scottish baronage—a type of faction which was to bedevil Scottish politics for many centuries to come. In 1255 Alexander was captured by an obscure official of large pretensions called the 'Doorward', who was supported by the Steward and the English king; in 1257 the opponents of English influence, led by Walter Comyn, carried him off in their turn. Comyn's death and the outbreak of trouble in England in 1258 simplified the situation for a time, and soon after Alexander himself took over the government. But faction within the kingdom with the threat of English intervention behind it had already given a presage of what was to come. For Alexander outlived his three children, and when his grand-daughter, the Maid of Norway, died in 1290, Edward I was called in to settle the claims of thirteen competitors for the Scottish throne.

1. Round disproved the legend of Stuart ancestry enshrined in Shakespeare's *Macbeth*, in his *Studies in Peerage and Family History* (1901), pp. 115ff.

CHAPTER TWELVE

RICHARD I AND JOHN

(1) RICHARD I, 1189–99

Few English kings have played so small a part in the affairs of England and so large a part in the affairs of Europe as Richard I. It may seem paradoxical to speak in this way of a man who has entered so deeply into legend as Richard 'Coeur de Lion'. But he visited England only twice as king, once for three months, later for two; and his reign was spent wandering restlessly about Europe and the Near East. disposing in grandiose fashion of gold, marriages, fiefs, kingdoms, and empires which had not the remotest connection with the English throne. His viewpoint was cosmopolitan and dynastic, and in this he resembled his brilliant enemy, the Emperor Henry VI. Richard disposed of England and half of France—his own inheritance; he went on Crusade and fought and arranged marriage alliances with Saladin; on the way he settled the affairs of Sicily, Cyprus, and Syria. Henry (King by inheritance of Germany and Lombardy) revised the settlement of Sicily, and won it for himself; imprisoned Richard and made England a fief of the Empire; schemed to become Lord of France as well. The reigns of the two powerful kings formed a fitting close to the glories of the twelfth century; but their dreams were short-lived. Both died young, Henry in 1197, Richard in 1199, and their empires rapidly disintegrated. Henry's fame soon came to be overshadowed by his even more brilliant son, Frederick II, the 'wonder of the world'; but Richard's place in English legend is undisputed. He is remembered as the great soldier, the crusader, and troubadour ; and the legend is substantially true.

Had he given his mind to it, Richard might have been a very able and successful monarch: he combined his father's shrewdness and strength with his mother's panache and sense of grandeur. But he made little effort to apply himself to ruling England. Immediately after his coronation, he pillaged the country for money for the third Crusade, and left behind him a regency so complex as to be unworkable. Two brothers had to be provided for. John was loaded with secular honours, Geoffrey (an illegitimate son of Henry II) was made Archbishop of York; both were then sent into exile. The chief man in the kingdom was the Chancellor and papal legate, William Longchamp, Bishop of Ely, who found that royal favour in the absence of the King was insufficient to compensate for the unpopularity which attached to a conceited *parvenu*; nor were Richard's arrangements sufficiently straightforward to give his deputy a free hand. But Longchamp and Walter of Coutances, Archbishop of Rouen, whom Richard sent to support or replace Longchamp according to circumstance, were both devoted and capable royal servants, and it is possible that Richard's scheme might have worked if his brother, John, had not had friends in England and France, and made skilful use of his opportunities for intrigue. In the event Longchamp was removed from office, and John prepared to follow up his victory by intriguing with Philip II of France for the throne itself.

In 1189 Richard left England ; in 1190 he set off for Sicily, whose government he reorganised. His brother-in-law, King William II of Sicily, had recently died ; and Richard's interest in the kingdom was among the most striking of many links between the two islands which the Normans had won in the ten-sixties. In the mid-twelfth century an Englishman had been Chancellor to King Roger II; and one of the leading Exchequer officials of Henry II, Master Thomas Brown, had served his apprenticeship in Sicily. Exchange of men and ideas was frequent.

While in Sicily Richard married Berengaria, a princess from Navarre. It was not until 1191 that he arrived in the East— at the siege of Acre, in time to join in the capture of the city. Richard's arrival and the capture of Acre led to the departure of the King of France, Philip II, who was always a reluctant crusader, and who had urgent business at home. One piece of business was the opportunity offered by Richard's absence to intrigue in Angevin affairs. Once Acre was captured and Philip gone, Richard became the effective leader of the Crusade. The purpose of the third Crusade was to restore the shattered kingdom of Jerusalem and to recover the Holy City itself, which after being for nearly ninety years in Christian hands (since its capture in the first Crusade in 1099) had fallen again to the Turks in 1187. Richard set about these tasks energetically. In September 1191 he defeated Saladin at the battle of Arsuf. At Christmas he was within twelve miles of Jerusalem itself, but could not risk the dangers of a siege. In the spring of 1192 he took a leading part in the negotiations which gave the kingdom of Jerusalem to his nephew, the Count of Champagne, and himself compensated the disappointed candidate with Cyprus. Finally, after a last, ineffectual effort to reach the Holy City, he made peace for three years with Saladin—after an unsuccessful attempt to marry a sister or a niece into Saladin's family—and in October 1192 set sail for home.

News of his exploits travelled ahead of him, and Richard was regarded as a hero in many parts of Europe, in spite of the failure of the essential purpose of the Crusade. But in the courts of Europe he had many enemies. His brother, John, was plotting with Philip II to prevent his return. Learning of this, Richard made his way up the Adriatic, presumably aiming to by-pass France to the north-east. It was too late in the year to cross the Alps in comfort, so he skirted round them and came to Vienna. In Vienna he was captured and imprisoned by an old enemy, the Duke of Austria, who was shortly afterwards constrained to hand him over to the Emperor Henry VI. The conscience of Europe was disturbed by such treatment of an honoured crusader, and the Pope was outraged. But Henry had captured a rich prize, and needed the ransom ; he also wanted to use Richard to forward grandiose schemes against Philip of France ; and he badly needed a hostage for dealing with Welf enemies in Germany (Richard's nephews) and the King of Sicily (Richard's protégé). The price was colossal. Richard was to further schemes for reconciling the Emperor and the Welfs and to pay £100,000 in ransom. The Welfs were reconciled ; the money was paid and went to finance Henry's conquest of Sicily ; Richard surrendered his kingdom and received it back as a fief of the Empire, and he and Henry concerted plans for humbling the King of France. At last, early in 1194, Richard was released. A month later he was back in England. In spite of all the confusion caused by his absence, he stayed for only two months. Then he returned to France to pursue his feud with Philip II ; and in France he lived for the remaining years of his life.

The most significant event of Richard's brief visit to England in 1194 was his re-coronation by the new Archbishop of Canterbury in Winchester Cathedral. It symbolised the establishment

221

of a new régime. The stigma of imprisonment was washed off; all men could see that Richard was king again in fact as well as in name; and the event sealed an alliance between king and archbishop under which England was governed until the accession of John. When Richard had lain in captivity, John and Philip of France had entered into a plot for the capture of Richard's kingdom. In 1193 John had rebelled. But the English leaders remained loyal. Aided by the dowager Eleanor of Aquitaine, now long accustomed to dealing with family difficulties, they rapidly disposed of John's supporters and prepared to subdue his castles. On Richard's release, John made a desperate bid to let Philip into Richard's French possessions before his brother was back in the saddle. It failed of its object—though it left Philip in possession of much Angevin territory—and John was compelled to throw himself on his brother's mercy. Meanwhile Richard's chief agent in England was now the former Bishop of Salisbury, Hubert Walter, an old royal servant, whom Richard had made Archbishop of Canterbury while he was still in prison (1193). Hubert was rapidly advanced to fill the place of William Longchamp. In Richard's last years he was Justiciar and papal legate. He was a distinguished lawyer—perhaps the author of the treatise on law which passes under the name of his old master, Ranulph Glanville; he was an administrator of unusual ability; he was evidently more tactful than Longchamp, and his own family was more distinguished. Hubert was a great man of the world; pious in his way, but his way was that of a business man, a lay patron, not of a churchman. He has left a mixed memory behind him; but for Richard he was ideal. Henry II's dream had come true; the chief offices in Church and state were combined in the hands of a single, devoted, royal servant.

From 1194 to 1199 Richard was repairing the damaged structure of his French empire and preparing doom for Philip of France. He reconquered lost territory, built up alliances, constructed castles—especially the famous Château Gaillard, which guarded the Seine as it twisted into Normandy. As always, he planned grandiosely and spent beyond his means. Early in 1199 he learned that treasure had been found in the Limousin ; and it was treasure that he needed above all for his schemes. He rode south in great haste ; but while he was attacking the Viscount of Limoges, he was wounded in the shoulder by an arrow, and after a few days was dead.

(2) JOHN, 1199–1216

Richard had made no firm settlement for his succession; and the customs of his various dominions allowed a claim both to his brother, John, and his nephew (son of John's elder brother, Geoffrey), Arthur of Brittany. The doyen of the Anglo-Norman baronage, William the Marshal, quoted Norman custom and declared for John; so did the Archbishop of Canterbury; both were echoing the dying voice of the late king. Thus John came to the throne with little difficulty, and after a tussle was able to make terms with Philip of France under which he received the whole inheritance; in return he recognised that his French dominions were fiefs subject to feudal law in the court of the French king, accepted a number of other restrictions and made a small concession of land. For the time John appeared to have won his ambition at last, and to hold virtually all that his father had held.

One might have thought that the constant absence of Richard I would have made his reign a comparatively insignificant episode. But the absence of the King had given the larger departments of government—the Chancery and Exchequer—an opportunity to live a life of their own; compelled them, indeed, to organise themselves more bureaucratically, more independently of royal control. This development was most conspicuous under the administrative genius of Hubert Walter, and so fully did John trust the Archbishop that Hubert's career suffered no check in 1199. 1199 was in fact a crucial year in the history of English administration. The first series of rolls on which copies were made of documents issued from the Chancery began in that year. These rolls—the equivalent of modern files—marked an epoch in record-keeping; the Chancery was beginning to take on the shape of a modern office. Nor was it solely a matter of book-keeping: the critical part which the Chancery played in thirteenth-century politics reflected in part the success of Hubert Walter's régime. The Chancery clerks had had a taste of semi-independence; the king was to become jealous of their independence; the magnates—having regard to the great diversity of legal and financial writs, which could affect their properties, rights, and finances, and which were to be bought in the Chancery—were increasingly anxious to keep a check on its activities.

No medieval English king save Richard III has been so much discussed in recent years as John, and many attempts have been made to salvage his reputation. They can hardly be said to have succeeded, but they have shown that the traditional picture of him as a monster of cruelty, alternating between fits of lethargy and outbreaks of wild activity, was overdrawn. This portrait was based almost entirely on the picture given in a single unreliable chronicle, that of the St Albans monk, Roger of Wendover, and repeated, with additions, by Matthew Paris. In recent years we have inclined to take a less favourable view of the personal characters of the rest of his line, and some have wondered whether John was really any worse than his father or brothers. To this it can only be answered that contemporaries clearly thought that he was. All the early Angevins were ruthless, despotic, and capable ; none of them was particularly moral. But Henry and Richard were trusted by their followers ; they respected the basic feudal code ; they were true leaders in the field, trustworthy in success and adversity, and they repaid loyalty by loyalty. Precisely what was wrong with John is very hard to say. But men did not trust him ; they refused to fight in his company ; they sought to exact unusual promises from him. It may have been a freak in his nature, allied to his ghoulish sense of fun. But it may have lain deeper. The trouble was not merely that he had plotted against Richard and intrigued with Philip of France—many men had done that ; to plot was a younger brother's birthright, and John had done little that Henry I had not done before acquiring the throne. John showed some deeper ground for distrust.

It would be unfair to blame John's flaws of character for all his failures. He was left a difficult legacy. Richard had spent far more than he could readily afford, and John was compelled to levy unpopular taxes to pay for his own wars. Nevertheless John's exactions were excessively arbitrary. His uncertain title to his lands enabled Philip to use Arthur as Philip had once used John ; and the clauses of the treaty between John and Philip gave the latter an easy handle to revoke it. John had subjected his French lands to the feudal jurisdiction of the French King's court; and he soon gave that court a chance to act. The county of La Marche was disputed by a man and a lady ; they arranged their differences by betrothal. In 1200 John put away his wife—their marriage had been technically illegal—and married the lady claimant to La Marche, who was also heiress of Angoulême. His rival rebelled, was suppressed, and given scant justice; he appealed to the French King. Philip was in no hurry to hear the appeal. He waited until his preparations were properly made, then heard the case; and his court gave judgment that John was to forfeit all his French fiefs. For half a century Capetian and Angevin had competed for power in north and central France, without either side gaining a decisive advantage. Suddenly, in 1202, the Angevins were condemned to lose all their lands; and, even more sensational, Philip was able to enforce a great part of the judgment. From the south of France neither he nor his successors could dislodge the English, though they could confine them to smaller territory than that of Eleanor's inheritance. The core of John's inheritance, Normandy and Anjou, was conquered by the French. The Angevin Empire had collapsed.

John never reconciled himself to the loss of Normandy and Anjou, and plotted and intrigued incessantly for their return. The *débâcle* continued. Anjou had gone in 1203; nor had the elimination of Arthur, who had plotted with Philip and been captured by John, helped John's cause. It is not certain how Arthur died, but it is generally thought now, and was generally thought at the time, that John was responsible for his death, and this belief led to the revolt of Brittany. In 1204 Normandy was lost, in 1205 the last castles in Anjou, in 1206 Brittany finally came into Philip's hands. John tried hard to raise an army in England for the recovery of his lost territories, and to raise enemies against Philip on the Continent. His difficulties were great. Once Normandy was lost, his English barons were unwilling to fight on the Continent. Most of them in any case no longer had Norman lands; a few, including William Marshal himself, had acknowledged Philip as their Norman overlord, and were pledged not to fight against him. For these and other reasons John's various campaigns were abortive, and it was not until 1214 that he was able to mount a serious offensive.

Meanwhile the two other disputes which dominated the reign of John had come to a head. From 1206 to 1213 John was embroiled with the Pope. The occasion of this violent disagreement was the election of a new archbishop to succeed Hubert Walter. Hubert had quarrelled with the monks, and they were determined to avoid another King Stork; the King was equally determined to replace him with a faithful royal

225

officer ; the English bishops, wishing to assert their right to a voice in the election beside the monastic chapter, sided with the King. The monks made a secret election of one of their number, and sent him to the pope to be confirmed; then under royal pressure they made a public election of the nominee of king and bishops, and sent again to Rome. By now a significant proportion of the monks was gathered in Rome. Pope Innocent declared both elections illegal and invalid, and set the monks to work again to elect a third candidate in his presence. Their choice was directed towards Stephen Langton, an English cardinal of great learning and prestige, but without recent experience of English affairs. In the end Langton proved himself a very effective primate. But for the time the King was outraged : his wishes had been totally disregarded. He refused the archbishop entry into England. The pope laid the kingdom under interdict, and subsequently excommunicated the King. This interdict meant that all the churches were closed : no masses sung, no marriages or funerals conducted. Only baptism and confession for the dying were permitted. For seven years the churches were silent, while pope and king and archbishop wrangled. In 1213 peace was arranged : the King surrendered. He was preparing for a final passage of arms with Philip Augustus, and needed all the support he could get. Furthermore, the pope was threatening him with deposition, and it was far from clear that the sentence might not prove effective. In 1213 John was absolved, in 1214 the interdict was lifted. From being the Church's enemy, John suddenly found himself in the unwonted role of its most faithful son. He even surrendered his kingdom to the pope and received it back as a papal fief : a gesture which did Innocent III little good, but strangely convinced him of John's sincerity. Stephen Langton was not so easily convinced, and no sooner was he established in England than he found himself falling out of favour with the pope.

In 1214 John made his last, supreme effort to recover his lost lands in France. He formed an alliance with his nephew, the 'Welf' Emperor Otto IV, who was still struggling to assert the Welf position in Germany against the rising star of the young Hohenstaufen, Frederick II.[1] Otto and his allies, with English reinforcements, were to invade France from the northeast, while John attacked through Poitou. But the great plan miscarried. John's campaign failed to achieve any serious penetration. He revived his power in Poitou and marched to

226

Angers, but soon found that his Poitevin vassals would not fight against the French king. In July, at Bouvines, the Emperor's army was heavily defeated. Bouvines was that rare event in medieval warfare, a decisive battle. Philip was rid of his enemies. The Welf Emperor suffered fearfully in prestige, and the success of Frederick II was soon assured. John's hopes of recovering Normandy were gone, and he returned to England to face discontent with an empty treasury and shattered prestige. An arbitrary king could not afford such a record of failure.

Already in 1213 the discontented barons had discussed the possibility of extracting from the King some guarantee that he would govern more moderately and predictably. In fact John was not much more despotic than his father and brother, but his manners and his misfortunes made him appear to be so, and the disasters of his reign encouraged men to resist him to his face. As yet they had little idea what they wanted. Something was wrong; the King, they argued, must have broken the customs of the kingdom. They looked into the past, and they found that Henry I had issued a charter at his coronation listing the abuses that he specifically wished to renounce. So the malcontents began to gloss Henry's charter and plan a new one of their own. The *débâcle* of 1214 gave them their chance, and early in 1215 rebellion broke out. In May the King knew he was beaten, and in June, in the meadow called Runnymede, John agreed that his seal should be set to Magna Carta.

The Charter was drawn up in the royal Chancery, and is a masterpiece of chancery drafting. It was drawn up after very elaborate consultations between the king, the rebel barons, and a few neutral figures of great prestige, such as the Earl Marshal and the Archbishop of Canterbury. Probably the swift solution of differences and some of the clauses in the Charter owed more to Stephen Langton than to the rebels. But the main choice of topics included in it must have been suggested by the barons themselves. It is a fascinating revelation of the views and horizons of the leading English barons of the day.

In form Magna Carta was a grant, in sixty-three clauses, of numerous rights and privileges and legal arrangements which the King guaranteed to observe. The Angevin monarchy at its height had been immensely powerful and arbitrary. John promised that it would accept the shackles of responsible custom. The assumption of the Charter was that there is or ought to be

227

a recognisable body of law covering all essential operations of royal government and the relations of king and subjects; and that royal government was tolerable only if this body of law was known.

These laws were extracted by the barons, and they stood to profit most from them; but other sections benefited too. As we read the Charter we are reminded how strongly the barons needed allies. In the years leading up to 1215 both sides had been looking for support; and the King had tried to make a name for himself for fair dealing and justice among lesser folk. Some members of all classes had suffered from his tyranny; but it is clear that the barons had to compete with the King for support outside their own class. The Archbishop and the Earl Marshal may have given them wise counsel, and seen to it that the Charter was not too narrow a document; but it is clear that self-interest also inclined the barons to be generous to other groups and interests. The English Church was to be free to obey the pope and canon law; the privileges of London and other boroughs were confirmed; merchants and all other travellers were to come and go freely; justice was to be done to Welshmen who had been dispossessed, and John's Welsh hostages were to be surrendered. The vaguest of all the clauses promised some measure of justice to the King of the Scots. Some clauses specifically, and many in practice, benefited all freemen. Many of Henry II's legal innovations were confirmed and (from the subject's point of view) improved; many unpopular taxes were abolished and arbitrary exactions by royal servants restrained. Substantial reductions were promised in the area of the royal hunting grounds, the much-hated 'forests', which had been governed by special restrictions against anything liable to damage the game or reduce their breeding grounds, enforced by savage penalties.

One clause must be quoted in full. 'No free man may be arrested or imprisoned or disseised or outlawed or exiled, or in any way brought to ruin, nor shall we go against him nor send others in pursuit of him, save by the legal judgment of his peers or by the law of the land.' The Charter did not specify what the law of the land was; but it none the less succeeded in doing very much more than protest against John's arbitrary condemnations. It stated very firmly that there was a law—which meant that there were recognised procedures, and that these must be followed. 'The King should be under God and the law,' wrote

228

the great judge of the next generation, Henry Bracton. Magna Carta does not quite say that—after all, in form these clauses are grants from the king, of his own free will. But the assumption is there. The great achievement of Bracton's age was to settle the main framework of an English legal system. In Bracton's day there were professional judges and something like a code, in marked contrast to the England of Henry II. The professional judge first appeared at the turn of the twelfth and thirteenth centuries ; the code was Bracton's own work, *On the Laws and Customs of England,* 'the crown and flower of English medieval jurisprudence' in Maitland's phrase, compiled in the twelve-fifties. Magna Carta helped to spread the idea that English law was reasonably fixed and knowable, and so to lay foundations on which men like Bracton could build.

It has often been discussed whether Magna Carta was the foundation of English liberties or a reactionary document extracted by a class or clique in its own interest. There is no simple answer. The majority of the clauses benefited the barons in some degree and a number specifically detailed ways in which relations between king and tenants-in-chief were to be subjected to fixed custom. When a tenant-in-chief died, the king could exact a 'relief'—a substantial sum of money—from his heir before the heir could succeed; this was to be limited to £100 for earl or baron. If the heir was under age, his lands were in 'wardship', that is to say the king, or whoever was granted the wardship by the king, became the guardian of the heir and had possession of his property; the king furthermore had the right to dispose of heirs and heiresses in marriage. These rights were limited and defined by the Charter, to ensure that the heir was not cheated by his guardian, nor married beneath him. In these and other ways the barons saw to their own interests; but many other interests and privileges were also protected.

By a long-standing tradition a new king swore at his coronation to keep Church and people at peace, to put down iniquity, and to show justice and mercy in his judgments. From time to time the coronation oath was developed into a charter, such as that issued by Henry I, which was known to the barons of Magna Carta; and from time to time kings repeated or developed their oaths on solemn occasions. In 1213 John himself had sworn a slightly altered version of the oath, which laid emphasis on the revival of good laws and the abolition of bad.

The novelty of Magna Carta lay not in the fact that the King bound himself to maintain good law, nor that he issued a charter of liberties ; but that the Charter should contain so elaborate and detailed a statement of important custom. We must not expect too much of it : it is a collection of clauses, not a rounded whole. But it was felt to serve a purpose ; to limit the monarchy by defining the law. The Charter included an elaborate clause providing machinery for its enforcement by a committee of twenty-five barons, to be called into existence if the king broke the Charter. But there was no suggestion yet that such a committee might not be a normal thing; that the duty of the King to consult his barons on important issues should or could be defined. Any such idea still lay in the future. The barons of Magna Carta felt they were dealing with an exceptional crisis; and when John himself was dead, the Charter was re-issued without any reference to the committee of twenty-five. From then on the Charter was often re-issued as a reminder to king and people that the king was not free to break these fundamental customs. A few changes were made ; the forest clauses, for instance, were carried off into a separate charter. But what could make sense was preserved ; and after 1225 subsequent re-issues showed virtually no further change.

By 1225 the Charter was accepted by all parties; but it had not been so in 1215. The Charter gave King John a breathing-space, which he used to obtain from the pope a bull condemning it as contrary to moral law and reprimanding the archbishop, and to gather forces to crush his enemies. There is little doubt that he would have succeeded, had not a fresh outbreak of rebellion attracted the support of the King of France. In an elaborate, if somewhat absurd manifesto, the French court announced that John was deposed; and the French Dauphin was sent to replace him. John made rapid attempts to deal with his enemies, but after a summer and autumn of marching and counter-marching, and after losing his baggage-train (including all his jewels and valuable relics) in a quicksand at the head of the Wash, he succumbed to sickness and died at Newark in October 1216.

1. The Welfs (or Guelphs) and the Hohenstaufen were the two families who competed for mastery in Germany in the twelfth and early thirteenth centuries. They were the descendants, respectively, of Welf IV, Duke of Bavaria (died 1101), and of Frederick of Hohenstaufen, Duke of Swabia (died 1105); and their rivalry had

its climax in the conflicts between Henry the Lion, Duke of Bavaria and Saxony (whose wife, Matilda, was daughter of Henry II of England) and the Emperor Frederick Barbarossa, and between Henry the Lion's son, Otto IV, and two Hohenstaufen—Frederick Barbarossa's younger son, Philip of Swabia, and Philip's nephew, the Emperor Frederick II.

CHAPTER THIRTEEN

HENRY III, 1216–72

When his father died Henry was a boy of nine. His position was exceedingly weak, and it was bound to be a number of years before the new King could rule on his own. But from some points of view his father's early death benefited his cause. Henry had no personal enemies. The Pope found himself guardian of a small child, which strengthened his determination to support John's dynasty. The more chivalrous of the barons gathered round him. Under the shrewd guidance of the legate Cardinal Guala and the experienced regency of William the Marshal, Henry's affairs prospered beyond expectation. Within two years Louis the Dauphin was compelled to abandon his attempt on the English throne and leave the country. The King's supporters had been notably successful, and their efforts to restore order and sort out the confusion caused by civil war helped to make England reasonably peaceful and prosperous.

It is notoriously difficult, however, for a group of regents to act together without friction. The skill of Guala and the prestige of the Marshal kept them in control at first. But Guala left in 1218 and the Marshal died in 1219. In the early twelve-twenties the leading role was played by the Justiciar, Hubert de Burgh, a royal servant well rewarded by John, who had risen from the ranks of the country gentry and was now made Earl of Kent and married to a Scottish princess. But he was not trusted by the greater barons, and his position would have been untenable but for the steady support of Archbishop Stephen Langton. Hubert and Stephen were at this stage very much trusted by the King himself, and they took advantage of this fact gradually to release him from tutelage—thereby in effect strengthening their own position. In 1223 the Pope (acting as Henry's overlord) allowed him the personal use of his own seal, under certain restrictions. Early in 1227 Henry declared himself of age and his personal rule effectively began. He was now nineteen and had been king for ten years.

Henry was lavish and artistic, he built palaces and castles

and adorned them with the best ornaments, hangings, and fur-
nishings that money could buy. He was also extremely devout.
His extravagance, sense of beauty, and piety were especially
concentrated on rebuilding and enlarging the Confessor's
church at Westminster. He consciously modelled himself on the
Confessor, he called his eldest son Edward, and in certain
respects he resembled his distant predecessor. Both were devout; shrewd in their way, but lacking the strength and brutali-
ty for consistent success in politics or for winning renown on
the battlefield. Henry was very self-conscious about his kingship, yet he was never able to throw himself into the
essential exercises of kingship as his father and grandfather
had done. He had serious weaknesses of character: he could
be obstinate, petulant, and mercurial, was extremely sharp-
tongued, rather ungenerous. Those whom he trusted, he trusted
implicitly; but he was suspicious of most of the world and
fearful of treachery. He was shrewd rather than subtle; his
piety lacked depth. To compensate for all this, there was a
certain quiet simplicity in his nature which prevented him
from being embittered or warped by the miseries and failures
of his reign. But he was not the sort of man whom the English
barons instinctively admired or trusted.

Henry's adult reign falls into two parts. Down to 1258 he
was, on the whole, in control of affairs, after 1258 government was often out of his hands, sometimes controlled by committees of barons, sometimes by the heir to the throne, the
Lord Edward. But through it all runs a single theme—conflict
between the efforts of Henry to maintain the near-absolutism
of his predecessors, and the efforts of his barons to control the
King, his council, and his ministers. There was never any question of abolishing the monarchy, even when the King himself
was in prison and Simon de Montfort was acting in his name.
Everyone assumed that government was the King's government. Indeed, the royal court was becoming increasingly the
centre of English life, the key to power and wealth. Profound
changes in society, and growing concern with the way in
which the great power of the Crown was wielded, led to constant unrest; failures in royal policy from time to time gave
excuse and opportunity for unrest to express itself. But the unrest was political. With the exception of the brief periods of
open civil war, the reign was a prosperous time for England at
large.

From 1227 until 1232 Hubert de Burgh remained Justiciar, and his power was undisputed. But his position depended on royal favour, and when the King grew weary and jealous of him, his fall was assured. In 1232 he was removed from office and imprisoned, and his place was taken by another old servant of John, Peter des Roches, Bishop of Winchester, whose son or nephew, Peter des Rivaux, became effective head of the royal administration. The new government was, so to say, purely bureaucratic: it consisted of trained civil servants. But the system was short-lived; in 1234 the two Peters were disgraced, and a largely baronial council, of which Hubert de Burgh was again a member, was re-established. The civil servants and the baronial council represented the two elements from which the royal council was selected. The King's attempt to rule entirely by the counsel of officials of his own choice, and the reaction against it which established a council of barons, were portents of greater events to come.

The next twenty-four years, from the crisis of 1234 to the crisis of 1258, witnessed no serious outbreak of trouble, but a succession of minor crises which failed to mature. The relations of Henry and the barons at large were never free from suspicion. Henry's minority had taught the barons what it meant to have a government which regularly consulted them, his later attempts to rule almost entirely through his own servants reminded the barons that they wished to be regularly consulted. The term 'royal council', applied at any date in the Middle Ages, is ambiguous. In the period covered by this book it might mean two things: it might mean the body of immediate councillors, barons, and royal servants, who attended regularly on the King and advised him on day-to-day affairs; or it might mean the Great Council, in which the leaders of the kingdom, lay and clerical—who regarded themselves as the King's natural advisers—met and advised the King on great issues of state. The composition of the Great Council was far from fixed; the King always had a fairly free choice as to which of the barons should be summoned, and although its deliberations were a traditional part of English government, strictly speaking there had been no obligation on the King to consult the barons on affairs of state. Henry III tended to arrange royal marriages and transact important business without consultation, and this was the more aggravating because the King's closest associates included several of the 'foreign' relations of his wife,

235

Eleanor of Provence, who were thought to encourage in Henry excessive concern for his claims in France, which threatened to commit the English kingdom to expensive adventures in which the English baronage had no interest.

Through the minor crises of Henry's middle years we can see developing something like a programme of reform, which the baronial leaders pressed on the King with growing insistence. Their first demand was usually for the re-issue of Magna Carta, which was quite readily granted. Their second demand was that they should be regularly consulted on important matters of state; that is, that meetings of the Great Council should be frequent and effective. They had come to see that the Charter alone was not enough; the baronial leaders never trusted Henry III, and they had slowly come to recognise the implication of this, that the King must be kept under constant surveillance. But the demand, in this precise form, was novel; and it was not until 1258 that it was pressed by a large party among the barons with any consistency of purpose; even then the demand was a temporary one, only intended to last for the lifetime of one impossible king.

The third demand of the barons was to have a say in the control of the great offices of state, the Chancery and Exchequer. Although the English monarchy had passed through several vicissitudes since the death of Henry II, the royal administration and the royal courts had developed steadily in authority and effectiveness. Government was a more elaborate thing, and the organs of state more powerful, than had been dreamed of even two generations before. The Chancery had followed the example of the Exchequer, and became a department with a fixed headquarters—it had gone 'out of court'. Developing power made the offices objects of suspicion to the baronage, and gave them many motives for wishing to have some say in their control, and their growing independence gave the barons some excuse for intervening in their working. It was much more difficult to object to the king's managing the affairs of his own household, and although the household itself was developing fast at this time, and an increasing share of royal revenue was being administered by the royal Wardrobe (a financial department which travelled with the king and was not under the control of the Exchequer), the barons attempted to interfere with household administration only in the major crises of 1258 and 1264. Thus the claim to a say in the appointment of Chancellor and Treasurer became a regular feature of baronial schemes for reform, and the barons sometimes tried to interfere also in the appointment of the head of the judiciary, the Justiciar. But before 1258 Henry never submitted to such proposals. He would pay lip-service at least to the principle that the Great Council should be consulted on important issues but he insisted that he must be free to appoint his own officers.

A minor crisis in 1238 brought to the front of the stage two of the leading figures of Henry's later years: his brother, Richard, Earl of Cornwall, and a notable from the south of France called Simon de Montfort, who was trying to claim the earldom of Leicester as his inheritance. In this year Henry consented to the secret marriage of his sister to Simon and the protest against the secrecy of the proceedings was led by Earl Richard. Henry agreed to amend his ways, and from that date had in Richard a steadfast supporter of great value to him, an able financier of immense wealth who on more than one occasion saved Henry's finances from disaster.

For a time, he also had a faithful supporter in Simon, who duly became Earl of Leicester in 1239; but a series of difficulties gradually alienated the brothers-in-law. Simon de Montfort was one of the most remarkable personalities of his day. He had many friends and many enemies in his lifetime, and he has had many of both since his death. There can be no doubt of his great ability and self-confidence, of his clear imagination, and of his skill as a soldier. He began as a foreign adventurer who won the liking of Henry III and married his sister. Like all the king's close associates, he found Henry an exasperating master. From 1248 to 1252 Simon was in charge of Gascony, which had been in a condition bordering on anarchy. He performed a difficult task with great energy and some success, and inevitably made enemies in the process. Henry expected (or claimed to expect) success more rapid and complete; feared (not wholly without cause) that Simon's tendency to arrogance was increasing the number of his enemies; and suspected Simon's semi-independent position. In due course Henry began to listen to Simon's enemies, and finally, in 1252, Henry summoned Simon home to answer his accusers in a trial at Westminster lasting five weeks. Simon in return was exasperated by Henry's failure to stand by him in his difficulties, and regarded the trial as an act of treachery. The trial opened, after a preliminary accusation by the Gascon representatives, with a violent attack on Simon by Henry himself. In the end the King was compelled to admit that the evidence told in Simon's favour, but he did not restore Simon to his command, nor could there be friendship between them again. Henry feared Simon, we are told, more than thunder and lightning, and Simon could never trust the King to act with sense and consistency or to stand by his friends.

The differences between Henry and Simon were enhanced by the fact that Simon, like many foreign-born settlers, had a much sharper vision of the true state of England, and a natural dislike of the muddle and confusion of Henry's mind. Simon was Henry's brother-in-law, he had no wish to see royal government abolished or even circumscribed, he wished to see it effective. In this he resembled Henry's son, the Lord Edward. Both wished to see government conducted in an orderly and rational way, on the basis of a harmonious understanding between King and notables. The difference was that Edward wished to keep the ultimate initiative in the King's hands, while Simon was prepared if necessary to imprison the King and act in his name. All this lay in the future in the early twelve-fifties: Edward was still a boy (he had been born in 1239), and Simon's views were only slowly forming. But it is clear that Simon was already one of the leading figures in a group of magnates who were seriously discussing methods of curbing the King's misgovernment. Simon's friends included Robert Grosseteste, the eminent and saintly bishop of Lincoln, and there are fascinating hints in the letters of their mutual friend, the Franciscan friar, Adam Marsh, that Simon was privy to some great scheme propounded by Grosseteste for the reformation of morals in England. Apparently the scheme had some bearing on secular as well as ecclesiastical affairs, though probably not directly on how government should be conducted. These glimpses of Simon's relations with Grosseteste show that Simon had a mind large enough for great schemes; just as a wealth of other evidence shows how precise a grasp he had on the practical details of government and administration and how well calculated was his cool, firm, sardonic manner to rouse Henry's temper.

In 1250 the Emperor Frederick II died, and the intrigues which followed his death involved the English royal family in endeavours even more grandiose than those of Richard I.

Frederick had been king both in Germany and in Sicily, and the popes were determined to prevent the two kingdoms from being united again; they were equally determined to complete the destruction of the Hohenstaufen dynasty. Complicated manoeuvres by the pope and by the leading subjects of the two kingdoms led Henry III in 1254 to accept the kingdom of Sicily for his younger son, Edmund, and Richard of Cornwall in 1257 to accept the kingdom of Germany for himself. Richard spent a number of years fruitlessly pursuing his phantom kingdom. Germany was relapsing into chaos, and a foreign potentate, however rich and able, had little hope of resolving its factions. Edmund amused himself for a while distributing titles and properties of his kingdom, but by the end of 1257 the whole of Sicily was in the hands of the Hohenstaufen Manfred, and Henry was left with nothing to show for the affair but an immense debt which was the pope's price for the kingdom. The Sicilian adventure, however, had two consequences of greater moment than itself: it persuaded Henry to prepare the way for a definitive peace with Louis IX of France, and it led to his surrender to a committee of barons in England in 1258.

The treaty of Paris marked the formal end of the Angevin Empire. Henry renounced his rights in Normandy, Anjou, and Poitou; Louis acknowledged Henry as his vassal in Gascony and other lands in the south. The treaty was on the whole generous to Henry; but its terms were so complex as to leave room for future trouble. For the rest of Henry's reign, however, France and England were at peace.

In domestic affairs, the events of 1257–8 started a crisis which lasted until 1265. Seven years of strife were followed by seven years of peace and restored royal government, ending in the King's death in 1272.

When Henry surrendered to the baronial opposition in 1258, a new system of government was established by the famous Provisions of Oxford, which reduced the King to little more than a *primus inter pares*. A new Council of Fifteen was established, consisting of seven earls (Simon de Montfort included), five leading barons, the Archbishop of Canterbury, the Bishop of Worcester, and one royal clerk; in all affairs of state the King had to consult the council. The three great officers of state, Justiciar, Chancellor, and Treasurer, were to be appointed by the Council and to be responsible to it; a baron was made Justiciar. In addition, the Provisions included a number of administrative reforms, particularly designed to ensure the Council's control over sheriffs, castellans (i.e. governors of castles), and lesser officials, and to reform abuses. The leaders in 1258, as in 1215, were a group of powerful magnates, and as in 1215, they needed to win allies by providing benefits for other classes than their own. But the reforms outlined in the Provisions of Oxford showed a far more coherent notion of how government was to be conducted than John's barons ever attained.

The Provisions of Oxford, supplemented by the Provisions of Westminster of 1259, remained the basis of English government until 1262. But government by a Council was too novel and elaborate an idea to win easy acceptance or to work smoothly. The Provisions of Oxford had been the fruit of co-operation between a number of leading magnates; gradually, as the years passed, they fell out among themselves. Personal differences divided Simon de Montfort from the Earl of Gloucester, the other dominating figure. Gloucester and others could not accustom themselves to ruling in evident disregard of the King's real wishes, and some of the reforms which had been instituted compelled the barons themselves to submit to unwelcome investigations of their own subordinates' abuses. In 1259 and early 1260 Henry was in France completing his settlement with Louis. Earl Simon, meanwhile, was coming to hold an increasingly dominant position in England. He had even come to an arrangement with the Lord Edward, who first appeared in 1259 as an important figure in English politics. Edward had put himself at the head of a group of young men, mostly of baronial families, who accepted his views or his leadership, and who came to form a small but important party. They were hardly a faction : they did not imagine that government could lie wholly in the hands of this or that group of barons—they knew it must be more widely spread : they respected the law of Magna Carta. In Edward they had a leader who would one day be king, and who would restore to the monarchy the kingly virtues, the prowess in tournament and battle which Henry so patently lacked. Unlike Henry, Edward would be trustworthy, competent, and a soldier. It was possible at this time for Edward and Simon to come to terms, both were prepared to maintain the Provisions of Oxford, even if Edward regarded the Council as essentially an advisory body, while Simon wished it to control the King.

The alliance between Edward and Simon aroused Henry's deepest suspicions; he seems to have suspected Edward of a plot to betray him, perhaps even to usurp the throne. Henry returned to England, asserted himself, and sent Edward into exile and then set to work to undermine the Provisions. Most of their makers were now lukewarm in their support, and by the turn of 1261 and 1262 Richard of Cornwall and a group of bishops were able to organise an arrangement between the King and the leading barons. In 1262 the Pope absolved Henry from his oath to the Provisions, Earl Simon went into exile and Henry was king again in fact as well as in name.

Henry's triumph was exceedingly short-lived. He failed to re-establish order in England, and he failed to come to terms with Simon. The barons who had welcomed a return to the more normal régime quickly remembered the distrust of Henry which had inspired the revolution of 1258. Discontent was widespread, but as in 1640–2 men differed on the distance to which it was possible or desirable to carry resistance to the King, and it was far from clear how many of the barons would support the King, how many oppose him if it came to war. The issue was decided by the prompt action of Simon de Montfort in 1263. He returned to England, put himself at the head of the insurgents, and forced the King to promise a return to the Provisions. Late in the year Earl Simon's supporters and the King agreed to submit their case to the arbitration of the King of France and in January 1264 St Louis, who was every inch a king, declared for Henry on every count and condemned the Provisions root and branch. This judgment, known as the 'Mise of Amiens', left the opposition barons no alternative but to submit or to fight for their cause; its effect was civil war, with both sides well supported.

In 1263 the Lord Edward finally decided that Simon's paths were too extreme, and when civil war broke out in 1264, Edward commanded the King's forces. On 14th May Earl Simon's army fell on the King's at Lewes in Sussex, attacking down a long slope into the town. Simon's left, consisting mainly of Londoners, was broken and pursued by the Lord Edward, but the rest of Simon's army quickly overwhelmed the bulk of the royal force. When Edward returned from his pursuit, he found the day lost. The King surrendered, and Edward became a hostage for Henry's good behaviour. From May 1264 till August 1265 Simon de Montfort was effective ruler of England.

Simon was in intention no dictator. He honestly believed that a return to the Provisions of Oxford was possible, and he strove to achieve it. Meanwhile, he and two colleagues, the young Earl of Gloucester (whose father had died in 1262) and the Bishop of Chichester, governed in the King's name, and chose to assist them a Council of Nine, with functions very similar to those of the Council of Fifteen of 1258–62, but more widely representative of the English upper classes. Simon had no wish to govern as the head of a clique, and for discussion of important matters of state he relied more than hitherto on the Great Council, at the same time trying to increase its solemnity and representative character.

The Great Council was reckoned to be a meeting of the leaders of the kingdom, lay and clerical, but the King had always had a fairly free choice as to which of the barons should be summoned. In the first half of the thirteenth century groups of lesser men, representatives of the knights and burgesses who were becoming increasingly active in the management of shires and towns, might be called to attend a council for a special purpose. Their presence was exceptional before the fourteenth century. But three times in Henry's later years, in 1258, in 1264, and in 1265, knights were called to represent the shires, and on the last occasion burgesses also attended to represent the towns. The dates are significant: one of these was the council which issued the Provisions of Oxford, and the others were the councils in which Earl Simon and his colleagues tried to reconstruct the government of the realm. The notion of the 'community of the realm' was gathering force. It was the strength of Earl Simon's position that he had won a considerable following among the 'gentry'. The weakness of his position was that his following among the barons was dwindling.

From the middle of the thirteenth century it became common to refer to the more important sessions of the Great Council as 'parliaments'. It was precisely in the years 1258–65 that the word 'parliament' was first commonly used. Originally the word simply meant 'parleying', a conference between king and notables. It was not an institution, but an occasion; an occasion when a meeting of a Great Council gave the king the opportunity to discuss with the magnates important affairs of state—the levying of taxation, the solution of tricky legal cases—or to receive petitions. Gradually men came to draw a distinction between Council and Parliament, to see Parliament as an institution, to know (or think they knew) who ought and who ought not to be summoned to it, how its procedure was to be organised, what kind of business it should transact, what powers it had. All this lay far in the future. In 1272 nobody knew or could have guessed that these conferences in Council were to grow into the central institution of English government. What Simon and his followers—and the Lord Edward— did know was that within the royal Council, and by broadly based discussion, vital aspects of royal government, jurisdiction, and administration could and had to be conducted.

Through the spring and summer of 1265 Earl Simon's position weakened. His chief associate, the Earl of Gloucester, had decided that royal government conducted by Simon could lead to no good result in the end. Late in May the Lord Edward escaped, was joined by Gloucester, and gathered an army in the Welsh march. On 4th August Simon's army was caught at Evesham in Worcestershire and quickly beaten. Simon himself was killed, and the King was once more restored to effective government.

Simon de Montfort's achievements were not buried with him. It is true that the idea of limited monarchy was a temporary expedient to deal with a crisis. But the idea that important affairs of state should be regularly discussed in Great Councils, and that there must be more continuous co-operation between the king and all the groups and interests among the English ruling classes had been firmly implanted in Edward himself, in his own followers, and in many others. The revolution of 1258 and the events of the following seven years had created precedents and started experiments which were not to be forgotten.

These seven years had also raised feuds and violent dissensions which it took many years to settle. Immediately after Evesham Simon's supporters were deprived of their lands, and the long guerilla warfare against the 'Disinherited', as they were called, began. They took refuge where they could, in fen and forest. Some of them organised bands of outlaws, and one of these (with its headquarters in Sherwood Forest) may have given rise to the famous legend of Robin Hood, but Robin more likely belongs to the early fourteenth century.[1] Eventually a fair settlement was devised and carried out on the basis of the firm but moderate document known as the Dictum of Kenilworth (1266) which was followed by the more elaborate

Statute of Marlborough (1267). This settlement was a triumph above all for the papal legate, Cardinal Ottobuono, but he found allies in Edward himself and in the Earl of Gloucester, neither of whom wished to see the positive achievements of the baronial plan of reform destroyed. Initiative in government was restored to the king, he was to be free to choose his servants and councillors, but Magna Carta was to be enforced and responsible government ensured by regular 'parliaments'.

The legate was not solely concerned to restore peace and good order to the kingdom, he had also come to preach a Crusade. The Sultan of Egypt was engaged in the piecemeal conquest of the surviving Christian outposts and principalities in Syria and Palestine. Although the crusading movement had lost the popular appeal which it had had in the twelfth century, the great effort of papal propaganda of the late twelve-sixties had quite a substantial effect. The Crusade, however, got under way very slowly. Ottobuono left England in 1268; it was not until 1270 that the English contingent, led by the Lord Edward himself, set sail. In the same year St Louis of France also set out on Crusade, to meet his death in Tunis before he ever reached the Holy Land. Louis' death severely weakened the Crusade, and Edward had to content himself with leading some raids on the Syrian coast, and helping in negotiations for peace with the Egyptian sultan, under which the coastal settlements round Acre and elsewhere were preserved until the sixteenth century. Late in 1272 Edward set out on his return journey, and had only reached Sicily when he received news that his father had died on 16th November 1272.

Edward's journey home was extraordinarily slow: it took him nearly two years to travel from Sicily to England, a space of time occupied in formal visits to the Pope and the King of France, in taking part in his last tournament, and in settling the affairs of Gascony. England, meanwhile was securely held by his friends. Edward had been accepted as king by hereditary right and by the will of the magnates immediately on his father's death. But it was not until 19th August 1274 that he was crowned in his father's choir in Westminster Abbey.

1. See Powicke, *King Henry III and the Lord Edward*, ii, pp. 529–30.

CHAPTER FOURTEEN

ENGLAND IN THE THIRTEENTH CENTURY

It is estimated that the population of England in 1086 was very roughly 1,500,000, in the late thirteenth century something over 3,000,000. These estimates are not very secure, but it is unlikely that they give a very false impression. The population had doubled, perhaps trebled. This was a substantial, even a sensational rise. The reasons for it are not entirely clear; but it seems likely that it reflects both a rise in the birth-rate and a decline in the death-rate. Throughout the Middle Ages expectation of life was far shorter than today. Many children died at birth, many more in the first year of life. Inadequate care and ignorance of nutrition prevented many children from surviving early childhood; if they grew up, accident and disease might carry them off at any age. Medieval medicine was primitive, neglect was often preferable to treatment, and supernatural cures—invocation of a favourite saint, touching by the king for scrofula ('the king's evil')—were usually more beneficial than was medical attention, at least they could involve no positive harm. The expectation of life was perhaps a quarter of what it is today but no figure would be of any significance. The important fact is that death was always near, life always insecure. If a man survived childhood and escaped a fatal illness or a fatal accident in early manhood, he might live to be eighty or ninety but a man entered old age soon after fifty and by sixty-five would have buried most of his contemporaries.

Two circumstances might gravely increase the death-rate: hunger and plague. It was not until the fourteenth century that bubonic plague came to carry off perhaps a third of the total population in one visitation. In earlier centuries famine was a more serious danger. The nearer people are to the subsistence level—the more they depend on what they themselves grow—the higher is the danger of famine. A bad harvest finds them without reserves to draw on, and without the money to buy food from more fortunate neighbours. The progress of money economy between the eleventh and thirteenth centuries reduced men's dependence on what they grew in each particular year, and so reduced the danger of widespread famine. This provided one of the conditions in which the population could rise; and increasing wealth, especially among the upper classes, coupled with some improvement in living conditions, no doubt enabled more of the population to survive childhood, to grow up and have children, and so contribute in their turn to the growth of population. But there was probably also a rise in the number of children born within the majority of families. The cause of this cannot be discovered now, but we can guess that the invasion of the Normans, already an extremely prolific people, had something to do with it.

The population had grown: so had the area under cultivation. The villages had spread; some had split into two or three, others had increased their area under the plough. In forest and fen, land had been cleared and drained and new villages founded. The lands laid waste so thoroughly by William the Conqueror had been resettled. The vale of York was thick with corn again before the end of the twelfth century. The small boroughs of Domesday Book had grown; many others had been founded to compete with them; new markets and new fairs had appeared, organised by merchants English and foreign. Exports and imports were no longer a tiny margin in an economy not far from the subsistence level. English wool went to Flanders and came back as cloth; English cloth and corn went to Norway, and timber and furs and many other supplies came back in their place; corn and herrings went to Gascony in exchange for many gallons of wine; from the Mediterranean came southern fruits, silks, sweet wine, raisins, and currants ('raisins of Corinth')—and the precious stones and spices—rubies, emeralds, pepper, ginger, cloves—which the merchants of Italy had brought from the Middle and Far East. England was far richer and more prosperous than it had been in 1086.

The wealth, however, was even more unevenly distributed than in the eleventh century. The large majority of the people were still peasants, and their standard of living had altered little. Indeed, rising population had increased the pressure on land, and land-hunger increased the dependence of many peasants on the goodwill of their lords. Freedom and unfreedom and all the complex rights of the manorial lord were being more closely defined by the lawyers and estate bailiffs. The life of the peasant remained hard and comfortless. But increasing national wealth, though it might bring little relief to the mass of the peasantry, meant a great increase in the opportunities which the few could take who prospered and saved. An active peasant could add field to field. No doubt this had always been possible; it was certainly easier and more common in the thirteenth century than before. A prosperous peasant could build up quite a substantial small property, endow his sons and give portions to his daughters from it, and still hope to leave a decent holding to support his widow and his heir.

Hand in hand with rising population went growing economic specialisation—still very small by our standards, but far beyond what the eleventh century could have dreamed. In particular, the fine wool produced by the English sheep tempted not only merchants from Flanders, but Italians in particular, who came to hold a preponderant place in English long-distance trade. The Italians owed their position in the first place to the large and growing papal taxes. The Italian merchants were the papal bankers. They collected taxes in money and in kind—and it was thus that they became accustomed to handling English wool on a large scale. The Italian merchants were often unpopular in England, but the country prospered in their hands. They taught English merchants their own more elaborate techniques, they provided capital and credit, they strengthened and simplified trade with the Mediterranean—especially in and after the late thirteenth century. It was papal taxation which brought capitalism and mercantile prosperity to England.

The Italians were not, however, the only merchants in England, nor must their initiative be exaggerated. The multiplication of fairs and markets meant a rapid growth in the number of English merchants. If much wool was exported, much was also manufactured into cloth in England itself; and weavers fullers, and dyers were increasing in numbers. Cloth-making was only one of many industries; iron, tin, lead, salt, and even coal were providing increasing numbers with a livelihood. More than ever were engaged in building. The urban classes had come to be an important element in English society. Some old boroughs, like Bristol, had been in the forefront of rapid development, especially on account of the wine trade with Gascony. Many new towns, like Lynn, an outlet for the fenland abbeys, Hull, the port of York and Beverley, and Newcastle, centre of the Norwegian trade, and also of the only important coalfield then exploited, grew and throve between the Conquest and the death of Henry III. But London remained far and away the greatest city in England. Now that new life was stirring in many corners of the country, it might have been supposed that London would feel the pressure of new competitors. But it retained its situation as the centre of the English road system, as a vast sheltered port convenient for continental shipping; and as royal government became more elaborate and more complex, more of its functions came to be performed in London and Westminster. In the days of Stephen, the Londoners had played an active part in national politics by expelling the empress and welcoming the queen. In 1191 the citizens formed a commune and claimed the right to a considerable measure of self-government; and although the 'commune' was never officially recognised by the king, the privileges of London slowly grew. By the thirteenth century the city oligarchy of mayor and aldermen was firmly established. London figured in Magna Carta; it played a decisive part in the events leading up to the battle of Lewes. Barons and knights were no longer the only powers in the land.

In 1086 a baron valued his land first and foremost for the knights they could supply. A man's prestige depended on the distinction of his retinue; his power depended on the number of men who would fight for him; his place at court and in royal favour depended on the behaviour of his contingent in war. By the thirteenth century the knights' fees had lost a great part of their importance. The cost of knightly armour had increased; the knight's fee could no longer support a fully armed knight. The quota was in process of being reduced. Meanwhile the fees had come to be subdivided and subinfeudated by all the changes and chances of 200 years. The exaction of the very elaborate and tiresome military service of early feudal days was no longer practical. Neither baron nor king could rely on the feudal levy any longer. From at least the early twelfth century the king hed depended largely on mercenaries; by the late thirteenth century the leading barons were no more than the officers of a mercenary army. King and barons had to tax their subjects to provide money to pay the royal host.

Other reasons also conspired to increase the barons' interest in cash. The wooden hall of eleventh-century days had given place to the great stone keep of the twelfth; and in the thirteenth century military necessity and the quest for comfort were increasing still further the dimensions of castles. Knights and barons were more often living in unfortified or semi-fortified houses as private war became rarer; large but simple, by our standards, with often no more than two rooms, but far more luxurious than the twelfth-century keep. The few pieces of solid furniture were beginning to be supplemented by more hangings and rugs, by glass for the windows and ornaments for the table. The great baron still had to have a castle, but usually reckoned to build a commodious house within large 'curtain' walls rather than suffer the discomforts of a dark keep. Curtain walls with ever more elaborate fortifications were being developed to separate the garrison more effectively from the new siege engines and their missiles. The climax of these developments can be seen in Edward I's great castles in Wales.

Within the baronial hall the greatest expense of the lord was not in furnishing, but in the lavish hospitality he had to keep up and the generosity he was expected to show to followers and guests. The decline of the knights' fees did not reduce the need for a lord to be well followed; very much the reverse. As the Middle Ages went on, retinues grew larger and the code of chivalry demanded ever more extravagant generosity. This reached its height perhaps in the fourteenth century, but chivalry was far from cheap in the thirteenth. The code demanded that a lord be brave (*preux*), loyal, and generous above all. A twelfth-century troubadour said that it was a disgrace for a man to live within his means. He ought to mortgage his estates and spend his substance entertaining and giving presents. The favourite form of entertaining for a rich man was to organise a tournament. This notable sport replaced private war as the favourite occupation of the warriors in the late twelfth and thirteenth centuries; though from private war it differed little, save that there were a few more rules to be obeyed. At first the tourney was a general mêlée. fought between two sides; only in the course of the thirteenth century did this begin to be replaced by jousting, by individual bouts between armed knights, which gradually acquired rules akin to those of modern boxing.

Two powerful social groups modified the nature of tournament and chivalry as time went on: the ladies and the Church. The status of women was still low. Under certain circumstances they could inherit land; a few great ladies, like the Empress Matilda and Queen Eleanor of Aquitaine, played a leading part in politics in their own right; but they were debarred from the two most respectable professions of the day —from the feudal host and from clerical Orders; only a few became nuns. A nobleman's sisters and daughters tended to be treated as pawns in the game of marriage alliances which he would be constantly playing. The lady's place was the home; her business child-bearing, which was probably at least as dangerous as war. Some wives were submissive; others were beaten; many, as in every age, dominated their husbands. But as long as marriage was a business, constant child-bearing the established custom, and education open only to the very few, the status of women could not be fundamentally altered.

New influences were at work to modify these traditions. The romantic ideal, incorporated into the courtly romances of the Arthurian and other cycles, was giving a new dimension to the code of chivalry. The romances were first written in the mid and late twelfth century; they were at the height of their popularity in the thirteenth. Their commonest theme was the lonely quest of the knight, in pursuit of adventures which might do honour to his lady. As expressions of earthly love, the romances varied from the trivial to the sublime. They brought into current use an attitude to women entirely new in European history—an attitude which has given us the word 'romantic'. At their best they incorporated this idea into a lofty ideal of knightly chivalry, most fully shown in some of the German and French stories of Sir Perceval or Sir Galahad in pursuit of the Holy Grail; and the romance made popular throughout western Europe some ancient stories, like that of Tristan and Iseult, hitherto confined to a single land. Tristan (Drystan) first meets us in Wales; but his story was later sung in many part of the Continent. The developed romance of Tristan was one of the few in which these tales rose to the height of romantic passion. The legend of Iseult was a constant protest against the actual status of medieval women.

The romantic ideal had its influence in the world of chivalry. Knights fought for their ladies' favour, and the ladies' gallery became an essential feature of a tournament. But the influence was slow to affect the married life of the ordinary world. Some of the men who sang that women were ethereal creatures, to be worshipped from afar, partially believed what they said;

and many of the women who heard themselves so described were disinclined to be treated as chattels and drudges. The presence of the ladies at tournaments helped to civilise the tournaments and, in the end, to civilise the world.

At first the Church condemned the tournament as it condemned private war; and until the reign of Richard I the king officially forbade them too. But a baron could not win men's respect unless he conformed to the fashion. When told on his deathbed to repay all that he had taken, that model of chivalry and honour, William the Marshal, replied: 'The clerks are too hard on us. They shave us too closely. I have captured 500 knights and have appropriated their arms, horses, and their entire equipment. If for this reason the kingdom of God is closed to me, I can do nothing about it, for I cannot return my booty. . . . But their teaching is false—else no one could be saved.'[1] In course of time, as the tournament became less violent, the Church's opposition weakened. Chivalry slowly became respectable. Meanwhile, it was extremely expensive; and the man who organised a tournament was liable to provide entertainment and gifts for an army.

To meet the royal taxes and the demands of his social position, the baron needed money. To some extent this could be provided by sound management of his estates. The thirteenth century was a great age of arable and sheep farming. Profits were high, techniques of estate management were developing, and by screwing higher rents out of his tenants and by exploiting some of his manors through his bailiffs a lord could hope to improve his income handsomely.

Some of the barons had immense estates. The baronage was no larger in the thirteenth than in the eleventh century— new blood had been compensated by the disappearance of old families. It was therefore, in general, much wealthier. But the increase in wealth had been modified by two circumstances: that the 'mesne' vassals (barons' vassals) and the knights—what were later to be called the 'gentry'—had much increased in numbers and had absorbed some of the new wealth; and that a large share of baronial wealth was concentrated in a few hands. Wealthiest of all was Richard of Cornwall, Henry III's brother, whose annual income would have been a fortune to a lesser man, who himself financed the currency reform of 1247, shored up the finances of the king and others by princely loans on many occasions, and was still a rich man after the costly attempt to establish himself in Germany. A few leading earls had incomes between £1,000 and £2,000 a year—incomes which, in modern terms, made them millionaires; most of the barons had incomes from land varying from £100 to £500 a year. The average annual revenue of King Henry III has been estimated at £34,000 to £35,000.

But we must not think of the economic position of the great lords purely in terms of their income. We are often told that wealth is power; and in a society in which armies were coming increasingly to consist of mercenaries this may seem on the way to being true. But in the thirteenth century it could equally well be said that power was wealth. The key to fortune lay as much in having influence at court as in good husbandry; and this was to be true of the English aristocracy for many centuries to come. Richard of Cornwall's wealth was only to a limited extent derived from his inheritance; royal favour showered properties and gifts on him—including the earldom of Cornwall, carrying with it much profit from the tin-mines, and the profits of the royal mint; in return Richard saved the crown from bankruptcy. The earls of Gloucester combined two of the best baronies of the Welsh march and substantial portions of other holdings. In theory this was the fruit of prudent marriages; but no lord could hope to acquire or keep fiefs on such a scale unless the king was behind him. There was one way in which the barons were even more closely dependent on the king for their livelihood. Several of the clauses of Magna Carta regulate the arbitrary use of feudal incidents—the money the king could levy from his tenants under a variety of conditions, especially for 'relief' when the baron died and his heir succeeded. Hitherto, when the king exacted fine or relief, he named the sum arbitrarily; and Henry I and John in particular—and all the English kings in some measure—had named fantastic sums. No-one expected these to be paid in full; the baron paid what he could from year to year, and was eventually forgiven the rest. The amount the king actually received depended on the baron's capacity to pay and on political circumstances. A powerful baron whose support the king needed might never pay more than a fraction of his fine. Unless the baron was particularly offensive to the king, he was unlikely to be broken by a royal fine. There are cases of barons who impoverished themselves in this period and sank to be small gentry or farmers; but in the

252

main the tradition was already established that a baron should be helped to maintain his station. The king rarely extracted more than the baron could afford; barons in difficulties might hope to receive grants of offices, sheriffdoms, castles, and even lands or money to assist them. It is estimated that sixty per cent of the barons owed money to the king in 1230; a number of them also owed money to merchants and money-lenders. The baronial class was not sinking under its debts. It no longer had the monopoly of power which had once been in its hands. But in reality it was richer and potentially more powerful than ever. Nor did debt make the barons sycophants of the king—after all, the king was as much in debt as they were. But it did ensure that the court played a large and increasing part in men's calculations. It was the chief source of wealth and social prestige for the upper classes. The two were intimately connected. Debt was a normal part of the evidence that a nobleman was leading a good life according to the code of chivalry.

One notable extravagance of the upper classes has still to be mentioned: their benefactions to the Church. The heroic days when barons founded new monastic houses on a grandiose scale were mostly past by 1200. But a few new foundations were made; smaller institutions, hospitals, and the like were still endowed; chantries were being established in the thirteenth century to ensure that a priest would sing mass for the founder's soul in perpetuity; and large and frequent expense on charity to the poor, the sick, and the Friars was expected of every rich man. Most barons had inherited an interest in one or more monasteries, to which they looked for prayers, and which looked to them for economic and political aid when it should be required.

The Church was wealthier than ever before; but its funds were almost as unevenly distributed as those of the laity. The basis of the Church's income lay in the revenues of parishes, derived from tithes and other 'gifts' due from parishioners to the parish clergy. Beyond that, bishoprics, cathedrals, and abbeys had been given extensive lands; the faithful contributed to the building and upkeep of churches and gave precious relics and ornaments to them. In efficient farming, Benedictine and Cistercian monasteries were often pioneers in the thirteenth century; and most monasteries were reasonably

253

well endowed and supported. The leading bishops were particularly well provided. The two archbishops and the bishops of Winchester, Ely, and Durham had incomes equal to those of the wealthiest of the barons. Like the barons, much was expected of them: a string of palaces, a large team of chaplains, and an immense household staff; open hospitality and princely generosity. Other bishops were not so well endowed; nor had the practice yet arisen which compensated a Welsh bishop for the poverty of his see by allowing him to hold an English deanery as well and to live in hopes of translation to a wealthier diocese. Below the bishops the possibilities of pluralism were being extravagantly explored. It has never been worse: Henry III's leading clerks amassed immense fortunes out of royal office and large pluralities. Later in the century Bogo de Clare, son of the Earl of Gloucester, put together church offices and rectories with the avidity of a collector. Pluralism was shortly to be tamed, so that its worst abuses could be avoided and such function as it had be carried out more efficiently. It was reckoned that tithes and parish dues produced more than enough money for many parish priests; yet the Church had no source of income for many of its other officials. How were clerics in the service of the king and of the bishops to be supported? The answer may seem obvious to us; but it did not seem obvious either to the king or to his clerks that they should live on their wages. Moreover, those engaged in learning and teaching in the rising universities could often only be supported by taxing this or that parish on their behalf. For reasons good and ill, the Church's wealth was being redistributed, as yet haphazardly and most unevenly; but there were not wanting men who wished to see this distribution more equitably and efficiently arranged, who cared first and foremost for the cure of souls.

The thirteenth century was a great age in the history of the medieval Church. The monastic Orders had lost much of their original fervour; the papacy, though far from forgetful of the source of its inspiration, was losing something of its original prestige as it grew increasingly powerful, increasingly involved in law and politics. But the thirteenth century saw an unusually high number of really distinguished bishops; saw Oxford and Cambridge grow and flourish and produce a number of the finest of the scholastics; saw the arrival of the Friars and the spread of the ideals of St Francis and St

254

Dominic in England; and saw the development of Gothic architecture—the flowering of the Early English style and the beginnings of the Decorated—culminating in the choirs of Westminster Abbey and Lincoln Cathedral.

After the death of Stephen Langton (1228), the English episcopate included three men of outstanding character: St Edmund of Abingdon, the saintly and earnest Archbishop of Canterbury (1234–40); St Richard Wych, a graduate of Oxford, Paris, and Bologna and a protégé of St Edmund, who was Bishop of Chichester (1245–53); and Robert Grosseteste, Bishop of Lincoln (1235–53). Grosseteste had been the leading teacher at Oxford and first Chancellor of the University; he was intimately associated with the early history of the Franciscan Friars in this country, though he never himself joined the Order. As bishop he was an ardent reformer. He attempted to enforce the methods and standards promulgated in the Fourth Lateran Council of 1215. Though always capable of taking an independent line, he was a faithful servant of the papacy. There was hardly an aspect of the Church's life which he did not touch; and if in the end he impresses us as a man of somewhat overbearing temper, the Church would have been much the poorer without him.

Oxford had been the seat of a school for about a century before Grosseteste came to study and teach there. Its formal development as a university came in his time; Cambridge was also beginning to emerge as a university in the first half of the century. Oxford had established its reputation as a centre for the study of law; Grosseteste's teaching gave it special distinction as a school of theology, but his own academic interests were immensely wide, ranging from the translation of Greek treatises through the diverse concerns of the books he was translating—mainly philosophical and scientific—to the study of the Bible and of theology itself. Perhaps he is most widely known as one of the first Western scholars to do any original thinking on scientific problems. His mind was encyclopedic and his activity ubiquitous.

In 1221 Friars of the Order of Preachers, the Dominicans, first came to England. They were intended to be an Order of instructed preachers, who could raise the standard of learning and orthodoxy in the Church, made up for the deficiencies of the parochial clergy in preaching and teaching and lead the counter-attack against heresy: it was in his tours among the heretics in northern Spain and southern France that St Dominic of Caleruega (*c*. 1171–1221) conceived the idea of his Order. Heresy was a very slight problem in England, but there was much work which an order of preachers might do; and the Dominicans immediately looked for a university town in which to establish their chief school in the country. Oxford was already the obvious choice; it was natural that the preachers should establish themselves there quickly, and that Grosseteste should be one of their earliest and most influential contacts.

Even closer was his friendship with the Order of Friars Minor, the Franciscans, who first arrived in England three years later than the Dominicans, in 1224. These two were the oldest and most eminent of the Orders of Friars. The way of life of the two Orders was similar: both were bound by oaths to poverty, obedience, and chastity; both lived by rules but not by monastic rules. The Friars were not monks: they were not confined within the walls of a monastery; they moved freely in the world and found their essential apostolate there; neither of the two Orders could hold any property of its own. Dominic's ideal was based on mature reflection by an experienced man on the special needs of the Church of his day. These needs influenced Francis, too, and led to changes in his Order; but its foundation was the result of an intense experience of conversion and illumination by an enthusiastic young Italian layman in his twenties. Francis was called to the life of the Gospel: his message was the message of Jesus to his disciples, to go out two by two, taking nothing for the way, 'neither gold, nor silver, nor brass in your purses . . . , neither shoes, nor yet staves: for the workman is worthy of his meat.' They were to do good, to preach, to work; and to live on charity, if necessary by begging. They were to be poorer and humbler than the poor.

The infectious gaiety of St Francis of Assisi (*c*. 1181–1226) still captivates us after the lapse of seven centuries. Nor was this quality lacking among the early Friars in England. 'The brothers were at all times gay and happy among themselves,' writes their chronicler, Thomas of Eccleston, 'so that when they looked at one another they could scarcely refrain from a smile. And so because the young Friars at Oxford laughed too frequently, it was ordained that as often as one laughed in choir or at table he should receive so many strokes of the rod.' And he goes on to tell the pathetic tale of the Friar who had

had eleven strokes and still could not keep a straight face.[2] The first two heads of the Franciscans in England—'ministers of the province of England'—Agnellus and Albert of Pisa, both seem to have been a nice mixture of sternness and good humour. Certainly they were men of distinction, and under their leadership the English province acquired a very good name. In certain respects it followed the founder's ideal very closely; but from the first, contrary to Francis's intentions, the Friars included scholars who cultivated their learning. The schools of Paris and Oxford were the centres of the movement which transformed the Order and provided it with a strong nucleus of learned men. Leading figures in this transformation were Albert of Pisa himself, who left England to become head of the Order in 1239, and the English Haymo of Faversham, who succeeded Albert as Minister General in 1240. Many of the great names among English Franciscans—Adam Marsh, the friend of Grosseteste and Simon de Montfort, John Pecham (later Archbishop of Canterbury), and Roger Bacon—remind us that the Franciscan School at Oxford was a vital centre of learning in the great age of scholastic thought. The Order was transformed in two ways: it acquired this learned nucleus, and it declined from its original fervour. But in 1272 we are still far away from the days of Chaucer's Friar.

Robert Grosseteste had been himself a leading influence in the development of Oxford and in the formation of the English provinces of the Order of Friars. That he played much part in the building of Lincoln Cathedral is less certain—though the nave at least may date from his time—but it remains one of the most remarkable monuments of thirteenth-century piety and art. The new Gothic forms, worked out in the twelfth century, were finding maturity in England as in France in the thirteenth. An austere and simple grace is as characteristic of Lincoln and the myriad churches which belong to its age, as the riot of line and ornament was characteristic of the early fourteenth century. These great churches are monuments to the wealth of English society: most strikingly Salisbury, where Bishop Richard Poore (1217–28) was able to conceive and in large measure execute the astonishing idea of moving cathedral, close, and the whole town bodily from its old hill fort to the banks of the Wiltshire Avon. These great churches were finely built, but not extravagant. Their height, their colour, their use of glass were restrained when compared with their contemporaries in France. To this the main exception was Westminster Abbey.

Westminster represents the personal taste of a king who had more artistic flair than political sense. In it French and English motifs were nicely blended; and the abbey choir, though hidden today by countless tombs, shorn of its colour by the Reformers and darkened by London's soot, can still make us see why it was reckoned in its day a masterpiece—to be imitated in the proportions and splendid sculpture of the Angel Choir at Lincoln and in many another English church. Westminster introduced a new idea of richness, of splendour in decoration into England.

'The new work at Westminster,' wrote Sir Maurice Powicke, 'was more than a royal tribute to a favourite saint, and much more than an embellishment of the London suburb where the king had his chief house and courts. It was the most strenuous and concentrated, as it was also the most gracious expression of a rich artistic life; and this life, fanned into intensity by the king, was in its turn the outcome of a social activity which engaged the interests of thousands of people, and meant more to them than all the political and ecclesiastical issues of the day. At one period in the course of the work some 800 men were engaged upon it, but these 800 had behind them the quarrymen who dug out the stone in Caen and Purbeck and many other places, the sailors and wagoners who brought it to Westminster, the woodmen in the forests who felled the oaks for timbers, the merchants who collected the materials for work in cloth and jewellery, in mosaic and metal, the tilers at Chertsey and other places where men made tiles, the financiers who advanced money for wages. Nor was the work at Westminster isolated; it was but part of a general activity.'[3]

Once again we are reminded of the critical importance of the court as a centre of artistic influence, as a vast exchange and mart where money was taken and received, where offices and land and marriages were granted out, where men were employed on a scale unequalled elsewhere. Men who counted and men who wished to count in English life—still an infinitesimal proportion of the total population—could meet and pursue their ambitions, their quarrels, and their friendships in the English court. But it was far as yet from monopolising English life. England was still a country of small communities, governed by intense local patriotisms. It is true that the natural

258

leaders of local society, the great barons, the knights of the shire, and the more eminent burgesses, were frequently acting as royal representatives for the countless activities of royal justice and administration in shire and borough and less frequently meeting in conference, parley, or Parliament under the shadow of the royal court. These communities were beginning to learn 'self-government at the king's command'. But the idea that local communities and central government must meet regularly if government is to be conducted with the consent of the people, still lay mainly in the future. In this and in other ways we must beware of looking forward too far. We are separated from what follows by the massive achievement of Edward I. But England was already far more populous, more wealthy, and more civilised than it had been 200 years before. The twelfth and thirteenth centuries saw great and fundamental changes, even if the way of life of the majority of the people had altered little. We can never say whether men were better or happier. We can only say that the choices of occupation and ideal open to most of them had increased; that they had larger opportunities. How they used them we can never hope, in detail, to know.

1. Quoted in S. Painter, *French Chivalry*, p. 89.
2. Thomas of Eccleston, *De Adventu Fratrum Minorum in Angliam*, p. 26. The story ends with a disturbing dream of the Friar, which led the brothers to behave more soberly.
3. *King Henry III and the Lord Edward*, II, pp. 572–3.

TABLE OF DATES

POLITICS (reigns of kings in italics)		THE CHURCH AND LITERATURE	
871–99	*Alfred*	871–99	Alfred's *Laws* and Translations
878	Alfred at Athelney, Battle of Edington, baptism of Guthrum	about 891	Oldest surviving copy of *Anglo-Saxon Chronicle*
		893	Asser's *Life of King Alfred*
899–925	*Edward the Elder*		
911–25	Re-conquest of Danelaw, first stage		
918	Death of Aethelflaed, Lady of the Mercians		
919	Raegnald, King of York		
925–39	*Athelstan*		
937	Battle of Brunanburh		
939–46	*Edmund*	940	St Dunstan, Abbot of Glastonbury
946–55	*Eadred*		
949 or 950	Death of Hywel Dda		
955–9	*Eadwig*	957	St Dunstan, Bishop of Worcester (London, 959; Archbishop of Canterbury, 960–88)
959–75	*Edgar*		
		961	St Oswald, Bishop of Worcester (also Archbishop of York, 972–92)
		963–84	St Ethelwold, Bishop of Winchester
		about 970	*Regularis Concordia*

973   Coronation of Edgar

975–8	*Edward the Martyr*		
978–1016	*Ethelred Unræd*	1002–23	Wulfstan, Archbishop of York
991	Renewal of Danish attacks: Battle of Maldon		

1012   Murder of Archbishop Aelfheah

261

1013–14	King Swein in England (died 1014)		
1016	Death of Ethelred and Edmund Ironside; triumph of Cnut		
1016–35	*Cnut*		
	1027 Cnut's pilgrimage to Rome		
1035–40	*Harold I*		
1040–2	*Harthacnut*		
1042–66	*Edward the Confessor*	1049–54	Pope Leo IX
1051	Exile of Earl Godwin	1051–2	Robert of Jumièges,
1052	Return of Godwin (died 1053)		Archbishop of Canterbury
1053–66	Harold, Earl of Wessex	1062–95	St Wulfstan, Bishop of Worcester
1055–65	Tostig, Earl of Northumbria		
1063	Death of Gruffydd ap Llywelyn		
1066	*Harold:* Battles of Fulford (20 Sept.), Stamford Bridge (25 Sept.), and Hastings (14 Oct.)		
1066–87	*William I, the Conqueror*		
1068–70	Rebellion in the north	1070–89	Lanfranc, Archbishop of Canterbury
1075	Rebellion of the earls; execution of Earl Waltheof	1073–85	Pope Gregory VII
1085	(Christmas) Planning of Domesday		
1086	Domesday Survey		
1087–1100	*William II, Rufus*	1093–1109	St Anselm, Archbishop of Canterbury
	1095–96 Preaching and start of the first Crusade		
		1097	Foundation of Cîteaux
1100–35	*Henry I*	1099–1128	Ranulph Flambard, Bishop of Durham

POLITICS		THE CHURCH AND LITERATURE	
1106	Battle of Tinchebrai; imprisonment of Robert, Duke of Normandy (died 1134)	1107	End of Investiture Dispute in England; Anselm's return from exile
1120	Wreck of the White Ship; death of William the Aetheling	1125	William of Malmesbury, *Acts of the Kings*
1128	Marriage of the Empress Matilda and Geoffrey, Count of Anjou (Henry II born, 1133)	1132	Foundation of Rievaulx and Fountains Abbeys
1135–54	*Stephen*	1138	Geoffrey of Monmouth,
1137	Death of Gruffydd ap Cynan		*History of the Kings of Britain*
1137–70	Reign of Owain Gwynedd	1139–61	Theobald, Archbishop of Canterbury
1139	Matilda landed in England	1139–43	Henry of Blois (Bishop of Winchester), papal legate
1141	Battle of Lincoln and imprisonment of King Stephen; imprisonment of Robert, Earl of Gloucester; release of King and Earl		
1144	Death of Geoffrey de Mandeville		
1144–5	Conquest of Normandy by Geoffrey, Count of Anjou		
1145–9	Geoffrey of Anjou, Duke of Normandy	1146	Death of Cardinal Robert Pullen
	1147 Start of second Crusade		
1147	Death of Robert, Earl of Gloucester	1147–67	St Ailred, Abbot of Rievaulx
1148	Matilda left England		

1149	Henry (later Henry II), Duke of Normandy (Count of Anjou, 1151; married Eleanor of Aquitaine, 1152; Duke of Aquitaine, 1153)		
1153	Duke Henry invaded England; Treaty of Winchester	1153	Death of St Bernard of Clairvaux
1154–89	*Henry II*	1154–9	Pope Adrian IV (Nicholas Breakspear)
1155–62	Thomas Becket, royal Chancellor	1159	John of Salisbury, *Policraticus* and *Metalogicon*
		1159–81	Pope Alexander III
		1162–70	Thomas Becket, Archbishop of Canterbury

1164   Council and Constitutions of Clarendon (January). Council of Northampton; flight of Becket (October)

1166   Assize of Clarendon

1170   Coronation of young King Henry (14 June). Murder of Thomas Becket (29 Dec.)

1176	Assize of Northampton	1173–4	William FitzStephen, *Life* of St Thomas Becket
1180–1223	Philip II 'Augustus', King of France	1177	Richard FitzNeal, *Dialogue on the Exchequer*
1183	Death of young King Henry	about 1187	'Glanville', *De Legibus et Consuetudinibus Angliae*
1189–99	*Richard I*		
1189–94	Richard I absent on third Crusade (capture of Acre, 1192) and in prison in Germany	1193–1205	Hubert Walter, Archbishop of Canterbury
1190–7	Henry VI, King of Germany and Western Emperor (crowned 1191)		

1197	Death of the Lord Rhys (ap Gruffydd)
	1198–1216 Pope Innocent III
1199–1216	*John*
1199	Beginning of Chancery rolls
1204	Conquest of Normandy by Philip II
	1207–28 Stephen Langton, Archbishop of Canterbury

1208–14   Interdict in England

1214	Battle of Bouvines
1215 (June) Magna Carta	1215 Fourth Lateran Council
1216–72	*Henry III*
1227	End of Henry III's minority
	1221 Arrival of Dominican Friars in England
	1224 Arrival of Franciscan Friars in England
	1226 Death of St Francis of Assisi
1240	Death of Llywelyn the Great
	1234–40 St Edmund of Abingdon, Archbishop of Canterbury
	1235–53 Robert Grosseteste, Bishop of Lincoln
1254	Henry III accepted the crown of Sicily for his son, Edmund
	1258 Thomas of Eccleston, *De Adventu Fratrum Minorum in Angliam*
1257	Richard, Earl of Cornwall, elected King of the Romans (i.e. of Germany)
	1259 Death of Matthew Paris
1258	Provisions of Oxford (denounced 1262)
1258	Llywelyn ap Gruffydd, Prince of Wales (died 1282)
1259	Treaty of Paris; Provisions of Westminster

1264	Mise of Amiens (January); Battle of Lewes (May)
1264–5	Government of Simon de Montfort
1265	Battle of Evesham and death of Simon de Montfort (August)
1272	Death of King Henry III

APPENDIX B

GENEALOGICAL TABLES

TABLE I KINGS OF WESSEX AND ENGLAND, before 1066

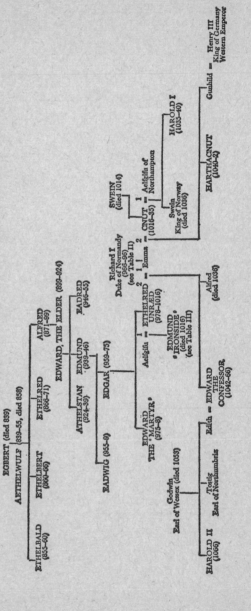

TABLE II THE NORMAN AND ANGEVIN KINGS

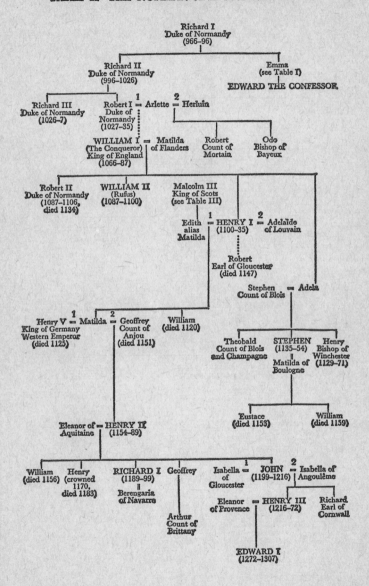

Richard I
Duke of Normandy
(966–96)

Richard II
Duke of Normandy
(996–1026)

Emma
(see Table I)

EDWARD THE CONFESSOR

Richard III
Duke of Normandy
(1026–7)

Robert I = Arlette = Herluin
Duke of
Normandy
(1027–35)

WILLIAM I = Matilda
(The Conqueror)   of Flanders
King of England
(1066–87)

Robert
Count of
Mortain

Odo
Bishop of
Bayeux

Robert II
Duke of Normandy
(1087–1106,
died 1134)

WILLIAM II
(Rufus)
(1087–1100)

Malcolm III
King of Scots
(see Table III)

Edith
alias
Matilda

HENRY I
(1100–35)

Adelaide
of Louvain

Robert
Earl of Gloucester
(died 1147)

Stephen
Count of Blois

Adela

Henry V
King of Germany
Western Emperor
(died 1125)

Matilda = Geoffrey
Count of
Anjou
(died 1151)

William
(died 1120)

Theobald
Count of Blois
and Champagne

STEPHEN
(1135–54)
=
Matilda of
Boulogne

Henry
Bishop of
Winchester
(1129–71)

Eustace
(died 1153)

William
(died 1159)

Eleanor of = HENRY II
Aquitaine   (1154–89)

William
(died 1156)

Henry
(crowned
1170,
died 1183)

RICHARD I
(1189–99)
=
Berengaria
of Navarre

Geoffrey

Isabella
of
Gloucester

JOHN
(1199–1216)

Isabella of
Angoulême

Arthur
Count of
Brittany

Eleanor
of Provence

HENRY III
(1216–72)

Richard
Earl of
Cornwall

EDWARD I
(1272–1307)

TABLE III THE KINGS OF SCOTS

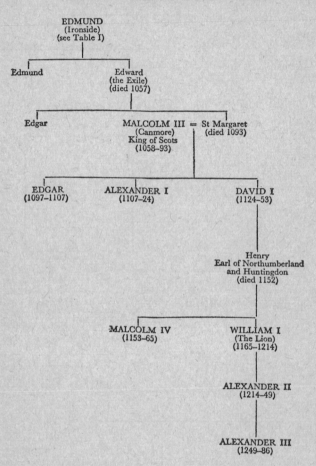

EDMUND
(Ironside)
(see Table I)

Edmund

Edward
(the Exile)
(died 1057)

Edgar

MALCOLM III = St Margaret
(Canmore)   (died 1093)
King of Scots
(1058–93)

EDGAR
(1097–1107)

ALEXANDER I
(1107–24)

DAVID I
(1124–53)

Henry
Earl of Northumberland
and Huntingdon
(died 1152)

MALCOLM IV
(1153–65)

WILLIAM I
(The Lion)
(1165–1214)

ALEXANDER II
(1214–49)

ALEXANDER III
(1249–86)

BOOKS FOR FURTHER READING

Fuller bibliographies will be found in the volumes of the Oxford History of England by Sir Frank Stenton, A. L. Poole, and Sir Maurice Powicke, and in *English Historical Documents*, I and II, listed below.

Maps

Useful maps may be found in many historical atlases: e.g. in Muir's (ed. R. F. Treharne and H. Fullard, 1962), W. R. Shepherd's (1956 ed.), or *Cambridge Medieval History,* volume of maps. For religious houses, see the Ordnance Survey's *Map of Monastic Britain* (North and South sheets, ed. R. N. Hadcock, 1950).

Sources

(in translation, or provided with translations, unless otherwise stated)

English Historical Documents, I, ed. D. Whitelock (1955), selected documents, *c.* 500–1042
English Historical Documents, II, ed. D. C. Douglas and G. W. Greenaway (1953), 1042–1189
R. W. Chambers, *England before the Norman Conquest* (1926)
Regularis Concordia, ed. and trans. T. Symons (Nelson's Medieval Texts, 1953)
Anglo-Saxon Chronicle, trans. G. N. Garmonsway (Everyman's Library, 1960) or D. Whitelock *et al.* (1961)
The Bayeux Tapestry (Phaidon Press, 2nd ed., 1965), new photographs with full commentary by Sir Frank Stenton, F. Wormald, and others
Eadmer, *Life of Anselm,* ed. and trans. R. W. Southern (Nelson's Medieval Texts, 1963), and *History of Recent Events in England,* trans. C. Bosanquet (1964)
Ordericus Vitalis, *Ecclesiastical History,* trans. F. Forester (1853–6)
William of Malmesbury, *Gesta Regum,* trans. J. A. Giles (1889)
William of Malmesbury, *Historia Novella,* ed. and trans. K. Potter (Nelson's Medieval Texts, 1955)
John of Salisbury, *Historia Pontificalis,* ed. and trans. M. Chibnall (Nelson's Medieval Texts, 1956)
Walter Daniel, *Life of Ailred,* ed. and trans. Sir Maurice Powicke (Nelson's Medieval Texts, 1950)
Dialogus de Scaccario, ed. and trans. C. Johnson (Nelson's Medieval Texts, 1950)

Walter Map, *De Nugis Curialium*, trans. M. R. James (Cymmro-dorion Record Series, 1923)

Autobiography of Gerald of Wales, trans. H. E. Butler (1937)

Jocelin of Brakelond, *Chronicle*, ed. and trans. H. E. Butler (Nelson's Medieval Texts, 1949)

M. A. Hennings, *England under Henry III* (1924), selected sources

Matthew Paris, *Chronica Maiora* (from 1235), trans. J. A. Giles (3 vols., 1852–4) (on this see R. Vaughan, *Matthew Paris* (1959); V. H. Galbraith, *Roger Wendover and Matthew Paris* (1944))

Thomas of Eccleston, *De Adventu Fratrum Minorum in Angliam* (Latin text ed. A. G. Little, 1951, Engl. trans. E. G. Salter, 1926)

W. Stubbs, *Select Charters* (9th ed., 1913). (Latin texts not translated; on this book and its author see H. M. Cam, 'Stubbs Seventy Years After', *Cambridge Historical Journal*, ix, ii (1948))

C. Stephenson and F. G. Marcham, *Sources of English Constitutional History* (1937)

G. G. Coulton, *Life in the Middle Ages* (2nd ed., 1954), selected documents

The European Setting

R. W. Southern, *The Making of the Middle Ages* (1953), a brilliant general survey from the tenth to the twelfth centuries

Z. N. Brooke, *History of Europe, 911–1198* (1938)

C. Petit-Dutaillis, *La monarchie féodale en France et en Angleterre* (1933, Engl. trans., 1936)

F. Kern, *Kingship and Law in the Middle Ages* (Engl. trans., 1939)

E. O. G. Turville-Petre, *The Heroic Age of Scandinavia* (1951)

P. H. Sawyer, *The Age of the Vikings* (1962)

J. Brøndsted, *The Vikings* (1965)

W. Ullmann, *The Growth of Papal Government* (1955)

C. H. Haskins, *The Renaissance of the Twelfth Century* (1927)

Cambridge Medieval History (8 vols., 1911–36), for reference

Cambridge Economic History of Europe (1941–   )

General and Political History

M. D. Knowles, ed., *The Heritage of Early Britain* (1952), a brief introduction, by a group of experts

P. Hunter Blair, *An introduction to Anglo-Saxon England* (1956)

Sir Frank Stenton, *Anglo-Saxon England* (Oxford History of England, 1943)

D. J. A. Matthew, *The Norman Conquest* (1966)

E. A. Freeman, *History of the Norman Conquest* (6 vols., 1867–79), an elderly classic

A. L. Poole, *From Domesday Book to Magna Carta* (Oxford History of England, 1951)

F. Barlow, *The Feudal Kingdom of England, 1042–1216* (Longman's History of England, 1955)

J. E. A. Jolliffe, *Angevin Kingship* (1955)

Sir Maurice Powicke, *The Loss of Normandy* (2nd ed., 1961)

Sir Maurice Powicke, *The Thirteenth Century* (Oxford History of England, 1953)

Sir Maurice Powicke, *King Henry III and the Lord Edward* (2 vols., 1947)

R. F. Treharne, *The Baronial Plan of Reform, 1258–1263* (1932)

R. F. Treharne, 'The Personal Role of Simon de Montfort in the period of Baronial Reform and Rebellion', *Proceedings of the British Academy*, xl (1954)

Wales, Scotland, and Ireland

W. Croft Dickinson, *Scotland from the Earliest Times to 1603* (1961)

R. L. G. Ritchie, *The Normans in Scotland* (1954)

I. F. Grant, *The Social and Economic Development of Scotland before 1603* (1930)

A. J. Roderick (ed.), *Wales through the Ages*, I (1959), a series of short essays by various experts

J. E. Lloyd, *A History of Wales from the Earliest Times to the Edwardian Conquest* (3rd ed., 2 vols., 1939)

J. G. Edwards, 'The Normans and the Welsh March', *Proceedings of the British Academy*, xlii (1956)

E. Curtis, *A History of Medieval Ireland* (4th ed., 1942)

The relevant chapters of G. W. S. Barrow, *Feudal Britain* (1956) are useful

Constitutional and Legal

W. Stubbs, *Constitutional History of England* (3 vols., 1874–8), the starting point of modern study; still a classic, though much of Stubbs's work has been revised, especially for the period before 1066

F. Pollock and F. W. Maitland, *History of English Law before the Time of Edward I* (2 vols., 2nd ed., 1898), Maitland's masterpiece

T. F. T. Plucknett, *A Concise History of the Common Law* (5th ed., 1956)

(Domesday Book and Feudalism)

F. W. Maitland, *Domesday Book and Beyond* (1897). (See p. 77)

J. H. Round, *Feudal England* (1895)

V. H. Galbraith, *The Making of Domesday Book* (Oxford, 1961), develops and corrects Round's *Feudal England* on the making of Domesday

V. H. Galbraith, *Studies in the Public Records* (1948), wider in scope than the title indicates

J. H. Round, *Geoffrey de Mandeville* (1892)

Sir Frank Stenton, *The First Century of English Feudalism, 1066–1166* (1932)

S. Painter, *Studies in the History of the English Feudal Barony* (1943)

(*Magna Carta and the Thirteenth Century*)

J. C. Holt, *The Northerners* (1961) and *Magna Carta* (1966)

G. B. Adams, *Origin of the English Constitution* (2nd ed., 1920), elderly, but a lively introduction to *Magna Carta*

S. Painter, *The Reign of King John* (1949)

F. Thompson, *The First Century of Magna Carta* (1925)

B. Wilkinson, *Constitutional History of England, 1216–1399* (3 vols., 1948–58)

(*Administration*)

S. B. Chrimes, *An Introduction to the Administrative History of Mediaeval England* (1952)

R. L. Poole, *The Exchequer in the Twelfth Century* (1912)

Social and Economic

E. Power, *Medieval People* (9th ed., 1950)

S. Painter, *William Marshall* (1933)

D. Whitelock, *The Beginnings of English Society* (Pelican History of England, 1952)

D. M. Stenton, *English Society in the Early Middle Ages* (Pelican History of England, 1951)

W. J. Ashley, *Introduction to English Economic History*, I (1909 ed.)

M. W. Beresford and J. K. S. St Joseph, *Medieval England, an Aerial Survey* (1958)

H. C. Darby (ed.), *Historical Geography of England before A.D. 1800* (1936)

C. S. and C. S. Orwin, *The Open Fields* (2nd ed., 1954)

P. Vinogradoff, *The Growth of the Manor* (2nd ed., 1911)

G. C. Homans, *English Villagers of the Thirteenth Century* (1942)

E. A. Kosminsky, *Studies in the Agrarian History of England in the Thirteenth Century* (Engl. trans. by R. Kisch, 1956), the work of an eminent Russian historian

E. Power, *The Wool Trade in English Medieval History* (1941)

E. M. Carus-Wilson, *Medieval Merchant Venturers* (1954)

Sir William Savage, *The Making of our Towns* (1952)

G. C. Brooke, *English Coins* (1932), for reference

A. L. Poole (ed.), *Medieval England* (1958), a collection of essays by various experts, on many aspects of English life

The Church

Dom David Knowles, *The Monastic Orders in England, 943–1216* (1940)

Dom David Knowles, *The Religious Orders in England, I, 1216– c. 1340* (1948)

Dom David Knowles and R. N. Hadcock, *Medieval Religious Houses, England and Wales* (1953), a catalogue, with an admirable introduction on monastic history

D. E. Easson, *Medieval Religious Houses, Scotland* (1957)

J. Armitage Robinson, *The Times of St Dunstan* (1923)

F. Barlow, *The English Church, 1000–1066* (1963)

R. W. Southern, *St Anselm and his Biographer* (1963)

Z. N. Brooke, *The English Church and the Papacy from the Conquest to the Reign of John* (1931)

Dom David Knowles, *The Episcopal Colleagues of Archbishop Thomas Becket* (1951)

C. R. Cheney, *From Becket to Langton* (1956)

D. A. Callus (ed.), *Robert Grosseteste* (1955)

R. L. Poole, *Illustrations of the History of Medieval Thought and Learning* (2nd ed., 1920)

H. Rashdall, *The Universities of Europe in the Middle Ages* (ed. Powicke and Emden, 3 vols., 1936)

H. Waddell, *The Wandering Scholars* (1927)

Art and Literature

W. P. Ker, *Medieval English Literature* (1912)

R. M. Wilson, *Early Middle English Literature* (1939)

T. S. R. Boase, *English Art, 1100–1216* (Oxford History of English Art, 1953)

F. Saxl and R. Wittkower, *British Art and the Mediterranean* (1947)

P. Brieger, *English Art, 1216–1307* (Oxford History of English Art, 1957)

G. Webb, *Architecture in Britain, the Middle Ages* (Pelican History of Art, 1956)

J. and H. Taylor, *Anglo-Saxon Architecture* (2 vols., 1965)

A. W. Clapham, *English Romanesque Architecture* (2 vols., 1930–4)

R. A. Brown, *English Medieval Castles* (1954)

M. Rickert, *Painting in Britain: the Middle Ages* (Pelican History of Art, 1954)

F. Wormald, *English Drawings of the Tenth and Eleventh Centuries* (1952)

A. Gardner, *English Medieval Sculpture* (3rd ed., 1951)

L. Stone, *Sculpture in Britain: the Middle Ages* (Pelican History of Art, 1955)

New Oxford History of Music, II, *Early Medieval Music to 1300,* ed. A. Hughes (1954 ed.)

INDEX

277

279

Cumberland, Cumbria, 28, 46, 63, 194, 197, 216

Cyprus, 219, 221

Damian, Peter, St, 156

Dane-geld, 71, 73, 84, 85

Danelaw, 52, 53, 63, 72, 78, 79; conquest of, by Edward the Elder, 61-3

Danes, 33, 38, 44, 45, 101, 110; bases of, 43, 81; conversion of, 38; customs of, 66; hosts, 43, 44, 45; invasions and raids, 20, 61, 78, 100, 203; first invasions, 49-50, 54-6, 58; second, 70-2; paganism, 69; settlement, 46, 52, 72-5, 103n, *and see* York; in Normandy, 105

Daniel, Walter, 155

David, St, 212

David I, King of the Scots, 175, 207, 215, 216

Dean, Forest of (Gloucestershire), 140

Deans, rural, 202, 212

Denmark, 101, 138; Kingdom of, 70-6; Kings of, *see* Cnut, Harold, Swein

Derby, 62, 81

Derbyshire, 140

Dermot, King of Leinster, 208, 214

Devon, 131, 140; sheriff of, *see* Baldwin

'Disinherited', the, 243

Domesday Book, Domesday Inquest, 190; making of, 102, 123-4; boroughs in, 135-6, 246; lordships in, 116, 117; manors in, 123-4, 131; salt industry, 140; social classes and society in, 22, 53, 77, 128, 132; waste in, 100

Dominic, St, of Caleruega, and Dominican Order, 255-6

Dover (Kent), 100; castle, 25

Down, 213

Dress, 26, 207

Dublin, 149, 213, 214

Duncan, King of the Scots, 207

Dunstan, St, Bishop of Worcester, Archbishop of Canterbury, 18, 66-9, 74, 118, 143, 151

Dunwich (Suffolk), 52

Durham, Bishops of, 162, 254, *and see* Flambard; Cathedral, 150, 151, 168; monks of, 133, 138

Dyfed, 211; King of, *see* Hywel

Eadmer, chronicler and biographer, 16, 17, 164

Eadred, King, 65

Eadwig, King, 66

Eadwulf, 63

Ealdormen, 79, 83; *and see* Brihtnoth

Earls (jarls), pre-Conquest, 72, 74, 75, 83, 94, 114, 115; post-Conquest, 100, 101, 117, 121, 183, 199; in Scotland, 215

East Anglia, 46, 102, 128, 131, 176; Earls of, 75, 101

Eddisbury (Cheshire), 62

Edgar, King, 16, 61, 65-9, 70, 81, 118, 161, 209; and Church, 67-9, 89, 118; coronation of, 66-7, 90; his laws, 73, 74

Edgar, King of the Scots, 166, 207

Edgar (the) Aetheling, 99, 161, 167, 207

Edington (Wiltshire), 54

Edith, Queen, 87, 94, 95; *see also* Matilda

Edmund, King, 64-7 *passim*, 205

Edmund Ironside, King, 72

Edmund of Abingdon, St, Archbishop of Canterbury, 255

Edmund, son of Henry III, 209, 239

Edward the Confessor, King, 101, 114, 115, 121, 201; career

282

Forests, 228, 230, 246
Forth, Firth of, 66, 194, 205
Fortresses, *burhs,* **55,** 62, 63, 110, 111, 122n, *and see* Castles, Towns
Fountains Abbey (Yorkshire), 155
France, 28, 29, 118, 137, 158, 194, 195, 209; Île de, 88; northern, 30, 58, 61, 97, 106, 125, 151, 195; southern, 225, 256; art in, 257, 258; learning and literature, 144, 157, 250; Edward the Confessor and, 143; William I and, 101; Henry II and, 178; Richard I and, 219, 221; John and, 109, 220, 226–7; Henry III and, 236, 239
France, Kings of, 88, 93, 109, 114, 122, 208, and see Louis, Philip; King's court, 224
Francis, St, of Assisi, 254, 256, 257; Franciscan Order, 18, 238, 256, 257; Minister General, 257
Franks, Duke of the, 64; Kingdoms, 79, 82, 109; Kings of the, 88, 105; Frankish Empire, 154
Frederick I, Barbarossa, King of Germany, Emperor, 159, 181, 184, 188, 231n
Frederick II, King of Germany, Emperor, 181, 219, 226, 238
Frederick of Hohenstaufen, Duke of Swabia, 230n
French, character of, 35, 36; monastic customs, 148, *and see* Cluny
Friars, 254–7
Frisian ships, 55
Fulford (Yorkshire), Battle of, 96
Fulling, 140, 141n
Furniture, 24, 26, 234, 249
Fyrd, 54, 55

Gaelic language, 197, 198

Galahad, Sir, 250
Gascony, 237, 239, 244, 246, 247
Geoffrey, Archbishop of York, 220
Geoffrey, Bishop of Coutances, 145, 146
Geoffrey, Count of Anjou, 173, 174, 193, 196n; as Duke of Normandy, 175, 178
Geoffrey, Duke of Brittany, 195, 223
Geoffrey de Mandeville, Earl of Essex, 176
Geoffrey of Monmouth and his *History of the Kings of Britain,* 33, 34, 122, 200
Geoffrey, son of Wimund, 119
Gerald of Wales, 212
German literature, 250; merchants, 140
Germany, 58, 221, 230n; Kings of, 88–91 *passim,* 122, *and see* Conrad, Frederick, Henry, Otto, Richard; monarchy, 68, 73, 239
Ghent, 68
Gild merchant, 136
Gildas, St, 213
Giso, Bishop of Wells, 87
Glamorgan, 209, 211, 212
Glanville, Ranulph, 192, 222
Glasgow, 215
Glastonbury Abbey (Somerset), 67, 68, 154
Gloucester, 102, 121; Earls of, 252, (Richard) 240, 254, (Gilbert) 242, 243, 244, *and see* Robert
Gloucestershire, 75, 140
Godric of Finchale, St, 138
Godwin, Earl of Wessex, 75, 94–6, 172, 199; house of, 99, 117
Gorze Abbey, 68, 154
Gothic architecture, 255, 257
Goths, the, 58

173, 178–9; career as King, 181–96; and Angevin Empire, 192–6; and the Church, 222, (quarrel with Becket), 17, 184–9; court of, 19, 25; family of, 181–2, 192–5, (daughter) 231n; law and administration under, 37, 79, 189–92, 228, 229, 236, (sheriffs) 120, (writs) 18, 118–9; and Ireland, 214; and Scotland, 216; and Wales, 204, 210

Henry, King, son of King Henry II, Duke of Normandy and Count of Anjou, 188, 192, 193, 195

Henry III, King, 20, 22, 29, 30, 233–44; personality, 233–4; and Scotland, 216; clerks of, 254; and Wales, 205

Henry VIII, King, 35

Henry I, the Fowler, King of Germany, 54

Henry V, King of Germany, Emperor, 170, 173

Henry VI, King of Germany, Emperor, 219, 221

Henry, Earl of Huntingdon and Northumberland, 216

Henry of Blois, Bishop of Winchester, 176–8 *passim*

Henry the Lion, Duke of Bavaria and Saxony, 231n

Hereford, Earl of, 101, 183, *and see* FitzOsbern, Ralph; Earldom, 209

Herefordshire, 95

Heresy, 146, 256

Hereward the Wake, 101

Hertford, 62

Hide, 82, 86, 116

Highland zone, 28, 130, 197

Hildebrand, *see* Gregory VII

Hohenstaufen, 226, 239

Hood, Robin, 243

Hoskins, Dr W. G., 131

Houses, 19, 24, 25, 125, 126, 137, 249

Howden, Roger of, chronicler, 17

Hubert de Burgh, Earl of Kent, Royal Justiciar, 233, 235

Hugh, St, Bishop of Lincoln, 154

Hugh, Earl of Chester, 164, 165

Hugh of Buckland, 119

Hull, Kingston-upon- (Yorkshire), 135, 247

Humber, river, 63, 65, 135

Hundred and wapentake, 78, 79, 81–4, 85, 123

Hungary, 143, 198, 207

Huntingdon, Earl of, *see* Henry; Earldom of, 215

Hwicce, Ealdorman of, *see* Leofwine

Hywel Dda (the Good), King of Dyfed, 64, 203–4

Iceland, 45; Icelandic sagas, 59n

Industry: cloth, mining and other industries, 140, 141, 246, 247, 258

Ine, King of Wessex, 56, 85

Infangenetheof, 83

Innocent III, Pope, 225, 226, 230

Interdict, 188, 226

Investiture, lay, 169–70

Irby (Cheshire), 46, 59n

Ireland, 183, 194, 197, 203, 207–8; Norse in, 46, 61, 63, 65, 207; and Normans, 197, 213–14, 214–15; trade with, 54; Lord of, *see* John

Irish people, 29, 210; Channel, 193–4; Church, 149, 213, 215, (scholars) 52; and Hebrides, 216; Kings, 64, Princes, 214

Iseult, 250

Islam, 38

Italian learning, 157; merchants, 247

Italy, 138, 144, 147, 148, 246; South, 157, 208; Arch-chancellor of, *see* Rainald; Normans in, 97, 106, 113, 118

Llandaff, see of, 212; Bishop of, *see* Urban; *Book* of, 212

Llywelyn the Great, Welsh prince, 204

Loire, river, 68

Lombardy, 219

London, 54, 62, 99, 100, 135, 136–8, 228, 258; as capital, 28, 30, 136–8, 209, 248; alderman of, 200; citizens of, 99, 241; Empress Matilda at, 176; Jews of, 164; Tower of, 25, 137

    Bishops of, *see* FitzNeal, Foliot, Robert; St Paul's Cathedral, canons of, 133, *see* Ralph; schools, 36

Longchamp, William, Bishop of Ely, 220, 222

Lorraine, Lotharingia, 65, 68, 69, 95, 143

Lothian, 66, 205, 215, 216

Louis the Pious, Emperor, 68

Louis VI, King of France, 169; as Dauphin, 166, 167

Louis VII, King of France, 178, 181, 195, 201; his heiress, 193

Louis VIII, King of France, as Dauphin, 29, 30, 230, 233

Louis IX, St, King of France, 239–41 *passim*, 244

Louth (Lincolnshire), 140

Low Countries, 133

Lowland zone, 28, 30, 209

Lynn, King's (Norfolk), 247

Macbeth, King of the Scots, 205; Shakespeare's *Macbeth*, 75, 205, 217n

Magna Carta, 22, 109, 227–30, 236, 240, 244, 248, 252

Magyars, 54

Maine, 93, 97, 101, 166, 169, 193

Maitland, F. W., 77, 80, 113, 115, 229

Malachy, St, 213

Malcolm II, King of the Scots, 205

Malcolm III, Canmore, King of the Scots, 205, 207

Malcolm IV, King of the Scots, 207

Maldon (Essex), 62; Battle of, 49–50, 70, 109

Maminot, Gilbert, Bishop of Lisieux, 147

Man, Kingdom of, 214

Manfred, King of Sicily, 239

Manor, manorial system, 31, 108, 110, 123–35; origin of, 125, 131, 132

Marche, La, 224

Margam Abbey (Glamorgan), 212

Margaret, St, Queen of the Scots, 161, 167, 198, 207, 215

Marie, Countess of Champagne, 201

Markets, 85, 133–6 *passim*, 141, 213, 246, 247; fairs, 133, 246, 247; market gilds, 136; *and see* Trade

Marlborough, Statute of, 244

Marsh, Adam, friar, 238, 257

Marshal, William (the), Earl of Pembroke, 214, 223, 225, 227, 228, 233, 251

Matilda, Empress, 250; as Empress, 173; as Countess of Anjou, 173; in England, 173–6 *passim*, 178, 210

Matilda (Edith), Queen, 161, 167, 172, 193, 199

Matilda of Boulogne, Queen, 172, 176

Matilda, wife of Henry the Lion, 231n

Mediterranean, 21, 106, 246, 247; lands, 143, 153

Mendip Hills (Somerset), 140

Merchants, 21, 138–41, 207, 210, 228, 247, 253

Mercia, 44, 63, 72, 78, 100; Ealdorman of, *see* Ethelred; Earls of, 95, *and see* Edwin,

Rémi, St, 145

Renaissance of twelfth century, 144, 146, 154, 156–60; and humanism, 158–60

Rheims, Archbishop of, 145; Council of (1049), 145–6 *passim*

Rhodri Mawr, Welsh king, 203

Rhys ap Gruffydd (the Lord Rhys), Welsh prince, 204

Rhys ap Tewdwr, Welsh prince, 204

Richard I, King, 136, 140, 202, 209, 219–22, 224, 238, 251; as Duke of Aquitaine, 193, 195; and Scotland, 216; as troubadour, 201; writs of, 18

Richard II, King, 208

Richard III, King, 224

Richard, Earl of Cornwall, King of the Romans (i.e, of Germany), 209, 237, 239, 241

Rievaulx Abbey (Yorkshire), 152–6; Abbot of, *see* Ailred

Ripon (Yorkshire), 155

Roads, 30, 248; Roman, 136

Robert I, Duke of Normandy, 93

Robert II, Duke of Normandy, 101, 161, 162, 163, 166–8 *passim*, 174

Robert, (Count) of Meulan, 168

Robert, Count of Mortain, 114

Robert, Earl of Gloucester, 175, 176, 210

Robert of Jumièges, Bishop of London, Archbishop of Canterbury, 95

Roger I, Count of Sicily, 113

Roger II, Count and King of Sicily, 113; Chancellor of, 220

Roger, Archbishop of York, 187, 188

Roger, Bishop of Salisbury, 120, 171, 175

Roger of Wendover, 224

Roland, Song of, 122

Rollo, Count of Normandy, 105

Roman de Rou, 183

Roman Empire, 109, 136; villas, 131

Romanesque architecture, 151

Rome, 32, 37, 212; pilgrimages to, 58, 75, 138, 201

Church of, papacy: 36–7, 38, 254; authority of, 36–7, 211, 228, 230, 255; and Crusade, 163; England a fief of, 226, 233; papal court, 97, 158, 226, appeals to, 146, 162, 185, 188; papal legates, 170, 176, 177, 213, 220, 222, 244; papal monarchy and reform, 143–9; papal taxes, 247

Rome, Popes, (eleventh century) 75, 76, 165, (twelfth century) 160, 170, 175, 177, 221, (thirteenth century) 233, 239, 241, 244, *and see* Adrian, Alexander, Gregory, Innocent, Leo, Urban

Rouen, 90; Archbishops of, 149, *and see* Walter

Round, J. H., 215

Roxburgh, 215

Runnymede (Surrey), 227

Russia, 45

Rutland, 81

Sac and soc, 83

St Albans Abbey (Hertfordshire), 224; monk of, *see* Paris

St Andrews (Fifeshire), 215

St Asaph (Flint), 211, 212

St Briavels (Gloucestershire), 140

St David's (Pembrokeshire), 149, 209; Bishop of, 178; see of, 212

Saladin, 219, 221

Salisbury (Wiltshire), (Old) 102, 151; (New) 257; Bishops of, *see* Osmund, Poore, Roger, Walter

Samson, Abbot of Bury St Edmunds, 17, 18

Walter of Henley, *Husbandry* of, 127

Waltheof, Earl of Northumbria, 100, 101

Wapentake, *see* Hundred

War, pre-Conquest, 45, 47; eleventh and twelfth century, 20, 110, 111, 118, 124, 170, 183, 202, (Battle of Hastings) 98–9; thirteenth century, 248–9, 252

Wardship, 229

Warenne family, 117

Warwick, 62

Wash, the, 230

Watling St, 54

Weald, the, 98

Wear, river, 138

Welf IV, Duke of Bavaria, 230n

Welf family, 221, 226–7

Wells (Somerset), Bishop of, *see* Giso

Werferth, Bishop of Worcester, 58

Wessex, 55, 100; army of, 62; Earls of, *see* Godwin, Harold; laws of, 56–7, 78; Kings and Kingdom of, 46, 54, 55, 56, 61, 63, 72, 81, 86, *and see* Aethelwulf, Alfred, Egbert, Ethelred, Ine; West Saxons, 43

West Town (Devon), 131

Westminster, 119; as seat of government, 32, 121, 166, 192, 212, 237, 248; Abbey, coronations in, 162, 167, 192, 244; and Edward the Confessor, 95; and Henry III, 22, 234, 255, 258; palace, 22, 25, 137; Provisions of, 240

Wherwell (Hampshire), 95

White Ship, wreck of, 172

Wigot of Lincoln, 119

William I, the Conqueror, Duke of Normandy, King, as Duke, 93–100 *passim*, 106, 161; as King, 16, 75, 79, 90, 99–103, 121, 123, 160, 246; and the Church, 118, 143–50 *passim*, 162; and Domesday Book, 22–3, 101–2; and the Jews, 138; and Wales, 204, 209; and the Norman settlement in England, 115–18 *passim*

William II, Rufus, King, 90, 118, 161–7, 168; burial of, 40; and the Church, 148, 163–6; and the Jews, 138; and Wales, 210

William I, the Lion, King of the Scots, 207, 216

William II, King of Sicily, 220

William d'Eu, 117, 118

William of Blois, son of King Stephen, 178, 184

William of Malmesbury, chronicler, 15, 16, 40, 157, 202

William of Aetheling, son of Henry I, 172

Wiltshire, 117

Winchester (Hampshire), 85, 102, 119, 121, 135; Bishop of, 184, 254, *and see* Ethelwold, Henry, Peter, Stigand; Cathedral, 40, 150, 151, 221; palace at, 25; Treasury at, 121, 137, 167

Wirral, peninsula (Cheshire), 46, 63

Witan, Witenagemot, 84, 89, 91, 99, 171

Wocca, 131

Woking (Surrey), 131

Women, status of, 249, 250, 251

Wool, 133, 141, 246, 247

Worcester, 143; Bishop of, 239, *and see* Dunstan, Oswald, Werferth, Wulfstan; diocese of, 116

Worcestershire, 75

Writs, 18, 87–8, 118–19, 191, 192, 200, 223

Wulfstan II, Archbishop of York, 74

Wulfstan II, St, Bishop of Worcester, 54, 116, 143, 150

MARIE ANTOINETTE
John Hearsey

In this fascinating biography, John Hearsey traces the development of Marie Antoinette from the irresponsible, arrogant and extravagant Queen living out her unreal existence at the Petit Trianon, to the tragic but courageous widow, who spent her last days in the prison of the Conciergerie under the shadow of the guillotine.

£1·25 *Illustrated*

LADY CAROLINE LAMB
Elizabeth Jenkins

A sensitive and colourful portrait of the wife of William Lamb, Viscount Melbourne and later Prime Minister, whose wayward disregard for convention made her the topic of conversation in fashionable salons throughout England.

45P

THE FALL OF THE HOUSE OF HABSBURG
Edward Crankshaw

A vivid portrayal of the history of the Habsburg monarchy from 1848 to 1918.
'Authoritative, lucid and utterly absorbing'
90p   *Evening Standard*

A GUIDE TO PREHISTORIC AND ROMAN MONUMENTS IN ENGLAND AND WALES
Jacquetta Hawkes

A detailed account, region by region, of the prehistoric as well as the Roman monuments to be found throughout England and Wales, enabling the visitor to find the most interesting sites and to understand the importance of what he sees.

£1·25 *Illustrated*

THE CENTURY OF REVOLUTION
1603–1714
Christopher Hill

In England between the years of 1603 and 1714 a transformation took place which embraced the whole of life, thought and taste. This book attempts to reassess what happened, penetrating below the surface of seventeenth-century events to show how our modern society began to take shape, and how England's position in the world was considerably altered. It outlines the changes which set England on the path of Parliamentary government, economic advance and imperialist foreign policy, of religious toleration and scientific progress, and shows the century as the greatest age in English literature.

While not setting out to provide an exhaustive compendium of facts, it considerably broadens and enriches our concept of a brilliant and bewildering century of change, heralding the modern world – 'the world of banks and cheques, budgets, the stock exchange, the periodical press, coffee-houses, clubs, coffins, microscopes, shorthand, actresses and umbrellas'.
6op

SCOTTISH KINGS AND QUEENS A.D. 1057 TO 1603

SOVEREIGN	MARRIED	Access.	Died
MALCOLM III (CANMORE)	Son of Duncan I....	1st Ingibiorg, widow of Thorfinn, Earl of Orkney; 2nd Margaret, sister of Edgar the Atheling.	1057	1093
DONALD BÁN............	Brother of Malcolm Canmore	....	1093	—
DUNCAN II............	Son of Malcolm Canmore, by first marriage.	....	1094	1094
DONALD BÁN........ (Restored)	....	1094	1097
EDGAR.	Son of Malcolm Canmore, by second marriage	Died unmarried.	1097	1107
ALEXANDER I	Son of Malcolm Canmore	Sybilla, natural daughter of Henry I of England.	1107	1124
DAVID I........	Son of Malcolm Canmore.	Matilda, daughter of Waltheof, Earl of Northumbria widow of Simon, Earl of Northampton.	1124	1153
MALCOLM IV (THE MAIDEN) ..	Son of Henry, eldest son of David I	Died unmarried.	1153	1165
WILLIAM I (THE LION)	Brother of Malcolm the Maiden	Ermengarde, daughter of Richard, Viscount of Beaumont	1165	1214
ALEXANDER II	Son of William the Lion	1st Joanna, daughter of King John; 2nd Mary, daughter of Ingelram de Coucy (Picardy).	1214	1249
ALEXANDER III	Son of Alexander II, by second marriage. ...	1st Margaret, daughter of Henry III of England; 2nd Joleta, daughter of the Count de Dreux.	1249	1286
MARGARET, MAID OF NORWAY	Daughter of Eric II of Norway, grand-daughter of Alexander III.	Died unmarried.	1286	1290
JOHN BALIOL	Grandson of eldest daughter of David, Earl of Huntingdon, brother of William the Lion.	....	1292	1296
ROBERT I (BRUCE)...........	Great-grandson of 2nd daughter of David, Earl of Huntingdon, brother of William the Lion.	1st Isabella, daughter of Donald, Earl of Mar; 2nd Elizabeth de Burgh, sister of Earl of Ulster.	1306	1329
DAVID II..........	Son of Robert I, by second marriage	1st Joanna, daughter of Edward II of England; 2nd Margaret, widow of Sir John Logie (divorced, 1369).	1329	1371
ROBERT II (STEWART)	Son of Marjorie, daughter of Robert I by first marriage, and Walter the Steward.	1st Elizabeth, dau., of Sir Robert Mure (or More) of Rowallan; 2nd Euphemia, dau., of Hugh, Earl of Ross, widow of John, Earl of Moray.	1371	1390
ROBERT III	(John, Earl of Carrick) son of Robert II.	Annabella, daughter of Sir John Drummond of Stobhall, niece of Margaret Logie.	1390	1406
JAMES I	Son of Robert III	Jane Beaufort, daughter of John, Earl of Somerset, 4th son of John of Gaunt and grandson of Edward III of England.	1406	1437
JAMES II........	Son of James I........	Mary, daughter of Arnold, Duke of Gueldres	1437	1460
JAMES III........	Eldest son of James II........	Margaret, daughter of Christian I of Denmark, Norway and Sweden.	1460	1488
JAMES IV......	Son of James III	Margaret Tudor, daughter of Henry VII	1488	1513
JAMES V......	Son of James IV......	1st Madeleine, daughter of Francis I of France; 2nd Mary of Lorraine, daughter of Duc de Guise, widow of Duc de Longueville.	1513	1542
MARY .... [of England 1603]	Daughter of James V, by second marriage ...	1st Francis, Dauphin of France; 2nd Henry, Lord Darnley; 3rd James, Earl of Bothwell.	1542	1587
JAMES VI (Ascended the Throne of England 1603)	Son of Mary, by second marriage	Anne, daughter of Frederick II of Denmark.	1567	1625

WELSH SOVEREIGNS AND PRINCES

WALES was ruled by Sovereign Princes from the "earliest times" until the death of Llywelyn in 1282. The first English Prince of Wales was the son of Edward I, and was born in Caernarvon town on April 25, 1284. According to a discredited legend, he was presented to the Welsh chieftains as their Prince, in fulfilment of a promise that they should have a Prince who "could not speak a word of English" and should be native born. This son, who afterwards became Edward II, was created "Prince of Wales and Earl of Chester" at the famous Lincoln Parliament on February 7, 1301. The title Prince of Wales is borne after individual conferment and is not inherited at birth; it was conferred on Prince Charles by Her Majesty the Queen on July 26, 1958. He was invested at Caernarvon on July 1, 1969.

INDEPENDENT PRINCES, A.D. 844 to 1282		ENGLISH PRINCES, SINCE A.D. 1301	
Rhodri the Great	844–878	Edward, b. 1284 (Edwd. II), cr. Pr. of Wales	1301
Anarawd, son of Rhodri	878–916	Edward the Black Prince, s. of Edward III. .	1343
Hywel Dda, the Good	916–950	Richard (Richard II), s. of the Black Prince	1377
Iago ab Idwal (or Ieuaf)	950–979	Henry of Monmouth (Henry V)	1399
Hywel ab Ieuaf, the Bad	979–985	Edward of Westminster, son of Henry VI. .	1454
Cadwallon, his brother	985–986	Edward of Westminster (Edward V)	1472
Maredudd ab Owain ap Hywel Dda .	986–999	Edward, son of Richard III (d. 1484)	1483
Cynan ap Hywel ab Ieuaf	999–1008	Arthur Tudor, son of Henry VII	1489
Llewelyn ap Sitsyhlt	1018–1023	Henry Tudor (Hen. VIII), s. of Henry VII.	1503
Iago ab Idwal ap Meurig	1023–1039	Henry Stuart, son of James I (d. 1612)	1610
Gruffydd ap Llywelyn ap Seisyll	1039–1063	Charles Stuart (Charles I), s. of James I	1616
Bleddyn ap Cynfyn	1063–1075	Charles (Charles II), son of Charles I	1630
Trahaern ap Caradog	1075–1081	James Francis Edward, "The Old Pretender" (d. 1766)	1688
Gruffydd ap Cynan ab Iago	1081–1137	George Augustus (Geo. II), s. of George I. .	1714
Owain Gwynedd	1137–1170	Frederick Lewis, s. of George II (d. 1751) .	1727
Dafydd ab Owain Gwynedd	1170–1194	George William Frederick (George III)	1751
Llywelyn Fawr, the Great	1194–1240	George Augustus Frederick (George IV). . .	1762
Dafydd ap Llywelyn	1240–1246	Albert Edward (Edward VII)	1841
Llywelyn ap Gruffydd ap Llywelyn. .	1246–1282	George (George V)	1901
		Edward (Edward VIII)	1910
		Charles Philip Arthur George	1958

THE FAMILY OF QUEEN VICTORIA

QUEEN VICTORIA was *born* May 24, 1819; *succeeded* to the Throne June 20, 1837; *married* Feb. 10, 1840 Albert, PRINCE CONSORT (*born* Aug. 26, 1819, *died* Dec. 14, 1861) ; *died* Jan. 22, 1901. Her Majesty had issue:—

1. H.R.H. Princess Victoria (*Princess Royal*), born Nov. 21, 1840, married, 1858, Frederick, German Emperor; died Aug. 5, 1901, leaving issue:—

(1) H.I.M. William II., *German Emperor* 1888–1918, born Jan. 27, 1859, died June 4, 1941, having married Princess Augusta Victoria of Schleswig-Holstein-Sonderburg-Augustenburg (born 1858, died 1921), and secondly, Princess Hermine of Reuss (born 1887, died 1947). The late German Emperor's family:—

(a) The late Prince William (*Crown Prince* 1888–1918), born May 6, 1882, married Duchess Cecilia of Mecklenburg-Schwerin (who died May 6, 1954) ; died July 20, 1951. (The Crown Prince's children:—Prince Wilhelm, born July 4, 1906, died 1940; Prince Louis Ferdinand, born Nov. 9, 1907, married (1938) Grand Duchess Kira (died Sept. 8, 1967), daughter of Grand Duke Cyril of Russia (and has issue four sons and two daughters); Prince Hubertus, born Sept. 30, 1909, died April 8, 1950; Prince Frederick George, born Dec. 19, 1911, died April 1966; Princess Alexandrine Irene, born April 7, 1915; Princess Cecilia, born Sept. 5, 1917).

(b) The late Prince Eitel Frederick, born July 7, 1883, married Duchess Sophie of Oldenburg (marriage dissolved 1926) ; died Dec. 7, 1942.

(c) The late Prince Adalbert (born July 14, 1884, died Sept. 22, 1948), married Duchess Adelaide of Saxe-Meiningen. (Prince Adalbert's children:—Princess Victoria Marina, born Sept. 11, 1917; Prince William Victor, born Feb. 15, 1919.)

(d) The late Prince Augustus William, born Jan. 29, 1887, married Princess Alexandra of Schleswig-Glucksburg (marriage dissolved 1920); died March, 1949. (Prince Augustus's son is Prince Alexander, born Dec. 26, 1912.)

(e) The late Prince Oscar, born July 27, 1888, married Countess von Ruppin, died Jan. 27, 1958. (Prince Oscar's children:—Prince Oscar, born July 12, 1915, died 1939; Prince Burchard, born Jan. 8, 1917; Princess Herzeleida, born Dec. 25, 1918; Prince William, born Jan. 30, 1922).

(f) The late Prince Joachim, born Dec. 17, 1890, married Princess Marie of Anhalt, died July 17, 1920 (leaving issue).

(g) Princess Victoria, born Sept. 13, 1892, married (1913) the then reigning Duke of Brunswick. (Princess Victoria's children:—Prince Ernest, born March 18, 1914, married Princess Ortrud von Glucksburg, 1951; Prince George, born March 25, 1915; Princess Frederica, born April 18, 1917, married Paul I., King of the Hellenes (*see* p. 215); Prince Christian Oskar, born Sept 1, 1919; Prince Welf Heinrich, born March 11, 1923, married Princess Alexandra of Ysemburg, 1960).

(2) The late Princess Charlotte, born July 24, 1860, married (1878) the late Duke of Saxe-Meiningen, died Oct. 1, 1919. (Princess Charlotte's daughter, Princess Feodora, born May 12, 1879, married (1898) the late Prince Henry XXX. of Reuss, died Aug. 26, 1945).

(3) The late Prince Henry, born Aug. 14, 1862, married (1888) the late Princess Irene of Hesse, died April 20, 1929 (issue, Prince Waldemar, born March 20, 1889, died May 2, 1945; Prince Sigismund, born Nov. 27, 1896).

(4) The late Princess Victoria, born April 12, 1866, married firstly (1890) Prince Adolphus of Schaumburg-Lippe, secondly (1927) Alexander Zubkov, died Nov. 13, 1929.

(5) The late Princess Sophia, born June 14, 1870,